CINEMATIC HYPERTEXT

Frontiers in Artificial Intelligence and Applications

FAIA covers all aspects of theoretical and applied artificial intelligence research in the form of monographs, doctoral dissertations, textbooks, handbooks and proceedings volumes. The FAIA series contains several sub-series, including "Information Modelling and Knowledge Bases" and "Knowledge-Based Intelligent Engineering Systems". It also includes the biannual ECAI, the European Conference on Artificial Intelligence, proceedings volumes, and other ECCAI – the European Coordinating Committee on Artificial Intelligence – sponsored publications. An editorial panel of internationally well-known scholars is appointed to provide a high quality selection.

Volume 122

Recently published in this series

Vol. 121. Y. Kiyoki et al. (Eds.), Information Modelling and Knowledge Bases XVI
Vol. 120. T.F. Gordon (Ed.), Legal Knowledge and Information Systems – JURIX 2004: The Seventeenth Annual Conference
Vol. 119. S. Nascimento, Fuzzy Clustering via Proportional Membership Model
Vol. 118. J. Barzdins and A. Caplinskas (Eds.), Databases and Information Systems – Selected Papers from the Sixth International Baltic Conference DB&IS'2004
Vol. 117. L. Castillo et al. (Eds.), Planning, Scheduling and Constraint Satisfaction: From Theory to Practice
Vol. 116. O. Corcho, A Layered Declarative Approach to Ontology Translation with Knowledge Preservation
Vol. 115. G.E. Phillips-Wren and L.C. Jain (Eds.), Intelligent Decision Support Systems in Agent-Mediated Environments
Vol. 114. A.C. Varzi and L. Vieu (Eds.), Formal Ontology in Information Systems – Proceedings of the Third International Conference (FOIS-2004)
Vol. 113. J. Vitrià et al. (Eds.), Recent Advances in Artificial Intelligence Research and Development
Vol. 112. W. Zhang and V. Sorge (Eds.), Distributed Constraint Problem Solving and Reasoning in Multi-Agent Systems
Vol. 111. H. Fujita and V. Gruhn (Eds.), New Trends in Software Methodologies, Tools and Techniques – Proceedings of the Third SoMeT_W04
Vol. 110. R. López de Mántaras and L. Saitta (Eds.), ECAI 2004 – Proceedings of the 16th European Conference on Artificial Intelligence
Vol. 109. E. Onaindia and S. Staab (Eds.), STAIRS 2004 – Proceedings of the Second Starting AI Researchers' Symposium
Vol. 108. V. Stefanuk and K. Kaijiri (Eds.), Knowledge-Based Software Engineering – Proceedings of the Sixth Joint Conference on Knowledge-Based Software Engineering
Vol. 107. F. Darses et al. (Eds.), Cooperative Systems Design – Scenario-Based Design of Collaborative Systems
Vol. 106. D. Bourcier (Ed.), Legal Knowledge and Information Systems – JURIX 2003: The Sixteenth Annual Conference
Vol. 105. Y. Kiyoki et al. (Eds.), Information Modelling and Knowledge Bases XV

ISSN 0922-6389

Cinematic Hypertext

Investigating a New Paradigm

Clara Mancini

Knowledge Media Institute, The Open University, Milton Keynes, United Kingdom

IOS Press

Amsterdam • Berlin • Oxford • Tokyo • Washington, DC

ISBN 1-58603-513-4
Library of Congress Control Number: 2005924284

Publisher
IOS Press
Nieuwe Hemweg 6B
1013 BG Amsterdam
The Netherlands
fax: +31 20 687 0019
e-mail: order@iospress.nl

Distributor in the UK and Ireland
IOS Press/Lavis Marketing
73 Lime Walk
Headington
Oxford OX3 7AD
England
fax: +44 1865 750079

Distributor in the USA and Canada
IOS Press, Inc.
4502 Rachael Manor Drive
Fairfax, VA 22032
USA
fax: +1 703 323 3668
e-mail: iosbooks@iospress.com

PRINTED IN THE NETHERLANDS

Cinematic Hypertext
C. Mancini
IOS Press, 2005

Preface

The non-linearity of hypertext has critical implications for scholarly discourse and argumentation, where it is commonly considered important to control the reader's exposure to the line of reasoning in order to communicate complex ideas and maximise rhetorical impact. The non-linearity of hypertext has been seen as a threat to authors' control over discourse order and the coherence of their argumentative discourse.

Existing hypertext paradigms offer different solutions to the problem of preserving user-defined navigation whilst maintaining coherence: page-based hypertext relies on the expressiveness of linear associative writing; semantic hypertext relies on the expressiveness of link taxonomies; spatial hypertext relies on the expressiveness of the visual features of hypertext. This research combines elements of these with new theoretical insights, to investigate a fourth paradigm referred to as Cinematic Hypertext. The problem of maintaining coherence is framed as the problem of representing and communicating discourse form in ways inspired by the mechanisms underpinning cinematographic languages for expressing coherently narrative relations.

Cinematic hypertext requires the consistent and concurrent use of the hypertext medium's formal features, grounded in structuring principles, in order to allow the emergence of a local language. For scholarly discourse, it is proposed that relational primitives based on Cognitive Coherence Relations (CCR) can be used as a structuring principle to define hypertext links, while the graphic features of the medium can be used to render these relational primitives. Relations between nodes are hence animated in principled ways as they are navigated, shaping discourse structure.

This dissertation articulates the theoretical basis for cinematic hypertext, proposes a prototype visual language to express a sub-set of CCR, provides experimental evidence that the visual results are meaningful, and specifies requirements for a cinematic hypertext environment.

Intended Audience and Scope

This work is intended for hypertext readers and producers, as well as analysts, because it proposes a way of thinking of hypertext as a medium. The concept of Cinematic Hypertext is presented from its theoretical ground to a first set of design guidelines, to the definition of a prototype language and its first evaluation. The work specifies the requirements for a cinematic hypertext environment. However, no implemented system is presented: the development of such an editor will be future work that can build on the results of this investigation. Here the main goal is the exploration and the proposal of a new approach to the electronic medium.

Acknowledgements

My research work and my individuality as a researcher owe a lot to the community of the Knowledge Media Institute, which has supported and nurtured me for years, in an intellectually stimulating and creative environment. Among the people of this community, above all I am grateful to Simon Buckingham Shum, who has been such an inspiring guide to me: his insightful advice and his close collaboration have allowed me to become the researcher I am today, and to successfully complete this work. I am also grateful to Marc Eisenstadt for the timely and perspicacious advice he has always offered me in key moments.

I would like to thank my colleagues Trevor Collins, Victoria Uren, Paul Mulholland, Peter Whalley, Arthur Stutt and Gary Li for making the time to discuss my work and offering me constructive feedback. And I would like to thank Damian Dadswell, Lewis McCann and Ben Hawkridge for offering me a lot of technical advice and material help. Thanks also to those who took part in my empirical studies for bringing a fundamental contribution to my work.

I owe a lot to the hypertext community in general, but in particular to David Kolb, Adrian Miles and Jim Rosenberg, who have always inspired me with their work and stimulated me with interesting discussions. Special thanks to David Kolb and Adrian Miles for kindly reviewing part of this work. And thanks to Elli Mylonas, David Durand and George Landow for their constructive feedback.

My gratitude also goes to Ted Sanders, who introduced me to his psycholinguistic community. He offered me fundamental advice and kindly reviewed part of this work. From the same community, I also would like to thank Henk Pander Maat and Alfons Maes and their colleagues for the helpful discussions they shared with me.

I am grateful to Frank Nack and Josie Taylor for thoroughly reviewing the whole of my work, providing me with stimulating and helpful feedback during discussions that will remain amongst the best memories of my academic life.

Finally, thank you, Anthony, for being so supportive: your creativity, your technical skills and your patience while I was completing this work have been most precious.

Contents

Cinematic Hypertext
C. Mancini
IOS Press, 2005

1. Cohesion and Coherence in Hypertext Argumentation: a Perspective

1. The Promise of a New Medium

At the beginning of the 1940s, Vannevar Bush (Bush, 1945) envisioned a machine that would be capable of working associatively like the human mind: large repositories of information made of inter-connectable units, where materials would be easily retrievable through logical and analogical associative trails laid down by end-users. The Memex constituted the first conception of what, two decades later, Engelbart described more systematically and first implemented in software (Engelbart, 1963), and, four decades later, Nelson (1981; 1987) dubbed hypertext: a new form of electronic text, structured as non-sequential writing, that allows the reader to go through it by choosing different reading paths. Years later, Landow (1992), working from a literary perspective, identified in the electronic hypertext the accomplishment of the poststructuralist idea of the text as a non-centred network of interconnected nodes (Barthes, 1960; Foucault, 1966), whose borders were permeable to other texts (Derrida, 1972). Hypertext, Landow observes, appeared as a reification of the Derridian concept of intertextuality implicit in all literature, while the largest hypertext of all, the World Wide Web, seemed to best represent Barthes' concept of textual network. Moreover, the characteristics of the new interactive medium were to transform the idea of both the reader and the writer.

The idea of a reader who is responsible for actualising his own text, finding his own closures, seemed to represent perfectly an emerging poststructuralist culture. In the post structuralist view, the subject's ability to know reality is partial, bound to his cultural context, but at the same time it is in the subject (or reader)'s interpretative act that the reality (or text) finds any possible sense, unification and closure. Reality itself is unstructured and fragmented, and it is only from a specific perspective and through the individual experience, as decentred and limited as it is, that the connection between these fragments becomes meaningful and takes shape. So, if on the one hand, the reader loses the possibility of producing 'the' interpretation and finding 'the' sense of a text, on the other hand, his interpretation is acknowledged almost as an act of creation that, through the individual reading experience, gives the text 'a possible' sense among the multiplicity of all possible senses.

Hypertext seemed to be the perfect reification of this new conception of humans and the cultural 'texts' that they write and read. As a new technology, it was promising to change the way in which for centuries we have been writing and reading, engaging with text, learning and even thinking, since the invention of Gutenberg's movable type (Kaplan, 1995).

Certainly, hypertext fiction authors like Michael Joyce finally have a medium to accomplish what many previous and contemporary writers had tried to achieve on paper.[1] Writers like Marcel Proust, James Joyce (Tolva, 1996; Theall, 2000), Marguerite Duras, Alain Robbe-Grillet or Claude Simon (Genin, 1998), had gradually adopted narrative structures whose linearity and space-time continuity were diminishing, and whose closure-less scenarios and situations would often evolve paratactically[2] through the juxtaposition or repetition of fragments open to multiple connections. But while in the linear medium available to these writers the increasing disarticulation of the narrative structure of their paper-based works was making them more and more difficult to read, hypertext authors could rely on a medium whose technical non-linearity and interactivity fully supported and valued the disarticulation and fragmentation of the narrative structure, as well as the multiplication of reading paths.

Hypertext has opened new horizons also in the world of non-fictional text. Encyclopaedic works - for instance Encarta[3] or Electronic Encyclopedia[4] - constitute hypermedia networks to be explored according to the paths of one's learning interests and needs. The rigid alphabetical order characterising traditional paper-based encyclopaedias is no longer the predominant criterion to organise information. The reader can more easily discover connections between things and build his own knowledge network no longer just through his cognitive activity, but through his very interaction with the system. Generally, hypertext seems to be changing people's approach and access to culture and cultural heritage.

Hypertext systems like D3E[5], VKB (Shipman et al., 2001) and Tinderbox (Bernstein, 2003) are beginning to change the way scholars do research and collaborate, making them both readers and writers, able not only to interactively navigate across information networks created by their colleagues, but even to manipulate those networks and create new ones of their own for others to navigate. With the advent of the Web, large scale initiatives such as the Open Archives Initiative[6] provide interoperable document archives, and efforts such as the Open Citation Project[7] and Citeseer[8] that automatically link inter-textual citations in electronic documents are establishing a new core hypertext-navigational infrastructure for researchers to browse the literature. Complementary to this are evolutions in the scholarly/scientific peer review process, with electronic journals such as Informattica Online (Baptista and Machado, 1999), EJournal[9], the Journal of Interactive Media in Education (JIME) (Buckingham Shum and Sumner, 2001), and the Journal of Digital Information (JoDI)[10] providing environments in which the individual author's discourse can be very easily supported (or challenged) and enriched through a network of argument, references and links to the discourse and artifacts of the wider scholarly community - as an example of a collaborative information space (Bannon and Bødker, 1991).

2. Argumentative Discourse and Hypertext

But how hypertextual are electronic journals and scholarly hypertexts in reality[11]? Do they actualise the idea of a network of discrete fragments multiply connected to one another, where the reification of countless explorative paths is possible? In fact, the structure of most electronic journals is not substantially different from the structure of paper-based journals: they gather articles from different authors, and the articles are in most cases organised as traditional papers, despite the presence of many links (JoDI) or annotation mechanisms (JIME). In the few available examples of hypertext essays, like Socrates in the Labyrinth (Kolb, 1995) or Writing Space (Bolter, 1991), where the hypertext structure is substantial, the minimal text unit more often than not still tends to be the equivalent of the paper page, with mostly referencing or elaborative links. In other words, for the most part, scholarly hypertext seems to still follow the papyrocentric paradigm (Harnad, 1991, 1997a, 1997b; Sumner and Buckingham Shum, 1998)[12].

The reason is that scholarly journals and scholarly texts are grounded in various forms of argumentation, and argumentation constitutes the one textual form and rhetorical function in which linearity, continuity and centrality are not surrendered by the author willingly, as in other genres of hypertext. As Carter observes (2000)[13], informative hypertexts – including technical documentation, encyclopaedias and educational materials – developed rapidly, exploiting the access, navigation, search and retrieval capabilities offered by the medium. Literary hypertext – including fiction, poetry and pedagogy – thrived on the ambiguity and inherent non-linearity of new reader-oriented narrative forms allowed by the medium. Expressive hypertext, which exploits the visual brainstorming and chunking capabilities of the medium, is also gradually developing. However, for persuasive hypertext, that is, argumentation, and in particular for its scholarly form, the characteristics of the medium almost seem to constitute a challenge to take on, rather than a resource from which to draw[14].

This should not be surprising in one sense, if we look at the characteristics and requirements of traditional argumentation. According to classical rhetoric, the aspects of argumentation are:

1) *inventio* or enuresis, which concerns the choice of the contents, what examples or evidence to bring in order to be persuasive; 2) *dispositio* or taxis, which concerns the arrangements of the contents and envisages four parts: *capitatio benevolentiae* (an opening that attracts the audience); *narratio* (the account of facts, which can start from the beginning – *ordo naturalis* – or in medias res – *ordo artificialis*); *confirmatio* (the account of the arguments); *peroratio* (the conclusion and appeal to the audience); 3) *elocutio* or *lexis*, which concerns the expression, the choice of the language and of the figures to add ornament to the discourse; 4) and 5) *memoria* and *actio*, which concern memorising and executing (in a theatrical sense).

Obviously, *memoria* and *actio* are not applicable to written argumentation[15]. However, out of the other three aspects, the hypertext author only has full control on the *inventio* and on the *elocutio*, not on the *dispositio*, which in fact represents a very important aspect. Although argumentation theory has evolved, and new theories (as discussed shortly) – such as Stasis Theory – de-emphasise the importance of discourse order in relation to other aspects, several theoreticians do question the adequacy of hypertext to mediate argument. Among them, Doug Brent:

"*Hypertext has proven itself an excellent medium for information retrieval and is rapidly catching on as a medium for fiction. However, there are relatively few argumentative pieces that truly take advantage of the medium. This may be just a matter of slow adoption, but it may also be that the medium itself just isn't very well adapted to either reading or writing intellectual argument...The essence of rhetorical argument is control--not intellectual tyranny but the ability to have a predictable effect. Even when the goal is not to foist a point of view on another but simply to create an image of the world as one sees it, the rhetor must be able to ration out the arguments she will make in order to present that point of view. Points of view are expressed in chains of argument in which ideas come first, second, third in order to achieve maximum argumentative weight*" (Brent, 1997).

According to a tradition that is as old as Plato's writings, Brent distinguishes between argumentative and exploratory rhetoric: the first being more reliant on a rigorous order, the second being by definition characterised by some degree of fragmentation and decentred-ness. For him, while hypertext lends itself to explorative rhetoric, the interactive medium is not as well suited for argumentative rhetoric, unless it is to deny its own mandate as hypertext.

David Kolb, a philosopher who has explored the use of hypertext for argumentation and who has written philosophical works in hypertext, acknowledges the main objection to the use of the interactive medium. In Socrates in the Labyrinth, he writes:

"*The principal argument against nonlinear web writing in philosophy is straightforward: philosophy necessarily involves argument, and argument necessarily involves a beginning, a middle, and an end. Thus a truly philosophical text needs a line* [...] *On this view, a philosophical argument (just as a mathematical proof) cannot be a cloud of disjointed statements. Hence the philosophical line cannot be dissolved in the way some have dreamed of dissolving the narrative line. And thus philosophical hypertext will have to respect the line by making arguments the units of presentation, and by maintaining an overall argumentative - hence linear - structure*" (Kolb, 1995).

On the same line speaks Charles Ess:

"[...] *the modernist paradigm of an author who seeks to convey meaning - in part, through logical and syntactical structures, including the linearity associated with print media - cannot be easily abandoned by even the most ardent proponents of poststructuralism and decentered hypertexts*[...] *My large point is that instead of accepting the either/or between modernism and postmodernism enjoined upon us by many postmodern enthusiasts - we as theorists, authors, and readers of hypertexts will be better served by a theory of hypertext which explicitly acknowledges the role of both paradigms*" (Esss, 1996).

This concern is reflected in different proposals that tackle the issue of non-linearity, and which seek to compensate for the lack of control on discourse order. Accordingly, Kolb describes different possible structures that could characterise argumentative ("*philosophical*") discourse in hypertext (Kolb, 1995), which characterise his own work. These range from linear and compact structures, to more non-linear and fragmented ones, seeking a balance between the paradigm of the closed line and the paradigm of the open network through the combined use of referencing, outlines, maps and explorative presentation with structured paths. Later on, in an essay on scholarly hypertext, Kolb (1997) proposed the concept of "*hypertext regions*" as complex semantic units in which the argument is structured within a single node whose connections to the surrounding nodes should reflect its internal structure. This technique is also described by Carter (2000), as one of the possible strategies to maintain the compactness and the order of argument in hypertext: he describes the use of overview nodes within which arguments are laid out linearly to be supported, elaborated and expanded by other nodes. This way the author can be sure that the reader will become aware of all the essential elements of the arguments and in the right order.

According to Stasis Theory, however, in a well-formed argument, the *presence* of the right elements is more important than their order of presentation. Carter proposes that, if order does not matter, then the linearity of the hypertext, and its implicit temporality, can be 'spatialised', and since hypertext is essentially a spatial medium (Tolva, 1996), these spatial dimensions provide important and reliable principles of discourse organisation. Carter continues "*In hypertext rhetorical 'moves' are not just figurative but literal, at least at a cognitive level*", arguing that navigational, and in general, spatial metaphors are particularly effective to describe the structure of discourse. Landow has emphasised how concepts like departure, arrival, path, network, etc., refer to a real practice and describe the activity of reading itself (Landow, 1991). Similarly, among the techniques to structure argument in hypertext, Carter, like Kolb, mentions the use of maps, schemas and outlines to help the reader understand and explore the *topographic space* that he is navigating (Bolter, 1991), to let him see what is where and how to reach it. However, while this spatialisation accounts for the representation of the argument's logical structure, it does not account for effects that order and temporality achieve in traditional argument. Furthermore, it leaves open the possibility that the reader may still decide not to visit certain nodes that the author considers critical to getting his point across, which may be an unacceptable risk for the author.

In a more linear approach, then, Carter mentions the use of a technique that exploits the effects of Primacy (people tend to remember better the piece of information that they have come across first) and Recency (people tend to remember the piece of information that they came across most recently). Unlike Stasis Theory and spatial approaches, this technique (well validated in cognitive psychology experiments) depends for its success on the order in which the reader will come across nodes. Another approach to the problem from the same perspective is the use of structural patterns. For instance, in the nine navigational patterns proposed by Bernstein for fictional hypertext, and for hypertext in general (Bernstein, 1998), links are arranged in such a manner that the reader is led down predefined paths from a starting point to a point of arrival – in effect, hypertext tours or paths that temporarily remove from the user the possibility of exploration (Hammond and Allison, 1987, Trigg, 1988). Within a single hypertext the reader can move through various, but predefined, series of nodes constituting navigational patterns. Bernstein's strategy is not to offer the reader a global view of the navigational space and to make sure that all the required elements of the argument are there, nor to centralise the argument in an overview node. Rather, his suggestion is to carefully design (and constrain) the hypertext navigation, imposing on it some kind of order. And again, the idea of linearity comes back into the picture – a return to route level navigation, rather than map level (Shum, 1990).

But whether it is through overview nodes, spatialisation metaphors, or navigational patterns, the final aim of these strategies is to return to the author's hands as much control as possible on the way their discourse comes across, on the way it takes shape before the reader's eyes, and ultimately on the way it coheres in the reader's mind.

3. Order, Cohesion and Coherence in Argumentative Hypertext

To summarise so far, hypertext's non-linearity and the lack of univocal order in discourse deriving from it, creates the crucial problem of discourse coherence, which concerns the expressive capabilities of the medium, and constitutes a major challenge for argumentative hypertext. The problem of *coherence* is relevant to hypertext discourse in general (Slatin, 1991), but it concerns hypertext argumentation in particular, precisely because argumentative discourse traditionally relies so much on the order of discourse parts, the uncontrollable and unpredictable multiplication of reading journeys around an argument affects its coherence, and its strength.

In cognitive terms, coherence is a characteristic of the mental representation that the reader constructs during the process of text interpretation[16]. Text comprehension depends on the reader's ability to construct a coherent representation of what (he thinks that) the text is conveying, and to do so the reader needs to be able to identify the conceptual relations (he thinks to be) holding between the set of discourse elements (whether these are sentences, paragraphs or entire text sections). Conceptual relations are primarily identified based on the content of the related discourse elements, but in linear discourse their identification is facilitated by connectives (explicit relational and referential phrases), which mark the conceptual content of the relation (e.g. *despite the fact that*, *in order to*, *because*, etc.). These connectives constitute an important element of discourse cohesion, but they can only be used when, as in linear text, discourse units are arranged in a predefined sequence, that is, in a univocal order. In hypertext, however, the use of textual connectives between nodes is problematic, because the order of access to hypertext nodes is not univocal: readers may or may not follow the links.

Furthermore, in linear discourse, whether it makes use of connectives or the construction is paratactic[17], the order in which discourse parts are presented constitutes a fundamental principle of coherence in itself, because it determines a univocal directionality upon the way discourse parts are related and interpreted, in the light of what comes before and what comes afterwards. In hypertext, however, the author can only partly control the order in which discourse parts will be accessed, and therefore he cannot rely on this principle for his discourse to convey a coherent representation. More precisely, he can only rely on order in a very local way: he can link a node to another node. However, the possibility of establishing a global univocal order through ordered extended structures is very limited in hypertext discourse[18].

In most informational hypertexts (encyclopaedias and other reference works), the lack of control on order is not a problem because it is the reader who establishes relations between nodes (discourse units) and constructs a discourse that coheres based on his personal requirements. The responsibility over discourse coherence resides almost entirely with the reader, whose interaction with the system aims at constructing his own discourse based on what he wants or needs to know[19]. In literary hypertext, the openness of the narrative order derived from the non-linearity of the medium creates an opportunity to play with fragmentation and ambiguity. The reader is indeed expected to interpret with a high degree of freedom the connections between the 'chunks' that the hypertext writer makes available for him, 'inventing' within the gaps of the narrative's texture, as the writer intends that he will do. In literary hypertext, therefore, the responsibility for discourse coherence is intentionally shared between the writer and the reader[20]. The effort of wrestling with the structure is part of the aesthetic experience of reading literary hypertext, which readers expect.

However, things are different with argumentation. If argumentation seeks to persuade and to convince the reader of the validity of one's idea (Carter, 2000), or to simply create an image of the world as one sees it (Brent, 1997), then the main responsibility over discourse coherence remains with the author - even if the author needs the interpretative work of the reader for the shape of his vision to be recognised and for his vision to come to life before the reader's eyes (see Chapter 2). To be able to fulfil that responsibility, the author needs control over the structure of discourse, or at least he needs to be able to shape his argument in a recognisable way. As we have seen, theoreticians like Kolb, Bernstein and Carter have put forward a number of possible approaches to shaping hypertext discourse that mediate between the open explorative network and the closed argumentative line. In different ways, the paradigms adopted in hypertext systems within hypertext research reflect this dialectic too, discussed next.

4. Representing Coherence: Structural Paradigms in Hypertext Systems

Different hypertext systems, for individual or for collaborative authoring, express different approaches to the task of the problem of coherence. What follows is a description of the three most representative paradigms and of the principles on which they are based: page-based hypertext, semantic hypertext and spatial hypertext.

4.1. "Page-Based" Hypertext

Historically, the first paradigm for hypertext, and still the most familiar and wide spread amongst scholars, is the "page-based" one, which already characterised Engelbart (1963) and Nelson's (1987) conceptions and implementations and which returned to dominate with the World Wide Web. In the html paradigm, the connectable object, the hypertext node, is the page[21], therefore the typical modality of visualisation is the page by page presentation rather than the node network visualisation, even when a navigational map of the site is provided somewhere. In general, as we will see, page-based hypertext does have ways of signalling discourse structure, but the result is very different to the discourse representation that takes shape in semantic networks and spatial hypertext configurations discussed below. On the other hand, in this type of hypertext, the connections between discourse parts are established between an element (usually a text element - word or phrase) within the page and another page altogether. That is, a new large discourse unit (i.e. the node) is opened up by a richly contextualised semantic element, which gives semantic value to the connection itself, by triggering the reader's 'semantic expectations'. As we will see, different forms of text can trigger different expectations about the link's target.

Another characteristic of page-based hypertext is that, being virtually endless pages, the discourse units that the reader can go through without ever having to activate any links may end up being very extended and articulated, structured just as paper based documents are with titled sections and paragraphs, and even chapters. At the same time, though, the medium supports connectivity at the finest granularity (individual characters, if desired), without requiring any particular 'structural' discipline or commitment to structure on the part of the author. That is, in theory, any single word of a Web page can be turned into a link to any other Web page - whether the target page contains one word or hundred thousand words - and the author does not need to commit to, or provide, any semantic definition for any of the links, even though he may rely on the expectations of the reader. For instance, if I come across a Web page in which the work of a scientist is discussed and I see that the names of other scientists who are said to have influenced his work are active links, I can reasonably expect that those links will take me to a page containing more information about these other scientists: who they are, what they have done, etc. (the conventionalised use of these 'predictable' connections is reported below).

Over time, Web designers have developed ways to differentiate for divers types of link, which have become the object of investigation in the study of Web based discourse structure (Moulthrop, 1992; Jackson, 1997; Haas and Grams, 1998; Nielsen, 1999; Carr et al., 2000; Miles-Board et al., 2002). In a recent study, Miles-Board (2003) examined the most representative Web and hypertext link taxonomies proposed over the years by different authors, comparing the existing typologies with the results of a very extensive investigation. His goal was to assess to what extent the Web shows signs of *Associative Writing*, by which the author means hypertext connections that "*interlink related concepts from the domain semantics, expose argumentation structures, add glossary functions or reveal instructional components*" (Miles-Board, 2003a).

What Miles-Board considers *Associative Writing* takes place in what he calls the content regions of the Web page, as opposed to the functional regions (a primary distinction in his classification). Functional regions provide navigation links – such as indexes, menus and navigation bars – exposing the primary structure of the site; they are graphically connoted, strongly structured, and visually recognisable. However, as Miles-Board observes, content regions, where the discourse's structure is articulated and proper *Associative Writing* reifies, remain largely unstructured and graphically poorly connoted. It is based on the linguistic information gathered from the text, on his conceptual categories and on his background knowledge that the reader can predict the discourse connections established by the links. However, in these regions, the discourse's structure as a whole is difficult to perceive, the system has no model to connote the role that each discourse part plays in it.

From the point of view of scholarly hypertext, if we look at the web pages of single scholarly works, their main structure tends to follow the traditional paradigm of linearity. In fact, *Associative Writing* – which especially characterises Web based scholarly work – is performed through four types of links: *structure links* target figures and different document sections; *citation links* target full citation details; *reference links* target pages containing further information about something mentioned in the source page; *glossary links* target kinds of dictionary definitions. None of these plays a role in the structure of the argumentative unit, that is, in contrast to semantic hypertext, these links are not of the explicit type *argument*, *rationale*, *evidence*, and so on. Among them, the link type that seems to have more associative potential is reference, and Miles-Board points out a Web example that makes a quite advanced use of it: the Astronomy Picture of the Day. This NASA site provides a daily abstract, which is expanded through links that target *background* and *elaboration* information to the main content, which in fact seems to reify the approach to hypertext described by Kolb (1997) and Carter (2000), as a way of maintaining the compactness of an hypertext argument in the interactive medium.

4.2. Semantic Hypertext

Another paradigm of discourse in hypertext, and approach to representing discourse coherence, is exemplified by semantic hypertext systems. Early examples (reviewed by Buckingham Shum and Hammond, 1994) included NoteCards (Halasz et al., 1987), gIBIS (Conklin et Begeman, 1988), SEPIA (Streitz et al., 1992) and Aquanet (Marshall et al., 1991), while current examples include Storyspace [22], Compendium (Selvin et al., 2001) and ClaiMaker (Li et al., 2002; Buckingham Shum et al., 2003). In these systems[23], grounded in the research traditions of knowledge representation and less formal concept mapping, hypertext nodes constitute instances of object classes and subclasses, depending on the node's content or function. Like ontological entities in knowledge modelling (Gruber, 1993), these classes are defined by specific properties as well as by properties inherited from classes that are higher in the hierarchy. Hypertext links become ontological relations between objects, and they are constrained by the properties that define the object classes. The relation's semantic content refers to the rhetorical relation holding between the nodes, that is, it describes the rhetorical function that one node has towards the other. The graphical result of a discourse modelling session is a net-like view of text nodes and labelled links, where the text nodes may or may not be characterised by additional visual features, such as icons, colours and fonts.

SEPIA's construction kit (Streitz et al., 1992), for instance, was designed precisely to tackle the problem of discourse coherence in hyperdocuments. It provided the hypertext author with a hierarchy of associated design object classes, defining nodes and links according to their function within the hyperdocument. In addition, it provided the author with a link taxonomy that allowed him to define the argumentative content of the relations established between nodes: *supports*, *contradicts*, *answers*, *justifies*, *criticises*, *rejects*, and so on. In the graphical representation of the hyperdocument network, these definitions appeared as labels marking the arrows connecting the various nodes. Nodes, in turn, were labelled with a short sentence referring to its content, and, depending on how they were classified as hypertext objects, they were attributed different representational features, for instance a different text box shape and a different spatial position. Also, any of the nodes could be opened to gain access to its full textual content. There were not, unfortunately, any user experience reports of SEPIA in real use.

Slightly different was Aquanet (Marshall et al., 1991), which was designed to support semiformal knowledge structuring tasks in a collaborative environment. As with SEPIA, the knowledge network that the system represented was made of basic objects and relational objects, respectively corresponding to hypertext nodes and links. Aquanet objects were made of a set of typed slots: in basic objects, all slot values had to be primitive data types (text, images, strings, etc.), whereas in relations, the slots could have either primitive data types or other Aquanet objects as values – and therefore they constituted structural entities that connected other entities in the structure. At the object level, basic object and relation types specified their own slots and constrained their slot's values; while at the structure level, different schemas defined different sets of allowable basic object and relation types, which could customise knowledge structures depending on the specific task. The graphical representation of these knowledge structures could make use of elements like lines, circles, squares, text labels, background colours, etc. Two different types of layout were possible: a network view and a spatial view; and both layouts allowed the user some degree of manipulation. In the spatial layout, objects appeared as coloured text boxes of different shapes, distributed in the working space and generating manipulable visual configurations.

ClaiMaker (Li et al., 2002; Buckingham Shum et al., 2003, Buckingham Shum et al., 2004) is a semantic hypertext system designed to represent scholarly argumentation by allowing scholars to make claims about the scientific material that they come across and use. The system allows the user to associate concepts with documents and to make connections between those concepts, which constitute linkable nodes. To link concepts, the user is provided with a rich ontology of argumentative relations, consisting of basic categories, further articulated in more specific 'dialect' links with 'user friendly' names (see Chapter 3, § 3.1, and Table 3.3). For instance, the category *supports/challenges* is articulated in links such as *agrees with, disagrees with, is consistent with, is evidence against*, etc. The idea underlying ClaiMaker's link taxonomy is that all scholarly fields make use of the argumentative relations' basic categories, but that within those categories they end up using different relations, constituting the argumentative 'dialect' of the field. On this basis, different communities should also be allowed to adjust the set of relations within the basic categories provided, according to their specific needs. Because ClaiMaker allows different users to associate different concepts to any piece of literature, at any level of granularity, what the system enables them to express are different interpretations and perspectives that develop within the scientific community, grounded in the scholarly literature available. The system can be used to work on digital libraries, generating from them a semantic network in which their fragmented material can be meaningfully connected ('hypertextualised'), also enabling a number of retrieval services (see Figure1.1.).

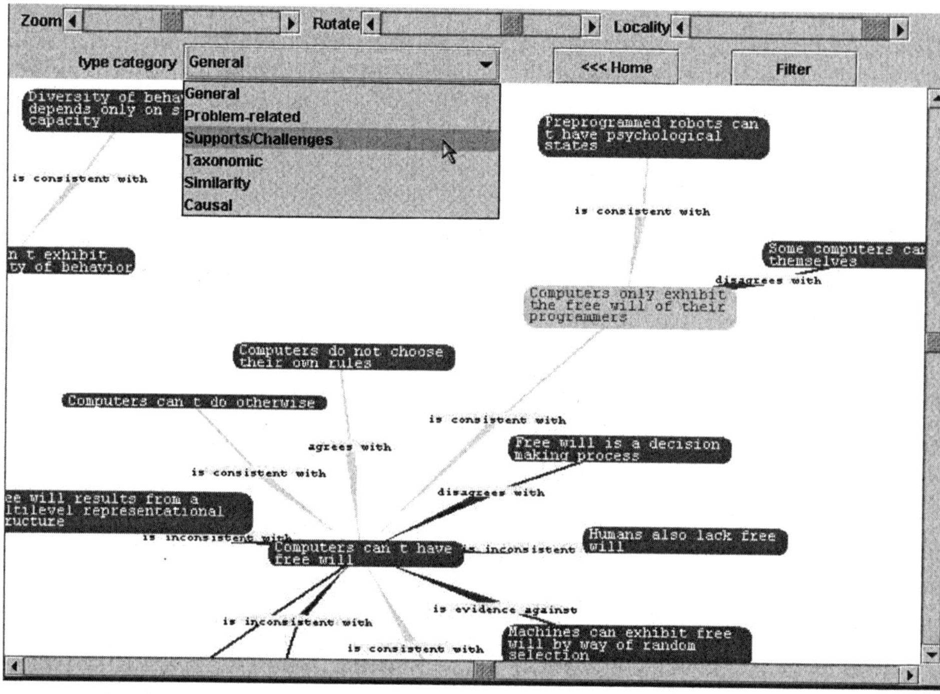

Figure1. 1. Visualisation of literature mapping in ClaiMaker (Buckingham Shum et al., 2003; Buckingham Sum et al., 2004). This example is taken from modelling the Philosophy of AI literature in the Turing debate, converting the large paper argument maps published by Horn (2003) into interactive Web versions.

At present, ClaiMaker is equipped to work mainly on text-based material, such as scientific papers. However, semiotic-aware architectures have been developed that enable one to handle multimedia material at different levels of signification (Nack and Hardman, 2001). Such architectures can potentially be integrated with ClaiMaker to enable it to represent argumentation in scientific fields such as cinematic theory. Other architectures designed for adaptive and dynamic hypermedia presentations (Rutledge and Hardman, 2000; Not and Zancanaro, 2000) can also potentially be integrated in a system like ClaiMaker.

4.3. Spatial Hypertext

A substantially different approach to the problem of coherence is represented by the concept of Spatial Hypertext (Shipman and Marshall, 1999) as exemplified by systems including VIKI (Marshall et al. 1994), HyperMap (Verhoeven and Warendorf, 1999), VKB (Shipman et al., 2001), and most recently Tinderbox (Bernstein, 2003). The idea of spatial hypertext was born from the experience of Aquanet itself and from other similar experiences that the authors had with interactive computer systems (Marshall and Rogers, 1992). They noticed that in the small-scale collaboration contexts in which Aquanet was tested, instead of expressing the connections between different objects by linking them through the use of relations, the users preferred to convey implicit relational structures through the use of spatial layout. That is, it turned out that people were at ease with categorising materials by grouping them, but rarely would they commit to the explicit expression of more complex relationships between objects, since this returned little extra value for the effort required. Instead, they made an individual and personalised use of spatial clues - like the object's position and graphic features - to establish implicit connections. Heuristic algorithms - developed after the analysis of the kind of structures that people were building - could then be used to recognise the resulting spatial structures, such as lists and piles of nodes (Marshall and Shipman, 1993).

Based on the visual/spatial metaphor for hypertext, VIKI was designed to support this method of interacting with information and the "*emergent qualities of structure*". Through the direct manipulation of nodes, it enabled users to create and navigate around objects and entire structures, while graphical features like colour, shape and border width could be used to differentiate nodes (Figure 1.2.).

As in Aquanet, objects were content holding entities, but were defined by slots that, in contrast to Aquanet, could be created as the user encountered and incorporated information that did not fit within the object's existing slots. Objects could be part of collections that could contain any number of objects in any spatial arrangement, and in which hierarchical structures could gradually emerge. As in Aquanet, both objects and collections could be instances of types, but in contrast, there were no inheritance mechanisms, which would be incompatible with the notion of emergent structure. Composites consisted of combinations of two or more objects or collections arranged in particular visual/spatial configurations. Patterns, such as vertical and horizontal lists of objects, objects stacks and composites, were recognised by a spatial parser that assisted the user in retrieval like functions to help consolidate emergent patterns as new, formally recognised structures.

These characteristics made VIKI useful as a tool for the practice of *information triage* for individual use – the interpretation process of sorting and organising materials to meet the requirements of a task (Marshall and Shipman, 1997). However, implicit spatial structures are problematic to understand and to work with when the user of these structures and the person who authored them are not the same. To address this problem, VKB, a second-generation spatial hypertext, provided new functions designed to support collaborative work, as well as those tasks requiring the specification of links. In VKB the graphical capabilities are greater than they are in its predecessor. Objects can contain multimedia materials, as well as URLs, which can be opened by clicking on the object's border. VKB also provides a navigable history, which allows the user to 'rewind' and view the stages of any spatial structure. Three types of navigational links are possible in the system: local, global and historical links. Local links connect an object or a collection to another object, collection or location within a collection of the same spatial hypertext. Global links connect an object within a spatial hypertext to another spatial hypertext. Finally, historical links connect an object within the hypertext to a point/stage in the history of the same hypertext - playing a contextualisation function. However, there is as yet little or no evidence of long-term use or reuse, or interpretation of existing spatial hypertext structures by new readers or authors - implicit structuring essentially remains the main goal of VKB.

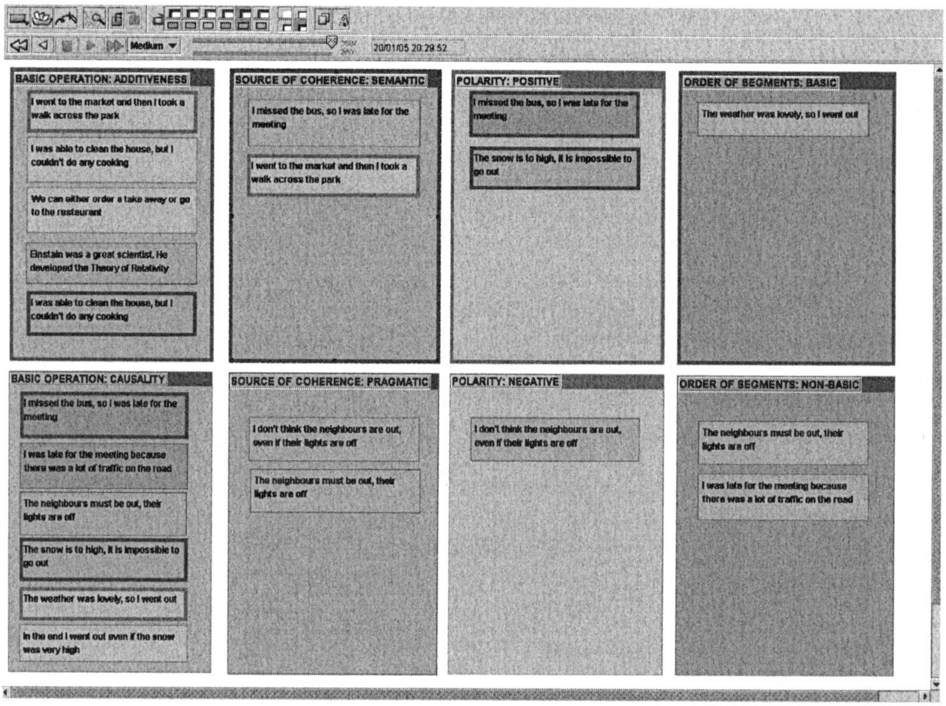

Figure1. 2. Screenshot from VKB, a second generation tool of Spatial Hypertext (Shipman et al., 2001). In this exercise, the tool is used to classify examples of discourse coherence relations.

The same can be said of combinFormation (Kerne et al., 2004), a digital engine that spatially displays the results of web queries by juxtaposing in a compositional space text sentences and images, which constitute hyperlinks to the source documents retrieved during the search. The user can manipulate the resulting *hypersign* collections, by selecting, reformatting and repositioning the *hypersigns* to shape personal compositions, in which multiple meanings are implicitly expressed at multiple levels of signification. This manipulation feeds back into the system new parameters for searching and integrating new *hypersigns* in the user's compositions. With the semantic richness of the image in its dialectic with text, and with a user-friendly mechanism of retrieval and composition, combinFormation does open interesting possibilities for spatial hypertext. However, at present the system does not support formal discourse structuring, its goal being to support the user's personal expression in order to promote individual creative processes of information discovery.

5. Advantages and Disadvantages of Three Different Approaches

To summarise, as we have seen, page-based hypertext, semantic hypertext and spatial hypertext are differentiated from one another by essential characteristics. Page-based hypertext's paradigm is the page-by-page presentation, in which structure is only suggested in functional regions through the spatial and graphical characteristics of the links, while in content regions links may be linguistically indicated or denoted, but do not provide any information about the hypertext structure. Semantic hypertext can be represented as a network of objects and connections, whose relations are defined and whose structure appears very clearly articulated. Spatial hypertext can be visualised as a configuration of graphically connoted objects, between which relations must be inferred using background knowledge not in the representation.

In page-based hypertext, even if linguistic signs suggest or even describe what the target page will present, the semantics of the relation itself is never explicitly defined. In semantic hypertext the relation between connected objects is always semantically defined and very often known by the reader - and often labelled. In spatial hypertext relations are implicit and no commitment to structure is required from the user. In page-based hypertext, even if certain sites may be programmed so that more windows open up at the same time, pages are not configured to work systematically in juxtaposition. In semantic hypertext this may or may not be the case, but in any case the articulation of nodes is visible on a map. In spatial hypertext the juxtaposition of individual objects in the visual field is the main modality of information organisation.

Finally, in page-based hypertext, connections are established anchor-to-node, which means that it is a specific and contextualised element of the source page to be linked to the target page, and not the source page as a whole, which in turn has implications for the specificity of the relation. In both semantic and spatial hypertext, connections are established node-to-node, that is, nodes are connected to one another as a whole.

The characteristics of page-based hypertext offer scholars a number of advantages. First of all, out of the three paradigms described above, this is the closest to the traditional form of argumentative writing, which – as we have previously seen – is still very dear to scholars. In contrast to traditional writing, Web based hypertext adds the potential for great flexibility in mediating between linearity and connectivity, to reflect exactly the "connective thinking" that characterises scholarly work. Moreover, creating links does not necessarily require committing to any relational semantics, which may be undesirable to some users. Linking and link representation conventions have instead developed over time to give functional links semantic connotations, but they constitute the only form of structure representation normally found in Web based hypertext.

These conventions provide little or no information about the discourse structure itself, and we have seen how, in content regions, *Associative Writing* does not make use of very structural connection types, whereas the structure that is exposed in functional regions has more to do with the organization of the document's material than with the discourse structure itself. In other words, page-based hypertext constitutes a flexible paradigm for discourse presentation, when the discourse's development tends to be linear. However this kind of hypertext does not effectively support the representation of non-linear discourse structures, that is, the Web does not yet offer tools to shape non-linear argumentative discourse. One could argue that providing tools to shape non-linear argumentative discourse is not needed, since the discourse's structure ends up being often linear any way, but if there were ways of structuring discourse in a recognisable manner, then Web discourse structure could become less linear and more hypertextual. If there were tools supporting hypertext discourse structuring on the Web, people could gradually develop the literacy that they need to take advantage of the functionalities offered by them, and of the potentiality of the Web's associativeness[24].

In this respect, semantic hypertext and spatial hypertext constitute more effective paradigms, even though they are not yet as flexible and easy to work with as page-based hypertext is. With respect to each other, however, they give very different answers to the need for discourse shaping in a non-linear medium. They both tackle two fundamental aspects of discourse representation: the expression of discourse connections and the construction of global structure. But they do it in very different ways: the former explicitly defines hypertext nodes connections as rhetorical relations, while the latter uses visual and spatial clues to implicitly suggest the existence of relations between nodes, with system support for incremental formalization towards more explicitly semantic structures; the former represents the discourse process in terms of 'moves' within an ontologically constrained network, while the latter supports the representation of emerging structure through visual and spatial features – the emergent design of the ontology.

Both approaches have advantages and disadvantages. The fact that in systems like SEPIA, Aquanet and ClaiMaker the semantic content of relations is explicitly defined and labelled, makes the relations themselves immediately intelligible, which ensures that they will be interpreted in the way the author wants the reader to interpret them. Moreover, the ontological definition of nodes and links as specific rhetorical relations and objects allows the representation of the discourse structure as a network, where all discourse components can be visualised all at once in an isomorphic configuration (or filtered, searched and re-presented in different ways by the system, which has a relatively fine-grained access to the 'semantics' of the structure). In this way the linear order of the argument turns into a visible layout where everything is there for the reader to see: through structure the author uncovers the process of his thinking; he displays his logical thread openly and directly, without leaving any ambiguities to the reader's interpretation.

This approach certainly allows the author to achieve a very clear representation of his argument, which helps the reader to construct a coherent mental representation of its content (van Gelder, 2003). However, by making the structure of his discourse explicit, the author does not necessarily bring the reader to embrace his 'vision'. That is, when discourse relations are outlined and explicitly defined, the reader gains access to the argument's structure all at once instead of just going through it step by step; he is allowed to access any of its parts in no particular order instead of having to go through its stages in a specific order. As we have seen, though, argumentation is based on the possibility of regulating the delivery of discourse contents to minimise the impact on the reader to lead him to the author's perspective, and not to just acknowledge his rationale. In traditional argumentation, that is, the author follows a gradual construction process, taking the reader on a journey whose goal is the achievement of a vision. If everything is explicitly structured and is made accessible in no particular order, such a process tends to turn into an acknowledgment exercise instead, while the vision tends to become a given rather than a goal[25]. As we have seen, Kolb (1995), Ess (1996) and Brent (1997) underline the importance of delivering information in a certain order - and not all at once – for the effectiveness of an argument, since the information that the reader accesses first sets the ground to receive the information that comes next. Similarly, in literature or in film, each paragraph or scene determines the way the next paragraph or scene will be interpreted, according to narrative strategies whose function is to lead the reader or viewer along a discovery path, to the final goal (Genette, 1972; Gardies, 1984). All traditional forms of narrative rely on information delivery strategies based on 'dosing' the amount of information that is made accessible at any given point, in order to successfully reach that final goal. In this respect, argumentation has a lot in common with narrative (literary or cinematic) text.

In fact, argument-modelling systems that make discourse relations and/or structure explicit are probably more suitable in phases of analysis or retrieval than in the phase of reading. They are very useful to represent an argument's structure for it to be understood as the result of an interpretation process that has already taken place. However, when the semantic network is used to generate automatic presentations, as in dynamic and adaptive hypermedia, the network's structure tends to turn into a linear or multi-linear sequence whose interactivity is limited on the basis of the designer's predefined criteria and whose underlying ontology cannot either be accessed or manipulated. A hypertext system for argument presentation - that is, an environment designed to assist the reading of hypertext arguments - could facilitate the understanding of the argument's content through shaping discourse relations and global structure, without necessarily having to make them univocally explicit (initially, at least)[26]. At the same time, though, whatever semantics and criteria were used to shape discourse structure, these could become accessible at some point, to allow the reader to take a step back, analyse what he has been reading, and maybe archive and reuse parts of it (activities that require visibility and manipulability).

This is partly the stance taken by spatial hypertext, where relations between nodes are marked - but not explicitly described - by spatial proximity and/or by visual features such as colour, shape, size, etc. This way discourse relations and discourse global structure are not put forward as a given, rather the reader is able to go through his own interpretation process and make his own interpretative choices. The emergence and the recognition of coherence is facilitated by a number of formal elements, however these elements do not constitute formalities committing node relations and discourse structure to any explicit semantics. That is, spatial distribution, colours, shapes, etc. provide a sense of differentiation and structure (as sense of syntax) but do not have predetermined meaning and can therefore be interpreted in different ways. At the same time, different users are also allowed to manipulate the formal features of each node in the discourse space.

This approach is particularly interesting in that it appeals to what characterises hypertext as a visual and spatial medium (Tolva, 1996), relying on visual clues as elements of discourse coherence, and therefore suggesting that hypertext could develop some form of visual language to shape argumentative discourse. However, the problem with this approach is that in the absence of predetermined semantics underlying the use of spatial and visual features, or rigorous criteria regulating the use of such features, their recurrence is not necessarily consistent. Visual shape is based on regularities and regularities require consistency to emerge. In other words, without consistency there is no language with which to shape discourse.

Another limitation of spatial hypertext for presenting arguments (or indeed any information) is that visual features are attributed to nodes on the basis of their content, and not on the basis of the role that nodes play as discourse elements. This aspect of spatial hypertext fails to represent one of the main characteristics of hypertext discourse: the multiplicity of roles that any one node plays within the whole of the discourse structure. In this kind of hypertext, the visual characteristics of an object, as well as its spatial position, tend to be defined as an 'absolute' (Rosenberg, 2002), which does not take into account the fact that any object is always part of - and occupies a position within - a context. This context is potentially determined by the set of the object's connections to other objects, and it is actualised by those connections, which are activated during each reading journey. But in order to represent discourse units as contextually grounded elements, rather than as absolutes, that is, in order to introduce conditional behaviour (as Rosenberg calls it), spatial hypertext needs to be extended with systematic presentation constraints, which would define a new intermediate form of hypertext between the semantic and spatial paradigms.

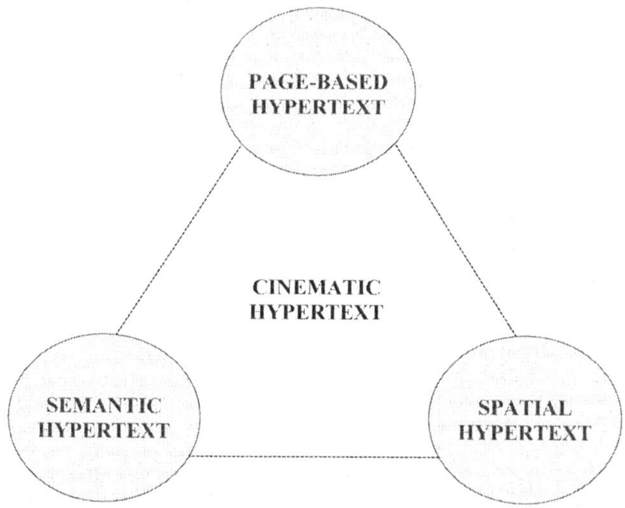

Figure 1.3. The three paradigms of hypertext to represent coherence: page-based hypertext, semantic hypertext and spatial hypertext. 'Cinematic' hypertext constitutes a fourth way to express coherence in hypertext, a hybrid which integrates characteristics of all the others.

6. Towards a Conception of 'Cinematic Hypertext'

Thus far, we have looked at the three most representative paradigms of hypertext and have seen how, from the point of view of scholarly hypertext, all three are characterised by interesting features. In this section we present Cinematic Hypertext, a fourth paradigm which integrates the ones described above, and in which their most interesting characteristics are combined to enable the implicit communication to readers of an argument's structure, based on principles that underpin cinematic language (Figure 1.3.). The objective is to achieve a definition of hypertext in which Associative Writing could be supported by tools that allow authors to increase the associativeness of their texts, in which the features of the medium could be more fully exploited and become elements of signification, and in which the connection between discourse parts could be expressed consistently but without requiring the author to commit to fine-grained ontologies of the sort reviewed above.

Page-based hypertext allows scholars to express connectivity in the most natural way, simply linking an anchor within a page to another page. In this way, the author can maintain the linearity of the discourse and, at the same time, create subtle kinds of connections at the finest granularity if they wish. Authoring environments like Storyspace allow the user to create and link nodes very easily, and even to make the availability of links dependent on the user's previous navigation, in the style of adaptive hypertext. It also offers users the possibility of navigating or authoring at the level of the single page, as well as at the level of the hypertext map. However, the hypertext map in Storyspace does not enable the author to express anything about the structure of the discourse, in the transitions between nodes at the moment of navigation. In other words, the system does not offer a language for associative writing, nor does it offer the author the possibility of forging one of his own.

Interestingly enough, an old system like Hypercard[27] offered a wide range of features that could be used to connote the transitions between nodes. Although this characteristic was not retained in the general development of hypertext authoring tools[28]. However, formal features in themselves do not constitute a language: if, together with the formal features, no criteria are offered to support their consistent and congruent use, at best they will only work as decorative elements, and at the worst they will generate disorientation and confusion (as, for instance, unprincipled use of fonts). Eventually they will be eliminated from the system and the users will not even notice or will be relieved.

The approach taken by semantic hypertext is the opposite: structuring criteria grounded in a formal ontology define hypertext connections explicitly and unambiguously, making the use of extra features simply superfluous. And the limitations of this approach for certain forms of sense-making analysis led to spatial hypertext, to free users from the need to commit to those semantics. With systems like VKB, spatial hypertext brings back the use of visual and spatial features as an alternative to link taxonomies, exactly because visual and spatial features support the expression of implicit relations and structure. However, we have seen the limitations of this approach and even those who most strongly support the cause of spatial hypertext are starting to realise that there could be another way.

Among them, Rosenberg - a strong advocate of implicit and emergent structure - has acknowledged that spatial hypertext would benefit from the adoption of structuring and representational rules. In his last essay on this subject, he recognises: "*It seems wrong to 'prohibit' agent rules from spatial hypertext due to an 'ideology' of implicit structure*" (Rosenberg, 2002). On the other hand, Rosenberg considers structuring rules even more committing than explicit structure, which makes their adoption appear like a substantial deviation from spatial hypertext's original 'vocation' to support activities where the declaration of explicit structure was intrusive. Clearly, when applying a structuring rule, one commits to some representational modality[29], but such rules become the 'raw material' with which one works in creative design. It would be as though one claimed that observing certain rules or codes in painting, dance, poetry, cinematography, etc., commits the artist to any structure. In fact, these rules and codes are at the service of his very expression; they simply make the creation of any complex and intelligible shape possible.

In other words, rules support the emergence of structure, but do not determine its final configuration, even though they obviously constrain it: it is the content of a work session that produces the final configuration of any structure. Nor is it necessarily the case that structuring rules make the resulting structure explicit, as opposed to implicit. They make it recognisable as a result, but it is a presentational design decision as to whether these rules are then made explicit to the end-user. That is, a structure emerging from a spatial hypertext session that follows certain representational modalities can be recognisable, and the reader may even be able to infer what it is meant to represent (particularly if it matches a pattern that has come to serve as an agreed template)[30]. However, for it to become explicit, the semantics codified by the rules must be explicitly disclosed to the reader in the user interface, as happens in semantic hypertext where relations are explicitly labelled through the use of natural language.

To summarise, it is true that rules that constrain the development of structure require a certain measure of commitment from the writer: without any constraints at all, a medium can hardly convey intelligible shape and what it conveys ends up being unreadable. The writer can of course bend or violate any conventional constraints and create shape, but without initial boundary lines, there is no space for creativity. However, in the context of hypertextual argumentation there are ways in which the commitment to structural constraints can be kept to a minimum.

6.1. Relational Primitives

First of all, these rules could be set to express very general relationships, that is, fundamental principles of discourse organisation that are as universal as possible, and therefore shared by many forms of discourse. These relations could be applied at the content level (if referred to the relation holding between two nodes' content - *semantic*) and/or at a discourse level (if referring to the relation holding between two nodes' rhetorical function - *pragmatic*). Rosenberg, for instance, indicates one of those principles as the *conjunction-disjunction* dichotomy (2001), which he applies at a discourse level. However, other principles can be identified as well, and indeed one purposes of this work is to identify these.

6.2. Role-Based Rendering of Nodes

Second, basing structure-conditioning rules on relational principles rather than on taxonomical principles, that is, shaping discourse based on relations rather than based on content, has the advantage that no nodes would be shaped once for all for what they contain, but their appearance would change depending on how they are related to other nodes. For instance, if the links along a certain path X are activated, and a particular node A finds itself in a specific position along that path, it is interpreted in the light of the nodes that come before it. It in turn conditions the interpretation of the nodes that follow it. In other words, the node A plays a specific role within that specific path, and it would be in playing that specific role that it would be attributed certain visual features, according to predefined representational parameters. However, if the links along a different path Y are activated, A finds itself in a specific position along another specific path, where it plays another role, which would be represented by the attribution of different visual features.

6.3. Temporality

The use of relational structuring principles has a third important consequence for spatial hypertext. As Rosenberg points out, conditional rules introduce in spatial hypertext the dimension of time, and therefore they reintroduce discourse order. That is, if I establish a rule according to which an action applied to an object (node) has as a consequence the modification of another object or even of a group of objects (a group of nodes), then I have established a *sequentiality* and therefore a *temporality*, according to which the discourse structure is going to be represented and/or modified. In turn, temporality opens the door to a development in the visual and spatial representation of objects, that is, it sets the ground for the dynamic representation of objects: *animation*. In other words, in order for the transformation operating on objects through conditional rules to be represented, the visual features characterising the objects need to be transformable themselves, so they become dynamic attributes. Such a change in spatial hypertext would enrich its expressive capabilities to a much greater extent, responding to the potential *affordances*[31] of the medium much more than it presently does, and it would exploit more fully the technical characteristics of the medium. Finally, it would allow hypertext authors to achieve a better representation of their discourse as a process rather than as a structure.

***

In brief, the proposed approach to rendering could offer a number of advantages. Discourse relations and structure would still be shaped through visual and spatial features, so that they would still remain implicit for the reader to recognise and interpret them. However structure would emerge based on relations rather than based on node content, so that the multiplicity of roles played by hypertext nodes within the network would be reflected in the formal changes that they would undergo during navigation. The use of primitive discourse relations as structuring principles would require a minimum commitment, while still leaving room for further and more specific interpretation (both by the writer and the reader in turn). Discourse structure would not end up being a global and static representation of the hypertext network[32], rather it would be represented as a dynamic entity activated locally by the reader's interaction. Finally, such dynamic representation could more fully take advantage of the visual and spatial characteristics of the medium, increasing spatial hypertext's ability to express the discourse's process[33].

This kind of hypertext could be constructed in user-friendly authoring environments, where writers could create their nodes and link them together as they are used to do, with the difference that they could differentiate the links that they create through the use of visual and spatial features whose consistent and congruent use would be supported, and therefore easy to maintain. If the conditional rules that they are allowed to work with are general enough and can even be broken when the author needs or wishes it, they would not demand a commitment to any specific semantics, allowing writers to be the creators not only of their hypertexts, but of the very languages in which they create them.

Thus far, the problem has been viewed through the lens of hypertext system paradigms. In the chapters that follow, theoretical and empirical research into diverse aspects of coherence are reviewed and discussed, to then deepen the exploration of design issues. This work is intended for hypertext readers and producers, as well as analysts, because it proposes a way of thinking hypertext as a medium. The concept of Cinematic Hypertext is presented from its theoretical ground to a first set of design guidelines, to the definition of a prototype language and its first evaluation. The work specifies the requirements for a cinematic hypertext environment, however, no implemented system is presented: the development of such editor will be future work that can build on the results of this investigation. Here the main goal is the exploration and the proposal of a new approach to the electronic medium.

7. Overview of Chapters

Following the perspective introduced above, the next seven chapters of this book explore the different aspects involved in the conception of a hypertext environment where the articulation of discourse structure would be regulated by basic relational principles and discourse relations would be rendered by visual and spatial features, exploiting more fully the inherent technical characteristics of the hypertext medium, which - it is argued - shares much in common with cinema.

2. Hypertext Coherence as Text Coherence. This chapter clarifies why the semiotic characteristics of natural language make it a very effective medium for conveying complex, abstract thinking, such that written text ends up constituting the backbone of scholarly hypertext argumentation, whether or not it is complemented by other media such as graphics, photography, film, sound, etc. Moving from this assumption, this chapter looks at the issue of discourse coherence in text, approaching the problem from a cognitive perspective and exploring related theories. These theories conceive text as a hierarchical structure made of spans whose content is related through basic cognitive concepts. Whilst theoreticians have not agreed on a specific set of relational concepts yet, nevertheless a number of fundamental relations - such as causality or additiveness - are universally accounted for. In the chapter it is proposed that these primitive relational concepts could be used in hypertext as principles of discourse articulation, that is, as principles to define representational conditional rules.

3. Applying Discourse Coherence Relations to Hypertext. Following the idea of using a particular approach called Cognitive Coherence Relations (CCR) to define representational conditional rules in hypertext, this chapter tries to account for argumentation link types in terms of cognitive coherence relations. Examples of link taxonomies from two semantic hypertext argumentation systems are analysed and mapped onto cognitive coherence relations, which brings interesting insights into the way these taxonomies could be composed and organised, and ultimately into the nature of the link types that they use. Subsequently, an example of a scholarly hypertext is analysed and its links are described in terms of cognitive coherence relations, whose application constitutes a CCR-based verification of the author's theoretical approach to structuring argument in hypertext.

4. Hypertext Coherence as 'Cinematic' Coherence. In this chapter the use of visual and spatial features in hypertext discourse is discussed from a cinematic perspective. Among the different theoretical frameworks that throughout the years have been used to analyse the hypertext medium, it is proposed that cinematic theory seems to best account for its linguistic potentialities. Therefore, theoretical work relating the cinematic approach to hypertext is presented and, based on the parallel between hypertext nodes and links on the one hand, and cinematic shots and edits on the other, the connection between cinema and hypertext is analysed in detail. Elements of cinematic theory are presented and a conventional set of cinematic rhetorical patterns is described. Based on the connection between cinema and hypertext, it is suggested that the way in which cinematic language rhetorical connections are signalled provides insights into the way, in turn, that hypertext could use visual and spatial features to mark discourse coherence relations and shape recognisable rhetorical patterns.

5. Applying Discourse Coherence Relations to Cinema. If coherence relations are a cognitive phenomenon, they should constitute a principle of discourse coherence not just in text, but in other media too, at least in those in which discourse is generated through the connection of discrete discourse units, as happens in cinema. Moving from this assumption, in this chapter the same cinematic patterns previously described are analysed in terms of cognitive coherence relations (mirroring the analysis in chapter 3 with link taxonomies). Following this, two cinematic sequences are taken as examples to be analysed in terms of coherence relations, interpreting the shot connections that the sequence's visual elements lead the viewer to make. The purpose of this exercise is to motivate the idea that hypertext discourse could be shaped in the same way as cinematic discourse is shaped, because transitions in both media can be expressed using coherence relations.

6. Visual Languages to Render Coherence Relations. The previous chapters tackled the issue of coherence in text and in a visual medium (cinema) that has many similarities to hypertext. In this chapter the connections between text discourse processing and visual discourse processing are presented and analysed. It is shown how certain principles of text cohesion have an equivalent in the principles of visual cohesion long established by Gestalt Theory. Therefore, it should be possible to 'translate' cohesive aspects or elements of textual coherence into graphic terms. With the objective of producing in hypertext a cohesive visual representation of coherence relations, this chapter also presents elements of semiology of graphics, which are then subsequently applied to designing discourse relations in hypertext.

7. Rendering Discourse Relations with Graphics and Animation. In this chapter the principles of visual perception and the variables of graphics presented in the previous chapter guide the design process of rendering cognitive coherence relational concepts through animated visualisations, for experimental purposes. A set of eight more basic and commonly acknowledged relations is selected to be graphically rendered, and its selection is motivated. The set comprises: causality, conditionality, conjunctiveness, disjunctiveness, similarity, contrast, elaboration and background relations. To render these relations, a minimum number of graphic variables is used, in order to keep any visual 'noise' as low as possible and to enhance the distinctiveness of the resulting representations: eight animated relational patterns.

8. Evaluating 'Cinematic' Discourse Relations: Empirical Study. This chapter describes and reports the results of the first empirical study designed to evaluate the expressiveness and effectiveness of the relational animated configurations whose design process was presented in the previous chapter. The methodology followed in the study, the experimental materials and the sample of the participants are presented, and the results of the test are analysed - quantitatively and qualitatively - from different perspectives. The limitations of the study are also discussed and possible improvements for future tests are suggested. Overall the results appear to be quite promising and motivate the continuation of this kind of research with further theoretical investigation, new empirical studies, and software support, described in the conclusive chapter.

9. The Form of Coherence in Hypertext Discourse: a Proposal. This final chapter retraces the steps that this work has taken towards the idea of 'cinematic hypertext', and it summarises the contributions that this work brings to the study of hypertext discourse and of the hypertext medium. It also discusses further steps that could be taken, both in terms of theoretical and empirical work, to advance further to the implementation of an environment for authoring. A functional specification is proposed that describes how a 'cinematic hypertext' system could work, and following that, how it could support the work of both scholars and students in the different situations in which argumentation is involved. Finally, the journey concludes with a reflection on the evolution of the language of visual media and on the possible evolution of hypertext's language.

Notes

[1] Hypertext authors can be found on sites such as the Electronic Literature Organization (www.eliterature.org) and Eastgate Publishing (www.eastgate.com).

[2] That is, where discourse parts (text spans or sections) are simply juxtaposed, without the use of connective devices.

[3] http://www.microsoft.com/products/encarta

[4] http://www.columbia.edu/cu/cup/cee/cee.html

[5] http://d3e.sourceforge.net

[6] http://www.openarchives.org

[7] http://opcit.eprints.org

[8] http://www.neci.nec.com/homepages/lawrence/citeseer.html

[9] http://www.ucalgary.ca/ejournal

[10] http://jodi.ecs.soton.ac.uk

[11] Let us distinguish between hypertext and hypertextuality. If *hypertext* is the medium, the concrete form which can only work in an interactive medium, *hypertextuality* we is a quality that any form of text (literary, film, etc.) may possess to different degrees. It is the possibility of reading paths or patterns that cross the linear or sequential distribution of text contents. Although a book or a movie is potentially hypertextual, due to the technical characteristics of the medium, hypertextuality finds itself reified only in interactive hypertext. A hypertext's hypertextuality is proportional to its interactivity, that is, to the freedom that the readers have to reify the hypertextuality of the text and to 'perform' hypertextual thinking (Mancini and Buckingham Shum, 2001, Mancini, 2003).

[12] Buckingham Shum (2003) shows how in fact already Nelson and Engelbart were particularly concerned with the arguments in hypertext.

[13] Here Carter cites Kinneavy's definitions (1980).

[14] Any new medium, in its early stages, encounters the inertia of people's cultural and behavioural models, which often blind them to the new possibilities introduced by it. If this has not been much the case with informative, literary and expressive hypertext, it has been the case for argumentation.

[15] However, they are relevant in that they show how the presentation of an argument is important for its effectiveness. Memorising the argument allows the speaker to present it in a seemingly spontaneous way, as if thoughts were naturally coming to his mind, instead of having been searched and organised with the purpose of persuading other people. Also, memorising allows the speaker to 'dramatise' his argument and look for an emotional contact with the listener that goes beyond rationality, so that the listener ends up adhering to the speaker's vision, not only because the contents of the argument and its logic are good, but also because its presentation is involving.

[16] For clarity of argument, concepts that are more extensively explored in chapter 2 are anticipated here.

[17] In paratactic construction, discourse parts are simply juxtaposed and the relation holding between them is only established based on the text's content.

[18] Unless, of course, one resorts to constrained paths, but the more constrained is the order of navigation, the less hypertextual is hypertext.

[19] With information retrieval alone there are different problems, having more to do with the possibility of finding information, and therefore entailing issues of 'information management', rather than issues of discourse coherence.

[20] This is an assumption on which the work of hypertext writers like Michael Joyce is based on (see Walker, 1999).

[21] In fact, HTML derives from SGML, a mark-up language for traditional documents.

[22] http://www.eastgate.com/Storyspace.html

[23] An historical review of argument mapping systems is given by Buckingham Shum (2003), tracing their lineage back to the hypertext pioneers Vannevar Bush and Doug Engelbart.

[24] We would like to suggest that the more links articulate the essential components of an argument, the greater their associative strength - but this seems to be a direction in which scholarly Web based hypertext still has to develop.

[25] It is true that in most hypertext systems, as content increases, it becomes impossible to present it all at once and therefore it has to be presented gradually, with some sequentiality. However, unless the order of presentation is predefined, it is much harder for the author to plan any journeys for the user. It is analogous to when a visitor is provided a topographic map, where every bit if information concerning the territory that he is about to explore is exactly codified through graphical signs and all the codification keys are provided in the legend at the bottom.

This kind of representation contrasts with the node-by-node presentation provided on most of the Web, or simply on paper. And in fact, Halasz defined systems such as gIBIS and NoteCards as systems where the map level browser is the primary view and mode of interaction: "*A second class of 'navigational' applications are the display-oriented representation tasks in which the network is centered around a single display, usually a browser, used to represent a structure being designed or studied. The goal of these tasks is to create and manipulate this display. In some sense, the network is secondary to the display and is used only to create the structure to be displayed and to "hide" unimportant details. In these tasks, information access occurs through the central display, with little direct card-to-card navigation.*" (Halasz, 1987).

[26] Natural language – which unlike other languages is the backbone of scholarly argumentation – provides a good model for argumentation presentation in hypertext. In natural language, discourse relations are marked by connectives, however normally they are not explicitly defined unless language is used in a descriptive or in an analytic way. For instance, in the sentence "*I went out with my umbrella because it was raining*", the connection between the two discourse parts is established by the connective "*because*", which marks – but does not explicitly describe the content of – a causal relation. However, if I was to analyse or describe the behaviour of the sentence's subject, I could say that "*the fact that it was raining caused her to go out with her umbrella*". (Chapter 2 describes research on text coherence in detail).

[27] http://www.wired.com/news/mac/0,2125,54365,00.html

[28] Interestingly some Web browsers are starting to offer page transition effects, such as those described at PageResource.Com: http://pageresource.com/dhtml/jdex5.htm.

[29] By representational modalities we refer to the formal features that could be used in hypertext systems to represent hypertext discourse components like nodes and links: colour, shape, size, spatial distribution, text format, etc. That is, the way the features defining the perceivable form of hypertext objects can be used to represent the discourse that they convey.

[30] In the analysis of cinematic language (Chapter 4) the establishing of local consistent visual devices turns out to be a key principle, which underpins the notion of cinematic hypertext.

[31] Defined by Gibson in the field of psychology of perception (Gibson, 1977; 1979), the concept of 'affordances' refers to the opportunities for action that an object offers to a subject. Expressing the relationship of the subject with the object, affordances are defined by the combination of the physical characteristics and capabilities of the subject and the characteristics and capabilities of the object. For psychological and cultural reasons, usually a subject only perceives a small part of all possible affordances offered by an object, which ends up restricting their action. The concept of affordences has been adopted since by other research fields, included educational technology (see Gaver, 1991; Laurillard et al., 2000).

[32] Because any part of the network, any hypertext node, would be represented in relation to its immediate neighbours and based on how (that is, from where) the reader encounters it.

[33] Of course this kind of representation and presentation of argumentative hypertext content could be complemented by the map-level representation and presentation that Halasz talks about (Halasz, 1987). Such representation could be made accessible in 'analysis' mode, as opposed to 'reading' mode.

Cinematic Hypertext
C. Mancini
IOS Press, 2005

2. Hypertext Coherence as Text Coherence

This chapter clarifies why the semiotic characteristics of natural language make it a very effective medium for conveying complex, abstract thinking, such that written text ends up constituting the backbone of scholarly hypertext argumentation, whether or not it is complemented by other media such as graphics, photography, film, sound, etc. Moving from this assumption, this chapter looks at the issue of discourse coherence in text, approaching the problem from a cognitive perspective and exploring related theories. These theories conceive text as a hierarchical structure made of spans whose content is related through basic cognitive concepts. Whilst theoreticians have not agreed on a specific set of relational concepts yet, nevertheless a number of fundamental relations - such as causality or additiveness - are universally accounted for. In the chapter it is proposed that these primitive relational concepts could be used in hypertext as principles of discourse articulation, that is, as principles to define representational conditional rules.

1. Coherence and Cohesion in Text: Definitions

The research and discussion on discourse coherence and cohesion has a long and well established tradition as far as text is concerned, and over time the question has been looked at from various perspectives. The notion of cohesion was first defined by Halliday and Hasan's *Cohesion in English*, back in 1976, and was accepted by the scientific community on that common ground since. The notion of coherence, however, has always been less defined and more controversial, and only in the two past decades has this concept become the focus of linguists' attention, pioneered by Fritz in 1982. However, nowadays, there is still not a definition or a theory of coherence that is generally accepted (Bublitz, 1999).

As previously anticipated (Chapter 1), from a cognitive perspective, text comprehension implies the construction of a coherent mental representation of the conceptual content conveyed by the text. The notion of coherence refers to the relationships between and among the concepts that constitute this representation. These relationships are formally represented by a number of linguistic indicators - like cue phrases and *deictics*[1] - which determine the *cohesion* of the text (Louwerse, 2001)[2]. While these indicators facilitate the recognition of conceptual relationships and therefore the construction of a mental representation, they do not generate *coherence* in themselves, and in fact the construction of a coherent mental representation would be possible even in the absence of any cohesion elements (Mann and Thompson, 1988; Sander et al., 1993; Knott and Dale, 1994)[3]. That is, the absence of connectives in the text would not prevent the construction of a coherent mental representation, if the content of the related spans allowed it.

To use Sanders and Spooren's words (2001), a constituting characteristic of texts is that they show connectedness, and coherence accounts for this connectedness, as a characteristic of the mental representation rather than of the text itself. Texts can present two types of coherence: *referential*, where discourse units are connected by reference to the same entity, and *relational*, where discourse units are connected by logical relations. Both referential and relational coherence are conveyed by linguistic indicators: *anaphoric* devices [4] indicate referential coherence, while *connectives* [5] indicate relational coherence. These indicators work as processing instructors (Givon, 1995) and evidence of their cohesive function is provided by a number of cognitive experiments that showed how the use of these indicators facilitates text processing (Sanders and Noordman, 2000).

Bublitz (1999) stresses the fact that, in contrast to *cohesion* (formally expressed), *coherence* is not given in a text independently from an interpretation and it is therefore based on additional information provided by the linguistic context, the socio-cultural environment, the interpreter's encyclopaedic knowledge. Also, coherence is not a state, but a process, in that it needs to be continuously checked against new information that the interpreter might gain access to and that may make it necessary to adapt the mental representation previously constructed. Finally, coherence is a cooperative achievement as it depends on both the speaker/writer and the hearer/reader, and on their willingness to negotiate coherence.

A last important aspect of cohesion and coherence is that they can be found at a local level, between adjacent clauses, as well as a global level, between groups of clauses. As we will see at the end of this chapter, this is very relevant to tackling the problem of coherence and cohesion in hypertext, since the possibility of defining cohesion at a global level constitutes the ground for the application of text coherence and cohesion theories to the hypertext's interactive network[6].

2. Different Approaches to Text Coherence

As introduced above, the question of discourse coherence has been studied from different perspectives and using different methods. Some studies are based on the analysis of linguistic indicators, that is, cohesive devices (Halliday and Hasan, 1976; Martin, 1992; Knott and Dale, 1994 - data driven, to use Louwerse's words). Other studies are based on the observation of underlying connective concepts, that is, coherence relations (Hobbs, 1985; Mann and Thompson, 1988; Sanders et al., 1993 - theory driven). In all of them, the study of discourse cohesion and coherence focuses on the study of discourse relations.

2.1. Relations as Hierarchic Connectors

Mann and Thompson's Rhetorical Structure Theory (RST) (Mann and Thompson, 1988) has been one of the most cited and applied in the field of computational linguistics and natural language generation. This is an analytical framework, applicable to written monologue, which allows an analyst to describe rhetorical relations between text spans in functional terms, and to identify the text's hierarchical structure. Within this framework, that is, each span of text is analysed in terms of the relation that it holds with other spans of text. Each pair of related spans constitutes a schema, where one of the spans plays the role of the nucleus and the other plays the role of the satellite. The structure of an entire text is defined in terms of the composition of schemas applications, which implies not only that relations can hold between sentences, but that the same relations can also hold between larger segments of text (see Figure 2.1.).

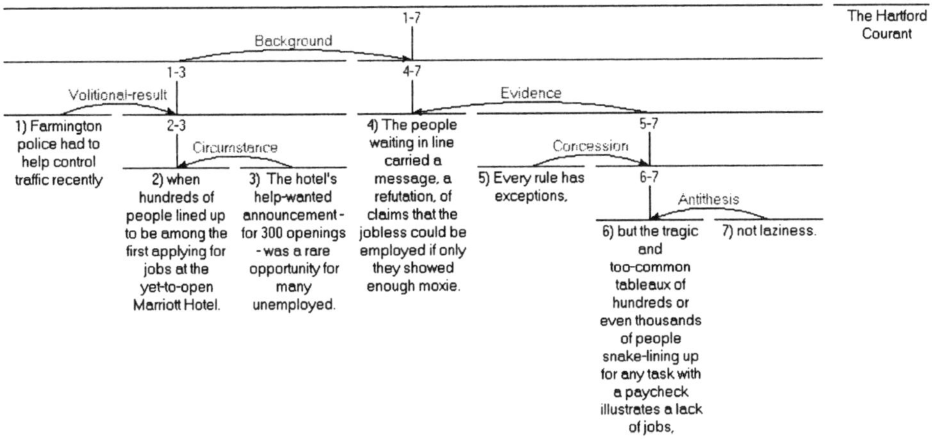

Figure 2.1. The example above is the structural map of the following text according to Rhetorical Structure Theory. Six relations are holding together the seven spans that make up the text, connecting to each other either single clauses or larger sections.

From *The Hartford Courant* (http://www.sil.org/~mannb/rst/unlazy/framer.htm).

1) Farmington police had to help control traffic recently 2) when hundreds of people lined up to be among the first applying for jobs at the yet-to-open Marriott Hotel. 3) The hotel's help-wanted announcement - for 300 openings - was a rare opportunity for many unemployed. 4) The people waiting in line carried a message, a refutation, of claims that the jobless could be employed if only they showed enough moxie. 5) Every rule has exceptions, 6) but the tragic and too-common tableaux of hundreds or even thousands of people snake-lining up for any task with a paycheck illustrates a lack of jobs, 7) not laziness.

This example is taken from William Mann's website devoted to RST (http://www.sil.org/~mannb/rst/).

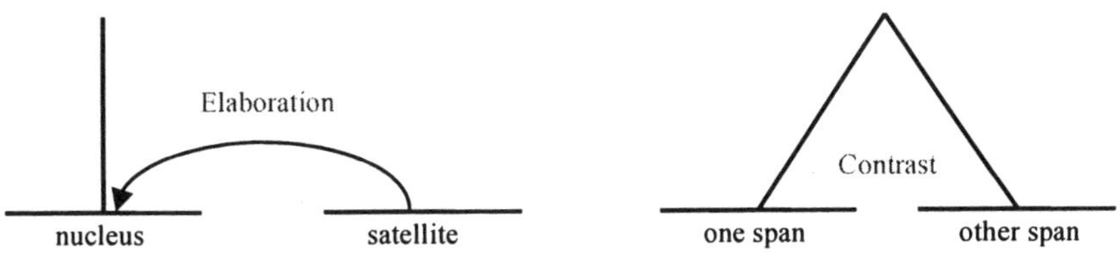

Figure 2.2. Example of Mann and Thompson's representational convention for relational schemes. The one on the left is the scheme of polarised relation (nucleaus + satellite), on the right is the scheme of a non-polarised relation (span + span).

The *nucleus* of a schema is the strongest term of the relation and it can stand alone, whereas the *satellite* is strictly dependent on the nucleus. A *relation* is defined by four parameters: constraints on the nucleus, constraints on the satellite, constraints on the combination of nucleus and satellite, and effect (on the reader) of such combination.

For instance, the sentence "*I work hard to buy a bigger house*" is composed of the spans "*I work hard*" and "*to buy a bigger house*". The first span constitutes the nucleus and the second span constitutes the satellite and between them, in RST terms, a *purpose* relation holds. For this relation, the constraint on the nucleus is that it has to present an activity; the constraint on the satellite is that it has to present an unrealised situation; the constraint on the combination between nucleus and satellite is that the satellite has to present a situation to be realised through the activity presented in the nucleus; finally, the effect on the reader has to be that the reader recognises that the activity presented in the nucleus is initiated in order to realise the situation presented in the satellite.

RELATION NAME	NUCLEUS	SATELLITE
Antithesis	Ideas favored by the author.	Ideas disfavored by the author.
Background	Text whose understanding is being facilitated.	Text for facilitating understanding.
Circumstance	Text expressing the events or ideas occurring in the interpretive context.	An interpretive context of situation or.
Concession	Situation affirmed by author.	Situation which is apparently inconsistent but also affirmed by author.
Condition	Action or situation whose occurrence results from the occurrence of the conditioning situation.	Conditioning situation.
Elaboration	Basic information.	Additional information.
Enablement	An action.	Information intended to aid the reader in performing an action.
Evaluation	A situation.	An evaluative comment about the situation.
Evidence	A claim.	Information intended to increase the reader's belief in the claim.
Interpretation	A situation.	An interpretation of the situation.
Justify	Text information.	Supporting the writer's right to express the text.
Motivation	An action.	Information intended to increase the reader's desire to perform the action.
Non-Volitional Cause	A situation.	Another situation which causes that one, but not by anyone's deliberate action.
Non-Volitional Result	A situation.	Another situation which is caused by that one, but not by anyone's deliberate action.
Otherwise	Action or situation whose occurrence results from the lack of occurrence of the conditioning situation.	Conditioning situation.
Purpose	An intended situation.	The intent behind the situation.
Restatement	A situation.	A re-expression of the situation.
Solutionhood	A situation or method supporting full or partial satisfaction of the need.	A question, request, problem, or other expressed need.
Summary	Text.	A short summary of that text.
Volitional Cause	A situation.	Another situation which causes that one, by someone's deliberate action.
Volitional Result	A situation.	Another situation which is caused by that one, by someone's deliberate action.
RELATION NAME	**SPAN**	**OTHER SPAN**
Contrast	One alternate.	The other alternate.
Sequence	An item.	A next item.

Table 2.1. Above the 23 rhetorical relations isolated by Mann and Thompson (1988) are described. 21 of them are mono nuclear relations (that is, they connect two spans of text that respectively function as nucleus and satellite of the relational schema. 2 of them, though, are multinuclear relations (that is, they connect spans of text that are equivalent to each other, so that neither of them plays the role of the satellite). The descriptions provided about nucleus, satellites or spans of the relations refer to their text's content. This table is taken from William Mann's website devoted to RST (http://www.sil.org/~mannb/rst/).

Apart from mono-polar relations, that is, relations between a nucleus and a satellite, there are bi-polar relations, which hold between two equivalent text spans. The difference is shown in Figure 2.2.

In total, Mann and Thompson describe 23 relations (summarised in Table 2.1). They motivate their set by arguing that the relations proved to be the most useful for the analysis of the data examined by them, but they also recognise that other relations may well be accounted for in a theory of text structure. In fact, in establishing what relations hold between the different parts of a text, the analyst has to make judgements that are determined by their knowledge of the context in which the text was written, and by the cultural conventions that they share with the writer. Also, at times rhetorical relations may be grammatically or lexically signalled, but they hold no matter whether they are signalled or not, offering the analyst no linguistic data on which to base a judgement. Because these judgements cannot be certain, Mann and Thompson define them as *plausibility judgements*.

The limits of Rhetorical Structure Theory are pointed out, among others, by Knott and Dale (1994): if the theory does not provide a method for specifying what counts as a relation, leaving the identification of relations to the judgement of the analyst, the set of relations identified by the authors can proliferate arbitrarily and indefinitely, and therefore become unusable or useless. In other words, if RST relations are purely descriptive constructs, they cannot provide any real insight into the working principles underlying text interpretation and interpretability.

2.2. Cohesive Devices as Evidence for Cognitive Categories

Like Mann and Thompson, Knott, Dale and Mellish (Knott and Dale, 1994; Knott and Mellish, 1996) approach the problem of text coherence from a computational linguistic perspective, but, unlike Mann and Thompson, they look at linguistic signs as a base for motivating the identification and isolation of cognitive categories. As the authors put it, they "use the cohesive devices of language as evidence for a psychological theory of text coherence" (Table 2.2.). The rationale behind this is that the structures of language are optimised for our communicative purposes, allowing the expression of our psychological reality. Language must therefore provide devices to mark our psychological constructs and these devices can be used as evidence for the identification of a set of cognitively-derived coherence relations. The authors call these linguistic marks of relations *cue phrases*, which they try to organise in a hierarchy through a series of *substitutability* tests[7], in order to produce a taxonomy of relational phrases.

In Knott and Mellish (1996), a series of substitution tests was conducted on a large number of English cue phrases, which led to the definition of a cue phrases taxonomy, which in turn led to the definition of a number of parameters describing the theoretical features of relations. When two cue phrases can always be used in the same context, they are said to be *synonymous*: *to begin with* can always be used in any context where *to start with* can be used, therefore they are synonymous, and the relation that they signal must present the same values of the same features. When two cue phrases can never be substituted for one another in any context, they are said *exclusive*: *to start with* and *alternatively* can never substitute one another, therefore they are exclusive, and the relation that they signal must present different values of at least one feature. When a cue phrase can be used whenever another can be used, but not vice versa, they are said to be *hypernym* and *hyponym*. As an example the author use the sentences "*Bill and Bob are quite different. Bill is a born optimist and Bob is perpetually gloomy*", and "*Bill and Bob are quite different. Bill is a born optimist whereas Bob is perpetually gloomy*". These show that *and* is a hypernym of *whereas*, because *and* can be used whenever *whereas* can be used, but *whereas* cannot be used whenever *and* can be used ("*I saw that Bob was gloomy and I went to talk to him*").

You can sit in the front seat,	*provided that* √ *if* # *even if*	you put your seat belt on.
I wouldn't vote for Major	*even if* √ *if* # *provided that*	you gave me thousand pounds.

Table 2.2. An extract from the materials used by Knott and Mellish (1996) for their substituability test. In the first sentence, the relational phrase '*provided that*' is the most specific, but '*if*' can also be used (√), whereas '*even if*' is definitely unusable (#). In the second sentence, '*even if*' is the most appropriate phrase, but '*if*' can still be used, whereas '*provided that*' is unusable. Since '*if*' can be used in both cases, because it is less specific, it constitutes a *hypernym* of both '*even if*' and '*provided that*'. Since 'even if' and '*provided that*' cannot be used to substitute each other, they are *exclusive*.

The features as obtained through the substitution tests were hypothesised to characterise the relations, and to describe the hierarchical taxonomy of cue phrases. Knott and Mellish express them in terms of preconditions necessary for the use of different cue phrases, and the communicative effects achieved by using them. They are defined as a set of bipolar parameters (see Table 2.3. and Table 2.4.):

Source of Coherence. Values can be *semantic*, when two situations are assumed to be connected in reality, or *pragmatic*, when two situations are assumed to be connected by inference: in "*it rained,* as a result *the streets were wet*" I report a situation that I observe in reality; whereas in "*the streets are wet,* it follows that *it rained*", I infer a fact from another on the basis of my general knowledge of the reality.

Anchor. Values can be *cause driven*, when a situation is presented as taking place as the cause of another situation, or *result driven*, when a situation is presented as taking place in order to achieve a result: in "*Bill had been up all night, so he looked pretty shattered*" the relation is cause driven; in "*Bill opened the fridge, and he had lunch*" the relation is result driven.

Pattern of Instantiation. Values can be *unilateral*, when the two related situations are presented on the same side with respect to the relation rule, or *bilateral*, when the two related situation are presented on the opposite side with respect to the relation rule: "*Bill lost the race last year,* but *he should win this year*" instantiates a bilateral pattern; whereas "*Bill should win the race this year. He lost last year,* but *they are running at altitude this time*" instantiates a unilateral pattern.

Focus of Polarity. Values can be *anchor-based* or *counterpart-based*: in "*Bob put his hands up, otherwise Bill would have shot him*" the transformation of the relation polarity from positive to negative is taken on by the anchor, the main action; in "*Bob kept his hands down, but Bill did not shoot him*" the transformation is taken on by the counterpart, the expected reaction to the main action.

Polarity. Values can be *positive*, if the rule defining the relation is confirmed, or *negative*, if the rule is defeated: in "*Bob shouted very loudly,* so *everybody heard him*" the causality rule is confirmed; in "*Bob shouted very loudly,* but *nobody heard him*" the same causality rule is defeated.

Presuppositionality. Values can be *presupposed*, when one of the two situations presented presupposes the other, or *non-presupposed*, when neither of the two situations connected presupposes or is subordinated to the other: in "*I used to have very long walks* when *I was living in the countryside*", the first situation presented presupposes the other; in "*We prepared dinner together. I cooked* and *he set the table*", neither of the two situations is subordinate to or presupposes the other.

Modal Status. Values can be *hypothetical*, when the verification of a situation depends on the verification of another situation which might or might not hold true, or *actual*, when the verification of a situation depends on another situation which certainly will happen: in "*This year I will visit a foreign country,* if *I have enough savings to pay for all the costs*" the relation is hypothetical; in "*I will give you a call,* as soon as *I will get home*" one situation will certainly verify because the other will certainly verify.

Rule Type. Values can be *causal*, when two situations are connected by causality, or *inductive,* when two situations are connected by induction: in "*Bob had trained a lot,* therefore *he won the marathon*" the relation holds by a causality rule; in "*Bill and Bob both like eating. Bill loves cakes,* and *Bob loves pasta*" the relation holds by an inductive rule.

NAME OF FEATURES	POSSIBLE VALUES	
SOURCE OF COHERENCE	semantic	pragmatic
ANCHOR	cause-driven	result-driven
PATTERN OF INSTANTIATION	unilateral	bilateral
FOCUS OF POLARITY	anchor-based	counterpart-based
POLARITY	negative	positive
PRESUPPOSITIONALITY	presupposed	non-presupposed
MODAL STATUS	hypothetical	actual
RULE TYPE	causal	inductive

Table 2.3. Knott and Mellish's 8 features, and their possible alternative value, which describe cognitive coherence relations and characterise the cue phrases that signal them in natural language (table taken from Knott and Mellish, 1996).

The strength of Knott, Dale and Mellish's work is that it tries to identify the cognitive categories that underpin the construction of discourse representation through the systematic analysis of objective data provided by the medium itself. However, the weakness is that language provides an extremely large number of cue phrases. To date, the authors have analysed only a small number of them, and it will take a long time to analyse them all. More seriously still, it is possible that, like Mann and Thompson's relations, the set of parameters so far obtained by Knott and Mellish might end up proliferating in order to account for all the cue phrases that a language can possibly provide. How usable or useful could a very large and complex set of parameters be?

And more to our point, how could it help to understand and handle the problem of coherence and cohesion in hypertext discourse?

CUE PHRASES	SOURCE OF COHERENCE	ANCHOR	PATTERN OF INSTANTIATION	FOCUS OF POLARITY	POLARITY	PRE-SUPPOSITIO-NALITY	MODAL STATUS	RULE TYPE
if A, B	-	-	-	count.-b.	-	presupp.	hypoth.	causal
A; despite this, B	pragmatic	cause-d.	bilateral	count.-b.	negative	non-pres.	actual	causal
even if A, B	-	-	-	count.-b.	negative	presupp.	hypoth.	causal
unless A, B	pragmatic	cause-d.	bilateral	anchor-b.	negative	presupp.	hyppth.	causal
until a, B	semantic	cause-d.	bilateral	anchor-b.	negative	presupp.	actual	causal
because A, B	pragmatic	-	bilateral	count.-b.	positive	presupp.	actual	causal
A in order that B	pragmatic	result-d.	bilateral	-	positive	presupp.	-	causal
A; as a result B	semantic	cause-d.	bilateral	count.-b.	positive	non-pres.	actual	causal

Table 2.4. A few examples of cue phrases and the values of the relational features associated to them (extract from a table in Knott and Mellish, 1996). The abbreviations mean the following: cause-d. = cause-driven, result-d. = result-driven; count.-b = counterpart-based, anchor-b. = anchor-based; hypoth. = hypothetical.

2.3. Coherence Relations as Basic Cognitive Primitives

In this respect, the work of Sanders, Spooren and Noordman (1993) - that directly informs Knott, Dale and Mellish's work (Knott and Sanders, 1998) - seems to be more promising. On the line of Hobbs' pioneering work (1985), the authors take a cognitive approach to the problem of text representation and they also treat coherence relations as psychological constructs. Like Hobbs but in contrast to Knott et al., Sanders et al.'s approach is theory driven, rather than data driven: they advance a psychologically plausible hypothesis which they are then able to subsequently support with experimental data. Like Knott and Mellish, they propose a set of parameters describing cognitive coherence relations, but unlike Knott and Mellish's set, their set consists of a small number of cognitively basic concepts, and in principle it is not subjected to proliferation exactly because it is based on primitive cognitive categories, which are properties common to all relations. This set is generated by the combination of four cognitive primitives (see Table 2.5.), describing relational meaning. These primitives are:

Basic Operation. Two discourse segments can be weakly connected, in which case they are related by *additiveness*, or they can be strongly connected, in which case they are related by *causality*; an additive operation exists if the two discourse segments are simply related by logical conjunction, whereas a causal operation exists if between the two discourse segments an implication relation can be deduced. For example: in "*I went shopping this morning. I took a walk in the afternoon*" the two discourse segments are related by additiveness. In "*This morning it was raining very heavily. I had to take my rain coat to go out*" the segments are related by causality. From this primitive, Knott and Mellish's *rule type* feature derives.

Source of Coherence. A discourse relation can be *semantic*, when the two discourse segments are related on the basis of their propositional content, or *pragmatic*, when the two segments are related on the basis of the illocutionary meaning of one or both of the segments; the connection between the two segments is semantic when it is presented as the result of an external observation of a situation, whereas it is pragmatic when it is presented as an inference based on personal knowledge. For instance: in "*It rained all day yesterday. The streets got flooded*" the relation between the fact that it rained and the fact that the streets were flooded is presented as an observation of a cause-effect phenomenon. In "*The neighbours must be out tonight. The lights in their house are all off*" the speaker infers a cause-effect phenomenon on the basis of the knowledge that he has that usually when people go out they switch off the lights - Knott and Mellish maintain this concept as their *source of coherence* feature.

Order of Segments. Two discourse segments can be related in a *basic* order, which corresponds to the order in which events are meant to actually verify in the described reality, or in a *non-basic* order, which does not correspond to the order of the described events. For instance: in "*I missed the bus this morning. I was late for the meeting*" the order of presentation of the events is basic, because it corresponds to the order in which they verify in the described situation. In "*I was late for the meeting. I missed the bus this morning*" the order of presentation is backward with respect to the event described and therefore the order of segments is non-basic.

Polarity. The relation between two discourse segments can be *positive*, when the two segments function directly and accordingly in the basic operation, or *negative*, when one of the segments denies the rule of the basic operation expressed by the other segment. For instance: in "*She did not sleep all night. In the morning she looked rather shattered*" the relation between the two discourse segments is positive, since the second segment is consistent with the basic operation set by the first segment, that is, the event described in the second segment is a consistent causal consequence of the event described in the first segment. In "*She looked as fresh as a rosebud, despite not sleeping all night*" the basic operation set by the first segment is contradicted by the second segment, that is, the expected causal consequence does not follow[8]. Polarity is positive or negative for all relations - This concept is referred to also by Knott and Mellish with their *polarity* feature.

PRIMITIVE CONCEPT	POSSIBLE VALUES	
BASIC OPERATION	additive	causal
SOURCE OF COHERENCE	semantic	pragmatic
ORDER OF THE SEGMENTS	basic	non-basic
POLARITY	positive	negative

Table 2.5. Sander, Spooren and Noordman's 4 cognitive relational primitives, isolated to describe discourse connections in text (from Sander et al., 1993).

The authors observe that the primitives described above also seem to be able to account for relations like, for instance, *goal-instrument* or *problem-solution* present in taxonomies like RST as proposed by Mann and Thompson (*purpose* and *solutionhood*). In fact, these relations result from the combination of two causal basic operations: in *goal-instrument*, causality exists between a state of affairs – as antecedent - and the action taken to change it – as consequent – and then between the action taken – as antecedent - and the resulting state of affairs – as consequent. In *problem-solution*, causality exists between the negative evaluated state of affairs – as antecedent – and the action taken to modify it – as consequent, and then between the proposed action – as antecedent – and its intended result.

Apart from their theoretical versatility, the validity of these primitives is also supported by experimental results, from which a number of interesting phenomena seem to emerge (Sanders and Noordman, 2000; Noordman and Blijzer, 2000; Sanders and Spooren, 2001). As far as the basic operation is concerned, causal relations appear to be easier and quicker to process than additive relations. Basic order relations appear to be easier and quicker to process than non-basic order relations. Positive polarity relations appear to be easier and quicker to process than negative ones[9]. The primitive source of coherence is the only one that has not gathered significant supportive evidence and that has been object of much discussion (Sanders, 1997; Knott, 1999; Dancygier and Sweetser, 2000; Pander Maat and Sanders, 2001) - but we will come back on this later.

BASIC OPERATION	SOURCE OF COHERENCE	ORDER OF SEGMENTS	POLARITY	CLASS	RELATION
causal	semantic	basic	positive	1a	*cause-consequence*
				1b	*condition-consequence*
causal	semantic	basic	negative	2	*contrastive cause-consequence*
causal	semantic	non-basic	positive	3a	*consequence-cause*
				3b	*consequence-condition*
causal	semantic	non-basic	negative	4	*contrastive consequence-cause*
causal	pragmatic	basic	positive	5a	*argument-claim*
				5b	*condition-claim*
causal	pragmatic	basic	negative	6	*contrastive argument-claim*
causal	pragmatic	non-basic	positive	7a	*claim-argument*
				7b	*claim-condition*
causal	pragmatic	non-basic	negative	8	*contrastive claim-argument*
additive	semantic	-	positive	9	*list*
additive	semantic	-	negative	10a	*opposition*
				10b	*exception*
additive	pragmatic	-	positive	11	*enumeration*
additive	pragmatic	-	negative	12	*concession*

Table 2.6. Sander, Spooren and Noordman's taxonomy resulting from the combination of the 4 primitives, and the prototypical relations that the taxonomy accounts for (table from Sanders at al., 1993).

In general, the great advantage of these primitives and of the relation set that results from their combination (Table2.6.) is that they express meaning that is independent from the discourse content and only concerns relations. Also, because these concepts are so basic and because the set that they generate is so restricted, they are likely to be more easily and fruitfully applied to hypertext discourse analysis then other taxonomies. However, the authors do recognise that other criteria could be added to the primitives that they propose, like *temporality* (to distinguish between simple *conjunction* and *sequence*), *hypotheticality* (to distinguish between *cause* and *condition*), *volitionality* (to distinguish between *reason* and *explanation*), and *specificity* (to distinguish between *specification* and *generalisation*) – we will return to this later as well.

2.4. Basic and Economic Parameterisation of Coherence Relations

Sanders, Spooren and Noordman's approach also informs the work of Louwerse (2001). Louwerse conducted a comparative study of the most influential taxonomies - Halliday and Hasan, 1976; Hobbs, 1985; Knott and Dale, 1994; Martin, 1992; Mann and Thompson, 1988; Sander et al., 1993 - and proposed an analytic and cognitive parameterisation of coherence relations, based on the similarities shared by the different sets.

TYPE	POLARITY	DIRECTION	EXAMPLES
causal	positive	backward	*A because B*
		forward	*A so B; because A, B*
		bi-directional	-
	negative	backward	*A although B*
		forward	*A nevertheless B; although A, B*
		bi-directional	-
temporal	positive	backward	*A before B; after A, B*
		forward	*A after B; before A, B*
		bi-directional	*A while B; B while A*
	negative	backward	*A until B*
		forward	*until A, B*
		bi-directional	-
additive	positive	backward	-
		forward	*A moreover B*
		bi-directional	*A similar B; B similar A*
	negative	backward	-
		forward	*A however B*
		bi-directional	*A alternatively B; B alternatively A*

Table 2.7. Above is Louwerse's analytic and cognitive parametrisation of coherence relations, derived from those categories that are represented in most text coherence theories (table taken from Louwerse, 2001).

Following Sanders et al's model, Louwerse found that all taxonomies account for causal, additive and temporal relations, as far as the parameter *basic operation* (which he calls *type*) is concerned; negative and positive relations, as far as the *polarity* parameter is concerned; semantic and pragmatic relations, as far as the *source of coherence* parameter is concerned; basic and non-basic relations (which he calls *forward* and *backward* relations), as far as the *order of segments* (which he calls *direction*) is concerned. Taking into account these similarities, the author proposes what he terms a "basic" and "economical" parameterisation.

As summarised in Table 2.7, Louwerse's model consists of three parameters: *type*, *polarity* and *direction*. The type parameter has three categories (or values): *causal*, *temporal* or *additive*. The parameter polarity has two categories: *positive* and *negative*. The parameter direction has three categories: *backward*, *forward* and *bi-directional*. Although the combination of all these categories results in 18 relations, the author's taxonomy only includes 13, since he claims that no instances exist of "*bi-directional causal*", "*negative temporal*", "*additive backward*", or "*additive bi-directional*" relations. Because it is the most controversial at the theoretical level and also the most uncertain from the point of view of experimental evidence, Louwerse excludes the parameter *source of coherence* from his taxonomy.

Among the linguists, this parameter has been accounted for by Halliday and Hasan (1976) and Martin (1992) as a dichotomy between *internal* and *external* use of conjunctions and relations; by Mann and Thompson (1988) as *subject matter* versus *presentational matter* relations; by Pander Maat (1994) as *content* versus *epistemic* and *interactional* relations; by Sweetser (1990) as *content* versus *epistemic* and *speech act* relations; by Van Dijk (1977) as *semantic* and *pragmatic* connectives; by Sanders and Spooren (1999) as *informational* versus *intentional*; by Knott (1999) as *semantic* and *intention-based* relations. The use of this parameter and its related categories in Sanders et al. (1993), and in Knott and Mellish (1996) is shown above. In Sanders (1997) an exhaustive dissertation can be found about this subject, so here this is only succinctly discussed.

As observed already in Knott and Mellish's and in Sanders et al.'s taxonomies, semantic relations (characterised by others as internal, subject matter, or content relations) refer to the connection between two events taking place in reality as it is observed from outside, according to the laws that are expected to rule that reality itself. That is, in semantic relations, the point of view on the described reality sets itself as objective and impersonal. In the sentence "*This morning the streets are flooded, because it rained all night*", I just make a detached observation about the connection between two physical phenomena, and my subjectivity does not come into place at all (see Dancygier and Sweetser, 2000; Pander Maat and Sanders, 2001). The relation expressed in the sentence is of the type *effect-cause*, which is mainly recurrent in descriptive text (Sanders, 1997).

In pragmatic relations (characterised by others as external, presentational matter, epistemic, or intended-effect), the connection between two events is presented as more subjective, as the result of a personal inference on the part of the speaker. That is, epistemic relations concern the beliefs of the speaker or what the speaker wants the reader to believe (Dancygier and Sweetser, 2000; Pander Maat and Sanders, 2001). In the sentence "*It must have rained all night last night, because the streets are flooded this morning*", I make a personal judgement, based on the assumption that when it rains for a long time the streets get flooded. In effect, I make a claim and bring an argument for it: the sentence expresses a relation of the type *claim-argument*, which is mainly recurrent in argumentative text (Sanders, 1997).

Finally, speech-act (interactional) relations express the connection between the speech act of the speaker and its justification for performing it (Dancygier and Sweetser, 2000). In the sentence "*What shoes are you wearing this morning...because it rained all night last night*", I perform a speech act, which consists in inquiring about my interlocutor's behaviour, and I provide a justification for doing so. Although it is accounted for by a few authors, this relational category remains the most controversial and the weakest of all. In favour of the distinction between *semantic* and *pragmatic*, however, there is some evidence (Sander et al., 1992; 1993; Noordman and De Blijzer, 2000), and in general different text types appear to be dominated by different types of relations, both in terms of quantity (there are more semantic relations in descriptive texts, and more pragmatic relations in argumentative text) and quality (pragmatic relations are dominant in higher text levels)[10].

As far as the relation parameter type is concerned, Louwerse observes that causal relations imply both temporality and additiveness, and temporal relations imply additiveness. In other words, additive and temporal relations are equivalent, except for the reference to time, and temporal and causal relations are equivalent except for the reference to causality. We have seen in Knott and Mellish (1996) and in Sanders et al. (1993) that causal relations are also assimilated to conditional relations through the parameter/category of *hypotheticality*. However, Meyer (2000) assimilates them through the criterion of *relevance*: the verification of an event depends on a number of conditions, not just on one cause, and it is a matter of deciding which one of the conditions (if any) is more relevant from the point of view of the observer (speaker/writer or hearer/reader).

To follow Meyer's example, consider the sentence: "*The man jumped out of the train in a rush. It was raining heavily and the pavement was very slippery. He ran up the stairs of the station. They were old and very steep. As he got to the last step, he slipped and fell*". What really caused the man to fall: the fact that he was running? The fact that he was in a hurry and therefore distracted? The fact that the stairs were steep? The fact that they were wet? According to Meyer, it is probably the concurrence of all these more or less relevant factors - conditions - that leads to the final event. This approach to causality tends to weaken the justification for including a parameter like *hypotheticality* in a coherence relation taxonomy. Moreover, the criterion of relevance, as well as the consequent conception of condition as a pre-existing element of the environment, seem to reveal the fact that conditional relations share something in common with background relations, as described in Mann and Thompson (1988).

In the condition relation, the satellite presents a situation that is prerequisite for the verification of the situation presented in the nucleus. In the background relation, the satellite presents information that is prerequisite to (or at least facilitates) the comprehension of the situation presented in the nucleus. The difference between the two relations is that in the condition relation what is enabled is the verification of an event or a situation, whereas in the background relation what is enabled is the understanding of an event or a situation – that is, of why an event or situation are true. In fact, background is one of the least specified relationships (together with elaboration), and it can take lots of forms, one of which is conditionality. Later on the common aspects between conditionality and background will become relevant (see Chapters 7 and 8).

As for additive relations, they connect two events or situations on the basis of some sort of equivalence, but the nature of this equivalence can be either conjunctive or comparative. In the first case, additive relations indicate the joint relevance of two situations, events or objects with respect to a whole or to a larger picture (Pander Maat, 1999). For instance, in the sentence "*I need to clean the kitchen and I need to dust the sitting room, before the guests arrive*", the equivalence is set with respect to the joint relevance of the two actions in order for the house to be ready to receive guests.

In the second case, though, additive relations also indicate the similarity between the connected situations, events or objects (Pander Maat, 1999). For instance, consider the sentence "*The trajectory of a projectile is determined by inertia, which makes it fly forward, and by gravitation, which makes it fall back into the ground. The trajectory of a planet around another planet is determined by inertia, which makes it move forward, and by gravitation, which makes it deflect from a rectilinear motion*". Here the equivalence is established by comparison between two situations that present structural similarities. Knott (1998) talks about comparison as based on inductive rules: on the basis of similarity in some respect, a comparison is drawn between two phenomena. If the similarity rule succeeds also in other respects that are relevant to the context, then we have a similarity relation; if the similarity rule is defeated in the other respects, then we have a contrast relation – which is a case of negative polarity additive relation.

3. Coherence Relations and Hypertext

From the preceding discussion we have seen how coherence relations hold together discourse parts and constitute its very structure. We have also seen that, according to certain authors, a small number of primitive concepts can account for basic cognitive coherence relations informing not only our representation of a text, but even our very perception of reality. These cognitive categories include concepts like causality, temporality, conjunction and similarity, negative causality, disjunction and contrast, but also specificity, hypotheticality and volitionality, and so on.

The fact that cohesion and coherence concern both the connection between single sentences and the connection between larger segments of text makes it possible to apply text coherence relations also to hypertext. That is, coherence relations can be used in hypertext to define the connection between nodes, which especially in argumentative discourse constitute significant text segments. And in fact, there are a number of examples of theoretical and/or empirical applications of coherence relations to hypertext - among them, Foltz's comparative analysis of hypertext and linear text strategies (1996) and Rosenberg's conception of conjunctive hypertext (2001), as theoretical applications; Thuring, Haake and Hannemann's hypertext design kit (1991), Not and Zancanaro's MacroNode Approach (2000), and Rutledge and Hardman's presentation generation system (2000), as empirical applications. The next chapter analyses a few hypertext link taxonomies, as well as an example of argumentative hypertext, showing how cognitive coherence relations can account for discourse connections proposed for semantic hypertext systems, as well as how they can be used to analyse hypertext arguments.

Notes

[1] Deictics are those linguistic indicators that refer the enunciation act to a speaker subject, to the time and place in which the enunciation act has taken place, and to the speaker's interlocutors. They are pronouns, and space-temporal elements (Benveniste, 1970).

[2] For instance, the connective '*because*' constitute a cohesive element between the text spans "*I wore my rain coat today*" and "*It was raining*".

[3] If the text spans "*I wore my rain coat today*" and "*It was raining*" were simply juxtaposed in absence of any connective, their juxtaposition still would make sense, that is, it would be possible to establish a coherent connection between them, although establishing that connection would be facilitated by the presence of a connective.

[4] Anaphoric devices are linguistic elements that refer to something that has been already mentioned or described in the text. They can be subjective pronouns, or space-temporal adverbs.

[5] Whereas anaphoric devices refer a piece of text content to another piece of text content, connectives connect two pieces of text content. They can be cue phrases like *and, because, afterwards, if*, etc. For instance, in the sentence "*Lisa took a shower, and then she went out*", the anaphoric device '*she*' is used to refer to Lisa without repeating her name, whereas the connective '*and*' is used to relate to one another the actions that Lisa made in a sequence.

[6] Because usually hypertext nodes are not made only by single text spans, but by whole paragraphs, global coherence, that is, coherence between larger sections of text (like paragraphs), is particularly relevant from the point of view of hypertext discourse coherence.

[7] The substitutability test consists in presenting to subjects pairs of text spans related by a connective. Each pair would be assigned three candidate connectives, one that was expected to be the best choice, one that could be used in that case without being the most specific, and one that could not be used at all. By substituting one connector with the other in turn, and in different pairs, the usability of each connector is tested for different relations and a classification of connectors is generated. See Table 2.2.

[8] Note that a paratactic construction, that is, a construction that does not make use of linguistic devices to signal the coherence relation, is more difficult to interpret with relations whose polarity is negative.

[9] Studies have also demonstrated that the ability of interpreting additive, non-basic and negative relations increase with age, that is, adults are able to interpret such relations more easily than children are (Sanders and Spooren, 2001).

[10] In fact, in a study about causal relations, Pander Maat and Degand (2001) propose a scalar approach to the question of the source of coherence in discourse relations. For them, semantic, pragmatic or speech-act relations should be considered as points on a continuum of relation types, rather than as alternative value of a discrete parameter. They call this continuum the *speaker-involvement scale*, and define it in terms of the degree of implicit involvement of the speaker in the construction of the relation.

Cinematic Hypertext
C. Mancini
IOS Press, 2005

3. Applying Discourse Coherence Relations to Hypertext

Following the idea of using Cognitive Coherence Relations (CCR) to define representational conditional rules in hypertext, this chapter seeks to account for argumentation link types in terms of cognitive coherence relations. Examples of link taxonomies from two semantic hypertext argumentation systems are analysed and mapped onto cognitive coherence relations, which brings interesting insights into the way these taxonomies could be composed and organised, and ultimately into the nature of the link types that they use. Subsequently, an example of a scholarly hypertext is analysed and its links are described in terms of cognitive coherence relations, whose application constitutes a CCR-based verification of the author's theoretical approach to structuring argument in hypertext.

1. Cognitive Coherence Relations and Hypertext: Scholarly Link Taxonomies

An approach to the problem of discourse coherence in hypertext is the definition of link taxonomies describing the quality of the relationship between discourse units, the nodes (Baron, 1996). The purpose of these link taxonomies is to provide a definition of the discourse role that any one node plays with relation to adjacent nodes, therefore accounting for their contextual function. In his review of various link taxonomies (Kopak, 1999), Kopak showed that there is a certain level of consistency in some of the link classes proposed by different taxonomies, like for instance links indicating the functions of *context*, *argument*, *cause* and *detail*. Here few of the taxonomies already analysed by Kopak, as well as the most recently delivered taxonomy developed within the ScholOnto project (Buckingham Shum et al., 2000), and used by the semantic hypertext system ClaiMaker (Buckingham Shum et al., 2002; 2004), are analysed in terms of CCR.

The aim of the analysis is to show that there is a large overlap between the categories of existing hypertext link taxonomies and the basic set of cognitive coherence relations identified by psycholinguistic research on text coherence, and that this overlap, as well as the fact that different link taxonomies present the same kind of relations, is to be explained with the cognitive categories that determine our discourse processes. In particular the overlap concerns exactly the categories identified by Kopak as recurrent in the link taxonomies that he analyses, which are interpretable as forms of the relational primitives already discussed. That is, coming from different places and following different routes, theoretical and empirical research on text coherence, on the one hand, and theoretical and empirical research on hypertext discourse structuring, on the other hand, appear to have independently produced similar results, identifying a number of - cognitive - discourse relations.

For instance, in the taxonomy proposed by Parunak (1991), constructed on the basis of grammatical structures, three classes of link types can be distinguished: *association*, *aggregation* and *revision* links. Among the association links, *word-proposition* link types indicate the relation between a piece of information and another piece of information that specifies the meaning of the former, which is the same function played by elaboration and evidence/justify relations. *Proposition-proposition* links, comprise four general types: *orientation links*, which indicate a relation between an event or situation and its context, and which could be identified with a background relation; *implication links*, which describe the logical connection between the propositions, and which could include causality and additiveness relations; *paraphrase links*, which connect pieces of information that say the same thing in different ways, and which can be interpreted as elaboration or restatement relations; *illustration* links, which connect propositions whose contents clarify one another by, for instance, comparison or contrast, and which could correspond to the similarity and contrast relations.

NORMAL LINKS		CCR EQUIVALENT	MOTIVATION
Citation	*Source*	N/A	It is a taxonomic relation.
	Pioneer	N/A	It is a taxonomic relation.
	Credit	N/A	It is a taxonomic relation.
	Leads	N/A	It is a taxonomic relation.
	Eponym	N/A	It is a taxonomic relation.
Background		Backward positive pragmatic causal in the hypothetical form.	It usually provides information that pre-exists the presented situation and that is condition for it to occur and be understood.
Future Work		Forward temporal positive semantic additive (sequential). Forward positive semantic causal.	It is usually related to present work that precedes it. It can simply be presented as coming afterwards, or to directly derive as a consequence of present work.
Refutation		Forward positive pragmatic causal associated with opposition.	It is a form of contrastive argument or evidence that supports going against a claim.
Support		Forward positive pragmatic causal.	It is a form of argument or evidence that supports a claim.
Methodology		N/A	It is a taxonomic relation.
Data		N/A	It is a taxonomic relation.
Generalize		Backward positive pragmatic additive in the form of specialisation.	It can be interpreted as a reverse form of elaboration in which previous information is reformulated in more general terms.
Specialize		Forward positive pragmatic additive in the form of specialisation.	It can be interpreted as a form of elaboration in which previous information is reformulated in more specialised terms.
Abstraction		Forward positive pragmatic additive in the form of abstraction. Forward positive pragmatic additive in the form of restatement.	It can be interpreted as a form of elaboration or restatement in which previous information is reformulated in more abstract terms.
Example		N/A	
Formalization		Forward positive pragmatic additive in the form of formalisation. Forward positive pragmatic additive in the form of restatement.	It can be interpreted as a form of elaboration or restatement in which previous information is reformulated in more formalised terms.

Application		Backward positive semantic causal. Backward positive semantic causal in the hypothetical form (conditional).	It can be interpreted as the consequence of a cause or condition represented by the piece of work that enables the application.
Argument	*Deduction*	Forward positive pragmatic causal via deduction.	It expresses the motivation for a claim, based on a deduction.
	Induction	Forward positive pragmatic causal via induction.	It expresses the motivation for a claim, based on an induction.
	Analogy	Forward positive pragmatic causal via analogy.	It expresses the motivation for a claim, based on an analogy.
	Intuition	Forward positive pragmatic causal via intuition.	It expresses the motivation for a claim, based on an intuition.
	Solution	Forward positive pragmatic causal via solution.	It expresses the motivation for a claim, based on a solution.
Summarization		Backward positive pragmatic additive in form of elaboration.	It can be interpreted as a reverse form of elaboration that succinctly refers to more detailed information.
Detail		Forward positive pragmatic additive in form of elaboration.	It is a form of elaboration with respect to more general, les precise, information already provided.
Alternate View		Forward negative pragmatic additive (alternative).	It presents alternative information or an alternative position.
Rewrite		Forward positive pragmatic additive in the form of restatement.	It is an addition that reformulate information already provided, presumably with some improvement.
Explanation		Forward positive pragmatic additive in the form of elaboration. Backward positive pragmatic causal (argument).	It can be interpreted as a form of elaboration when it adds clarifying information that expands a concept already expressed, or as an argument when it motivates a claim.
Simplification		Backward positive pragmatic additive in the form of elaboration.	It can be interpreted as a reverse form of elaboration that reformulates previous information in simpler terms.
Complication		Forward positive pragmatic additive in the form of elaboration. Forward positive semantic causal associated with opposition.	It can be interpreted as a form of elaboration, when is used to say that further complexities are added to an existing situation, or as an obstacle that potentially causes a desired result no to happen.
Update		Forward positive pragmatic additive in the form of elaboration. Forward temporal positive semantic additive in the form of elaboration (sequential).	An update can be looked at either as constituting the further elaboration of a present piece of work or application, or it may be looked at as simply coming after the present piece of work.
Correction		Forward positive semantic causal.	A correction addresses a mistake, by which it is motivated.
Continuation		Forward temporal positive semantic additive (sequential). Forward temporal positive semantic causal.	Like future work, it is usually related to a present work or situation that precedes it. It can simply be presented as coming afterwards, or to directly derive as a consequence of present work.

Table 3.1. Trigg's normal link taxonomy (from Trigg 1983), analysed in terms of Sanders et al. (1993) and Louwerse (2001)'s relational parameters.

What are called *normal* link types in TEXTNET's taxonomy (Trigg, 1983; Trigg and Weiser, 1986) (see Table 3.1), also seem to represent quite closely Sanders and Louwerse's set of CCR (Chapter 2, § 2.2.3, 2.2.4). As Kopak (1999) points out, the normal link types are to connect nodes that constitute the main thread of the hypertext discourse, and have a rhetorical nature, as they connect nodes on the basis of the discourse structure. Among them, *background*, *refutation*, *support*, *application*, *argument* and *correction* are causal or derivatives of causal relations. As previously discussed (Chapter 2), *background* (which corresponds to the background relation as it is described in Mann and Thompson, 1988) is a type of pragmatic conditional relation, which is a pragmatic causal relation associated with the criterion of hypotheticality. *Refutation* is a type of pragmatic causal relation associated with an opposition (additive negative forward) or contrast (additive negative bi-directional) relation: refutation is an argument or a piece of evidence that goes against a claim, or that supports a claim that is opposed to the first claim. Instead, *support* is a type of pragmatic positive causal relation, which holds between a claim and an argument or between a claim and a piece of evidence. *Application* can be interpreted as a conditional relation, that is, as a hypothetical semantic or pragmatic causal relation, if it is possible to infer that the fact that B applies A also means that B would not be possible (or would not verify) unless A was applied. The five types of *argument* links are obviously forms of pragmatic causal relations, for which the logical operation holding between claim and argument can be an *induction*, a *deduction*, a *solution*, (supposedly) an *intuition*, and even an *analogy*. Finally, *correction* is referrable to causality in a similar way as the dichotomy problem-solution is: an evaluated negative state of affairs (what needs to be corrected) causes the action taken to modify it (the correction) (see Chapter 2, § 3).

The other relations of the taxonomy are all derivatives of additive relations (except few taxonomic relations). *Future work* and *continuation* are both additive temporal, that is, sequential relations, although one could argue that both are a type of causal relation, since both the future work and the continuation of whatever research work is caused by the work results that come before. This is also a possibility, and the choice between the two really depends on the context in which the relations are used. *Generalise* and *specialise* are backward and forward additive relations associated with the criterion of specificity (Chapter 2, § 3). The pairs *summarisation* and *detail*, and *simplification* and *complication* are interpretable as respectively backward and forward additive relations associated to a criterion of elaboration as explained in Mann and Thompson (1988). *Explanation* and *rewrite* are similar to the previous ones, where the latter can be interpreted as a form of elaboration and the former as a form of restatement, a 'zero degree' elaboration. Similar considerations can be made about the *update* link type, and even for *abstraction* and *formalisation*. Differently from the others is *alternative view*, which corresponds to a negative additive relation, a contrastive one. Finally, among the normal links of the taxonomy there are some taxonomical ones, like all the ones included in the category *citation*, *methodology*, *data* and *example* - although about this one it could be said that it may happen to play the function of evidence, in which case it would denote a pragmatic causal relation. Since taxonomical relations are not object of investigation here, they are not discussed.

Apart from the group of normal links, TEXTNET's taxonomy also includes a large group of commentary links (Table 3.2). With only few exceptions, this group's links enable the specification of judgements on hypertext nodes, and therefore are content focused rather than relation focused.

COMMENTARY LINKS		COMMENTARY LINKS (cont/d)	
comment	*critical*	*thesis*	*inelegant*
	supportive		*simplistic*
related work	*misrepresents*		*arbitrary*
	vacuum		*unmotivated*
	ignores	*argumentation*	*invalid*
	is superseded by		*insufficient*
	is refuted by		*immaterial*
	is supported by		*misleading*
	redundant		*alternative*
problem posing	*trivial*		*straw man*
	unimportant	*data*	*inadequate*
	impossible		*dubious*
	ill-posed		*ignores*
	solved		*irrelevant*
	ambitious		*inapplicable*
thesis	*trivial*		*misinterpreted*
	unimportant	*style*	*boring*
	irrelevant		*unimaginative*
	red herring		*incoherent*
	contradict		*arrogant*
	dubious		*rambling*
	counterexample		*awkward*

Table 3.2. Trigg's commentary link taxonomy (from Trigg, 1983).

Another example is offered by ClaiMaker's link taxonomy (Buckingham Shum et al., 2002). The fact that the taxonomy was constructed with a partial reference to CCR, means that at least the categories derived from cognitive coherence relations will constitute link types referable to them – and if it was possible to build a fully functional set of rhetorical links for argumentation based on CCR, this is already proof of their validity in hypertext. However, all the link types of the empirical ontology developed to capture scholarly discourse relations can be described in terms of CCR (Table 3.3).

In the taxonomy there is a class of links called *similarity*, and in fact all the link types included in it constitute forms of additive, similarity or contrast, relations (that is, positive and negative comparison relations). Like for all the other links, in ClaiMaker the relations have a weight, which defines the degree of additiveness or causality expressed. For instance, *is-identical-to* weighs more than *shares-issues-with*, both having positive polarity; whereas *has-nothing-to-do-with* and *is-not-analogous-to* represent a kind of zero weight relations, whose polarity is neutral; finally, *is-the-opposite-of* weighs more of *is-different-to* on the scale of negative polarity, which expresses a different degree of contrastiveness.

Likewise, the class of link types called *causal* includes links that express causal and conditional semantic relations, both positive and negative, with two exceptions: *predicts* and *envisages*, which can be interpreted as pragmatic causal relations. These two relations, that is, are based on the assumption (in turn based on experience) that a future event will – probably – occur because some signs are there to allow the prediction. As I infer that "*it must have rained*" from the fact that "*the roads are wet*", I can equally predict that "*it will rain*" from the fact that "*there are black clouds in the sky*". In that sense, one could say that black clouds predict rain, in the same way as wet roads signal the fact that it rained. Apart from these two, the other causal relations of the class are semantic ones. *Causes* is the most straightforward case. *Is-capable-of-causing* and *is-prerequisite-for* are both conditional relations, that is, both relations express a potentiality, a possibility, but not necessarily a given fact (as it happens in pure causality). In the former we have the expression of a sufficient condition (A is sufficient condition for B to occur), in the latter we have the expression of a necessary condition (B does not occur unless A is there) – in this context, Meyer's (2000) approach to causality and conditionality well explains these hypothetical relations.

RELATION CLASS	DIALECT LABEL	P/W	CCR EQUIVALENT	MOTIVATION
General	*is about*	+/1	Forward positive pragmatic additive in the form of elaboration.	It indicates elaboration of something being presented or mentioned.
	uses/applies/ is enabled by	+/1	Backward positive semantic causal. Backward positive pragmatic causal in the hypothetical form (conditional).	It expresses the result of a cause or condition that makes it possible for such result to happen.
	improves on	+/2	Backward positive semantic causal.	Similar to solution-problem.
	impairs	-/2	Forward positive semantic causal, associated with opposition.	It causes something not to happen. Or it obstacle its happening.
Problem Related	*addresses*	+/1	Backward positive semantic causal.	Similar to solution-problem.
	solves	+/2	Backward positive semantic causal.	Similar to solution-problem.
Supports/ Challenges	*proves*	+/2	Forward positive pragmatic causal.	Because of it, something can be assumed or claimed.
	refutes	-/2	Forward positive pragmatic causal, associated with opposition.	It supports or proves that something cannot be claimed.
	is evidence for	+/1	Forward positive pragmatic causal.	It supports an assumption or claim.
	is evidence against	-/1	Forward positive pragmatic causal, associated with opposition.	It supports the negation of an assumption or claim.
	agrees with	+/1	Bi-directional positive pragmatic additive.	It adds elements to the same view.
	disagrees with	-/1	Bi-directional negative pragmatic additive.	It adds contrastive elements to a view.
	is consistent with	+/1	Forward positive pragmatic causal. Forward positive pragmatic causal, associate with enumeration.	It motivates an assumption or claim. Or it adds to something else that motivates an assumption or claim.

Supports/ Challenges Cont/D	*is inconsistent with*	-/1	Forward negative pragmatic causal. Forward positive pragmatic causal, associated with opposition.	It fails to motivate an assumption or claim. Or, it contrasts something else that motivates an assumption or claim.
Taxonomic	*part of*	+/1	N/A	It is a taxonomic rel.
	example of	+/1	N/A	It is a taxonomic rel.
	subclass of	+/1	N/A	It is a taxonomic rel.
Similarity	*is identical to*	+/2	Bi-directional positive semantic additive in the form of similarity.	It is the highest degree of similarity.
	is similar to	+/1	Bi-directional positive semantic additive in the form of similarity.	It is a simple similarity.
	is different to	-/1	Bi-directional negative semantic additive in the form of contrast.	It expresses the negative result of a comparison.
	is the opposite of	-/2	Bi-directional negative semantic additive in the form of contrast.	It expresses the highest degree to which a comparison can fail.
	shares issues with	+/1	Bi-directional positive semantic additive in the form of similarity.	It is a mild degree of similarity.
	has nothing to do with	-/1	Bi-directional 'zero degree' semantic additive in the form of similarity or contrast.	It expresses a case in which two objects are not even comparable.
	is analogous to	+/1	Bi-directional positive semantic additive in the form of similarity.	It expresses a similarity and a successful comparison.
	is not analogous to	-/1	Bi-directional 'zero degree' semantic additive in the form of similarity, or semantic additive contrast.	It is either a non-similarity or the negative result of a comparison.
Causal	*predicts*	+/1	Forward positive pragmatic causal.	It is an assumption based on present signs.
	envisages	+/1	Forward positive pragmatic causal.	It is an assumption based on present signs.
	causes	+/2	Forward positive semantic causal.	It causes something to happen.
	is capable of causing	+/1	Forward positive semantic causal in the hypothetical form (conditionality).	It constitutes a sufficient condition.
	is prerequisite for	+/1	Forward positive semantic causal in the hypothetical form (conditionality).	It constitutes a necessary condition.
	is unlikely to affect	-/1	Forward 'zero degree' semantic causal.	It does not cause anything.
	prevents	-/2	Forward positive semantic causal, associated with opposition.	It causes something not to happen.

Table 3.3. ScholOnto (Buckingham Sum et al., 2000) and ClaiMaker's link taxonomy (Buckingham Shum et al., 2002; 2004), analysed in terms of the relational categories proposed by Sanders et al. (1993) and Louwerse (2001).

However, not all the causal and conditional relations accounted for by the taxonomy are included in the class of causal link types: two of them are to be found in the class of *general* link types and they are called *impairs* and *is-enabled-by*. Impairs can be interpreted both as a causal or a conditional semantic positive relation (although its meaning expresses a negative concept): in its causal form, the relation can be interpreted as meaning that an event A causes an event B not to occur (causal form); in its conditional form, it can be interpreted as meaning that if A occurs, then B does-not occur (which is different from a negative causal or conditional relation, where 'even if' A occurs, B does not occur; or even if A does not occur, B does occur). *Is-enabled-by* (isolated by Mann and Thompson as enablement) is interpretable as a positive conditional relation, which can be interpreted as meaning that A is a necessary but not necessarily sufficient condition for B to occur, that is, B is allowed to occur only if and when A occurs. In the same link category, the relation *uses/applies* (given as a possible alternative expression for *is-enabled-by*) could also be interpreted as a conditional relation, but (like in Trigg) only in the case in which conditionality was clearly implicated, that is, in all those cases in which it was clear that the fact that B uses or applies A also means that B would not be possible (or would not occur) unless A was used/applied (in other words, it would have to be clear that B exists only because A is used/applied) - in all the other cases, uses/applies expresses a different relation, as we see below.

Causal relations are also expressed by most of the link types included in the *support/challenge* class. Precisely, they well represent pragmatic causal relations, both positive and negative, which typically describe the connection between a claim and its arguments. There are two exceptions: *agrees-with* and *disagrees-with*, which in CCR terms seem to correspond to similarity and contrast, or additive and opposition (negative additive) relations. In fact, agreement in itself does not constitute support, but it expresses similarity of perspective or opinion, whose addition to one another can constitute a reinforcement of that perspective itself. That is, if my friends agree with me that "*the prime minister of our country is not a good statesman*", our agreement does not support our opinion that he really is a bad statesman. However, if one of us provides good arguments to motivate the claim, or better, provides evidence that the prime minister is a bad statesman, then the claim is supported[1]. In the same class, *proves* can be described as a case of pragmatic causal relation in the form of claim-evidence, whereas *refutes* as a case of negative pragmatic causal relation in the same form, where the assumption of supportiveness fails. The same can apply to the pair *is-evidence-for* and *is-evidence-against*. Even if less evidently, *is-consistent-with* also expresses a causal (that is, a necessary) relation: a bunch of data or a piece of evidence A can be consistent with a claim (model, theory, etc.) or argument (explanation, justification, etc.) B, in which case A directly supports B, in which case we would have a pragmatic causal relation; alternatively, data, or a piece of evidence, A can be consistent with another set of data or piece of evidence B with respect to a claim (model, theory, etc.) or argument (explanation, justification, etc.) C, in which case a pragmatic causal relation would be implicated in association with a similarity relation. For *is-inconsistent-with*, we could say that the assumption of consistency, that is, of supportiveness fails, so we have a negative pragmatic causal relation.

The remaining link types of the taxonomy included in the *problem-related* class could be interpreted in coherence relation terms as different forms of solutionhood relations as described in Mann and Thompson (1988). *Solves* and *addresses* would both express forms of causality where an initial situation A being evaluated negatively causes it to be addressed or solved by B. In the class of *general* links, instead, *is-about* could be loosely interpreted as a form of elaboration relation, that is, as an additive relation associated to an elaboration criterion. *Improves-on* could also be interpreted as a temporal (sequential) additive relation in form of elaboration, where the elaboration is judged to bring positive change. When not utilised in the way discussed above, *uses/applies*, could also be interpreted as an elaboration relation, in which case the elaboration is constituted by the result of the use or application (whether a concept or a method). In some cases, though, uses/applies could also be interpreted as an evidence (pragmatic causal) relation, and precisely in all those cases in which the use or application B constitutes an empirical example or expression of the abstract entity A.

Finally, at times, the evidence relation could also describe the *example-of* link type, included among the taxonomic link types. In fact, any example has also the function of providing evidence for an argument or claim. For instance, I could say that apes are examples of primates, but I could also say that primates have a frontal vision and bring the example of apes as evidence for what I am saying. However, in its taxonomic function, though, example-of is equivalent to all taxonomic relations, like *part-of* and *subclass-of*, which are not the object of analysis here.

The description of various link taxonomies and semantic hypertext relation ontologies in terms of cognitive coherence relations constitutes a first analytic verification of the applicability of CCR to scholarly hypertext. As we have seen, for the most part the set of cognitive coherence relations proposed by Sanders and Louwerse accounts for the link types that appear in the analysed taxonomies. However, there is a number of links that do not seem at first solely interpretable in terms of Sanders et al. and Louwerse's set of primitives (see Chapter 2, § 2.3-4), but require the use of additional relations. These additional relations are *background, elaboration* (Mann and Thompson, 1988), *specification* (Sanders et al., 1993), *abstraction, formalisation, restatement*, etc. They all seem to partly work on the basis of the CCR primitives, but partly they require the assumption of additional explanatory criteria. It is difficult to provide any exhaustive and definitive explanation for this fact, because most relations are the object of ongoing study. However, we can conclude that these links can still be analysed in the light of the CCR primitives, as complex versions or variations of the CCR primitives themselves. It definitely seems valuable continuing the investigation on cognitive coherence relations and their derivatives, and their applicability to the analysis and construction of hypertext link taxonomies.

The next section analyses a hypertext essay in order to show how CCR can be used as analysis tool with a piece of work that has not been written with the corpus of the cognitive coherence relations in mind.

2. Cognitive Coherence Relations and Hypertext: a Scholarly Hypertext Example

The following analysis of a hypertext argument aims at verifying how easy it is to apply CCR to hypertext when the argument has not been built relying on any link taxonomy, and what their application reveals about the argument's structure. "Hypertext and Suburbs", a dissertation from David Kolb's scholarly hypertext *Sprawling Places* (2004)[2], is used here as an example for this kind of application.

This dissertation draws the parallel between hypertext and suburbs, as a way of understanding both hypertext and suburban spaces, outlining both similarities and contrasts between the virtual spatiality of the new medium and the physical reality of suburbs. Part of a complex argumentative hypertext about places, this relatively contained essay is circumscribed around a specific subject and is therefore rather independent from the rest of the work. Its argument develops over thirteen rather large nodes connected by twenty-nine links.

CCR are used here to analyse three different levels of discourse connections: the connections between hypertext nodes, the connections between paragraphs in a node, the connections between text spans in each paragraph containing links. The full text of the thirteen nodes that compose the dissertation, the hypertext's map and the full analysis of the relations holding at different levels are presented in Appendix. The analysis' results are, however, presented and discussed in the next section.

2.1. Analysis' Results and Interpretation

The differentiated analysis carried out, originally aiming at verifying the applicability of coherence relations to hypertext discourse, reveals that at different levels the plausibility of the judgements (Mann and Thompson, 1988) that can be made about discourse connections varies, as well as the recurrence of relation types that hold between nodes, paragraphs and text spans. The findings for all the nodes at the three levels are summarised in Table 3.4 below and subsequently discussed.

DEFINING PARAMETERS			SPECIFIC FORM	BETWEEN NODES	BETWEEN PARAGRAPHS	BETWEEN TEXT SPANS
causal	semantic	positive	cause			11
			condition			2
		negative	contrastive cause			2
			contrastive condition			2
	pragmatic	positive	argument	3 (elaboration?)		8
			background	7 (elaboration?)		2
		negative	contrastive argument			1
additive	semantic	positive	similarity		6	4
			list			5
		negative	contrast		12	2
			alternative		1	4
	pragmatic	positive	enumeration	1	3	19
			elaboration	16	8	34
		negative	concession		2	11
total relations for each level of connections				**27**	**32**	**107**

Table 3.4. Results of the application of CCR to the analysis of discourse connections between nodes, between paragraphs and between text spans in Hypertext and Suburbs, from *Sprawling Places* by David Kolb (2004) (http://www.dkolb.org/sprawlingplaces/suburbsa.html).

In general the subject of the argument, the particular approach to hypertext adopted by Kolb and the very fact that it is an argument seem to determine the recurrence of certain relations and discourse patterns. That is, the fact that the argument develops around a comparison is responsible for the recurrence of the several similarity and contrast relations within nodes; the fact that elaboration and background relations tend to prevail between nodes depends on Kolb's 'regional' approach to hypertext argumentation (Kolb, 1997 - Chapter 1, § 2); and the fact that this piece of hypertext is an argument determines the presence of so many pragmatic relations. However, each of these aspects ought to be explored more in detail. As said above, apart from analysing in terms of CCR the relations between nodes, the relations between the different paragraphs of single nodes, and between the text spans of single paragraphs are analysed - and the recurrence of different relations between and within nodes, and between nodes and the text spans surrounding links are compared - to verify their distribution.

As shown in Table 3.4, of the 107 relations holding *between the text spans* of the paragraphs containing links, the greatest number consists of elaboration relations (34), followed by enumeration relations (19), concession and cause (11), argument (8), list (5), similarity and alternative (4), contrastive cause, condition, contrastive condition and contrast (2), and contrastive argument (1). The fact that elaboration and enumeration relations are very numerous with respect to the others shows how the argument develops by progressive accumulation of argumentative elements, as well as showing its level of articulation and potential richness from the content point of view. In general the various relations that one would expect to find in argumentative discourse can be detected at this level of analysis. In particular, the fact that a good number of causal relation types is observable at this level shows that here is where the logical structure of the argument properly articulates: as we have seen (Chapter 2), causality constitutes the strongest kind of connection between two discourse parts, which makes each one more dependent on the other. Also, at this level the discourse articulation is often indicated by connectives, which makes the interpretation of relations more straightforward.

At the level of relations *between paragraphs within a single node*, however, the picture seems to be different. Of the 32 connections identified in total between paragraphs, 12 could be interpreted as contrast, 6 as similarity, 8 as elaboration, 3 as enumeration, 2 as concession, 2 as argument, 1 as alternative. Causal relation types seem absent at this level, whereas, in proportion to the total number of relations, similarity and contrast have greatly increased, indicating that it is at this level that the construction of the parallel between hypertext and suburbs is articulated. Despite being additive relations, contrast and similarity constitute powerful elements of text coherence, as they trigger effects of conceptual juxtaposition that help the reader construct a strongly structured mental representation of the argument. In this case, for instance, the pattern of the comparison presenting both similarities and contrasts works as an axis along which the conceptual structure of the discourse develops. In general, partly because the argument is constructed along a parallel, and partly because the related discourse units are still rather short, the relations between text chunks are still easily interpretable.

At the level of relations *between nodes*, the picture changes again. Of the 28 links inter-connecting the hypertext's nodes, 16 seem interpretable as elaboration relations, 7 as background relations, 3 as possible argument relations, 1 as enumeration. That is, almost all the connections between nodes seem to consist of elaboration or background relations, with the exception of the links originating from the starting node. In this node, in fact, the hypertext author succinctly lays out all the elements of his argument - the parallel between hypertext and suburbs, without supporting any of the claims that he makes, which are being supported by the arguments provided in the nodes connected to the starting node. Moreover, one of the two elaboration links from the starting node leads to a dead end node, from which the reader has to return, while the other elaboration link leads to a node that reformulates the parallel between hypertext and suburbs in more general terms, restating its usefulness, this time from the point of view of suburbs (as opposed to the point of view of hypertext)[3]. Apart from this beginning, the rest of the nodes seem to provide for each other elaboration or background information, which helps the understanding of claim-argument structures presented within single nodes, and that are echoed and reinforced by the background and elaboration information provided by the connected nodes. In general, though, making plausibility judgements about each connection is less straightforward than it is at the other levels of analysis, for a number of reasons, due to the lack of explicit connectives, aggravated by the size and complexity of the nodes.

From these data, it seems that the main structural moves of the argument are kept compact within any single node (except for the links originating in the starting node, in the way that we have seen), leaving the connections between nodes to elaborate the main concepts and comparisons drawn within the nodes, and to provide one another with the appropriate context. This means that each node constitutes a relatively accomplished and independent argumentative unit. The starting node presents the main claims and counterclaims of the dissertation, each corresponding argument being contained in the nodes immediately connected to the first one. In turn, then, the content of those nodes is elaborated or provided with a context by other nodes, in a movement of progressive argumentative expansion.

This analysis of the hypertext's structure exactly reflects what David Kolb himself describes as his approach to hypertext (Kolb, 1997 - Chapter 1, § 2). Relations that are structurally more important for the development of an argument tend to be expressed within single nodes - because they connect discourse parts that are subordinate to each other and therefore dependent on each other, that is, because they constitute the logical passage from one stage to the other of the reasoning. This tendency to maintain the integrity of the text fragment containing those relation types reduces the occurrence, between nodes, of such structurally important relations. Instead, less structural, and therefore weaker, relation types tend to characterise the connections between nodes – because they hold between logically non-subordinated discourse parts and therefore are non-dependent on each other. The fact that these are 'looser' relations, though, makes their recognition or definition less straightforward.

We have seen how hypertext argument writers are not too reliant on the medium's interactivity and non-linearity (Chapter 1, § 2). This example shows very well that hypertext writing still tends to be 'textual' - as opposed to hypertextual - since writers tend to choose not to establish structurally essential relations outside the single node, that is, outside the single hypertext discourse unit: in so doing they would expose their discourse to the risk that the reader might not come across passages that are structurally essential to the coherence of discourse, which would compromise the integrity of the argument structure and therefore its effectiveness[4].

As described by Carter (2000), a strategy to handle the fragmentation of hypertext argumentation consists of producing relatively self-sufficient nodes, that is, nodes that contain the crucial connections and passages of the argument within themselves already. The result is that the connections between nodes end up being less structurally critical, while their role is rather to produce a "reinforcement" effect through which the content of single nodes would be amplified and expanded. This way, different nodes tend to be more like variations, explorations, amplifications of one another, rather than constituting one another's structural completion. Consequently, the argument seems to progress across discourse units that produce resonance effects with one another, in a motion of progressive expansion, as exemplified in the analysed example.

A consequent aspect of this approach is that nodes tend to be rather large and quite articulated (as in the analysed example), which, as we have seen, makes it more difficult to determine what relation exactly holds between two nodes. In other words, the longer, more complex and more autonomous the related units, the more general the relation becomes that can be inferred between them. And among the different relations that we have found, background and elaboration are the most generic of all, the ones in which the related units are most structurally independent from each other. Ultimately, this aspect is also a consequence of the paratactic construction that often characterises the connection between hypertext nodes, where the interpretation of relations cannot count on the information provided by connectives, and therefore it may be more plausible to infer background or elaboration relations rather than other more committing relation types. This could explain what Miles-Board et al. (2002; Miles-Board, 2003) observed about connectivity in *content regions* on the Web: the fact that *Associative Writing* is mostly expressed in form of elaboration and background relations (through what he calls *reference* links) – between a page in which a subject is presented and a target page containing elaboration or background information that expands or contextualises the information provided in the source page.

3. Expressing Hypertext Coherence Relations

In sum, these analyses suggest that cognitive coherence relations constitute an effective analysis tool. Their application reveals relevant elements of the argument construction and confirms important aspects of the argumentation strategy adopted by the author. If cognitive coherence relations can be productively applied to the analysis of hypertext link taxonomies and arguments, then they could be used as structuring principles in hypertext discourse representation. As far as semantic hypertext is concerned, cognitive coherence relations could support the construction of link taxonomies for semantic hypertext systems, to make sure that all the important relations are represented at least at the general level and that their organisation follows rigorous criteria. As far as web based hypertext is concerned, cognitive coherence relations could be used to offer scholars broad typologies of discourse connections to refer to in their *Associative Writing* (Miles-Board et al., 2002). As far as spatial hypertext is concerned, cognitive coherence relations could be used in their primitive form to define minimally committing conditional rules to support the emergence of hypertext argumentation structures (see Chapter 1, § 6).

Finally, as far as this work is concerned, cognitive coherence relations could be used to define basic hypertext discourse connections, not with the purpose of labelling the links between nodes - as it happens when link taxonomies are used - nor of indicating link types within nodes' text - as it happens in most web based hypertexts - nor with the purpose of classifying nodes' content - but rather, with the purpose of defining alternative ways of consistently representing such basic discourse relations in hypertext in general, and in argumentative hypertext in particular.

We have seen (Chapter 2) how in text the recognition of coherence relations is facilitated and driven by cohesive devices, through which writers can formalise the cognitive connections holding their discourse together. However, such linguistic facilitators cannot be used as easily (and in fact they tend not to be) in hypertext: linguistic cohesive devices can properly be used in linear text, since they indicate the connection between two specific discourse segments that find themselves in a certain order, within a specific hierarchy, whose parts are all visible to the reader; moreover, in text each discourse part is univocally connected to the others, whereas in hypertext a single node can be the target of several links coming from different source nodes. In other words, in hypertext, a node may find itself connected to different nodes and different readers may come across it through very different paths, which makes the use of both anaphoric and connective devices problematic (see Chapter 1, § 3). It is not by chance that in the hypertext example that we have analysed connective and anaphoric signs are not used at all to establish connections between nodes - and this is all the more true for nodes that are multiply connected. Therefore, if cohesive signs are to be used at all in hypertext, they cannot really be part of the node's text, rather they have to characterise the connection between nodes through features that remain "external" to the nodes themselves.

These features, though, do not necessarily consist of labelling links, as in semantic hypertext systems (for instance, Thuring et al., 1991; Streitz et al., 1992; or Marshall et al., 1991). It is true that, according to the cognitive approach, coherence relations are a type of 'necessary' inference that a reader needs in order to achieve coherence and to interpret the relation intended by the author, and when he misses the intended coherence relation or gets it wrong, he has not understood the text (Sanders and Spooren, 2001). However, the text still leaves the readers space for making decisions, especially when the construction is paratactic. Again, according to the cognitive approach, the whole relation interpretation process is influenced and steered by connectives and other relational signals to assist the reader in producing the correct interpretation. However, signalling a relation (as normally happens in text) is not the same as enunciating it (as happens in semantic hypertext), that is, the types of signals used in text still require the interpretative work of the reader. In fact, to produce certain rhetorical effects, many times non-specific connectives are used in argumentative texts, which lend themselves to different interpretations[5]. In cases in which the discourse construction is paratactic, as often happens in hypertext and as we have seen in the example that we have analysed, this interpretation work on the part of the reader becomes more of an enterprise.

In other words, if *coherence* is a cognitive phenomenon that characterises the process of building and maintaining a mental representation of a text rather than the text itself; if it is a cooperative achievement between the writer and the reader; if it is based on the linguistic context, the cultural context and encyclopaedic knowledge of the reader (Bublitz, 1999 - see § 1 of this Chapter); then, text relations are inherently susceptible to being interpreted in different ways. This susceptibility, this irreducible openness, is crucial for the fruition of the discourse conveyed by the text, and, for the reasons discussed above, it ultimately constitutes a crucial characteristic of hypertext discourse. It was previously suggested that leaving space for the reader to deliberate over the relations holding between text parts is important to gain the reader's adherence to the author's vision (see Chapter 1). Because, despite the fact that, given such space, the reader might misunderstand the text and miss the author's point, the gradual and progressive, back and forth, constructive work that the reader engages in allows him to actively re-construct the journey to the author's vision. Therefore, at least in the phase of argument reading, this interpretative space, this ambiguity, ought to be preserved.

On the basis of these observations, it is here proposed that in hypertext discourse, and in particular in argumentative hypertext, 1) cohesive devices could be used to suggest a sense of structure between the nodes, 2) these cohesive devices could be "external" to the text content of the node, and 3) the meaning of each cohesion sign could be left to individual interpretation, that is, the individual could be given the space for making interpretations about the hypertext connections. The next chapter shows how a different set of cohesive devices are at work in cinematic discourse, how the hypertext medium shares fundamental affordances with the cinematic medium, and how the way discourse coherence is achieved in film provides a picture of how it could be achieved in hypertext discourse presentation.

Notes

[1] In other words, an argument or a piece of evidence can support a claim or a position, however, agreement or disagreement have to be supported by an argument or by a piece of evidence, in order to support or challenge any claim.

[2] http://www.dkolb.org/sprawlingplaces/suburbsa.html

[3] Since the work is about urban places.

[4] Unless, of course, the hypertext system could enforce link following.

[5] For instance, we have seen that a high level connective like *and* can be used both for signalling additive or causal relations: if I say "*Yesterday it was raining and the streets got all wet*", *and* is probably signalling a causal relation; however, if I say "*Yesterday I went to the hairdresser and I did some shopping*", *and* is probably signalling an additive sequential relation. Finally, there can be ambiguous cases in which the relation signalled could plausibly be either additive or causal: if I say "*Yesterday I picked up my pay cheque and I paid the bills*", *and* can signal both an additive sequential relation (because I might simply be accounting a sequence of actions that I made yesterday), as well as a causal conditional relation (because the fact that I was able to pay the bills depends on the fact that I received my pay cheque). In cases like this, contextual factors that are external to the text (and not just internal ones) can determine the reader's decisions.

4. Hypertext Coherence as Cinematic Coherence

In this chapter the use of visual and spatial features in hypertext discourse is discussed from a cinematic perspective. Among the different theoretical frameworks that throughout the years have been used to analyse the hypertext medium, it is proposed that cinematic theory seems to best account for its linguistic potentialities. Therefore, theoretical work relating the cinematic approach to hypertext is presented and, based on the parallel between hypertext nodes and links on the one hand, and cinematic shots and edits on the other, the connection between cinema and hypertext is analysed in detail. Elements of cinematic theory are presented and a conventional set of cinematic rhetorical patterns is described. Based on the connection between cinema and hypertext, it is suggested that the way in which in cinematic language rhetorical connections are signalled provides insights into the way, in turn, in which hypertext could use visual and spatial features to mark discourse coherence relations and shape recognisable rhetorical patterns.

1. The Roots of the Connection between Hypertext and Cinema

Over time the connection between cinema and hypertext has been established in a number of ways. However, this connection has often only been superficial, as - to quote Miles (1999) - it has either concerned the exploitation of the "*pictorial qualities*" (p.217) of hypertext or simply the use of images "*to embellish and add 'depth' to otherwise monocultural textscapes*" (p.218) (like in Joyce and Moulthrop). Even in more advanced hypertext work that presents a "*cinematic allure*" (p.218) (like Hypercafé; and textMorphs), Miles still identifies the limits of a literal reduction of the cinematic into a medium whose theory and practice are already dominated by the "*linguistic and grammatical order of the word*" (p.218).

Similarly, a number of commonly used computer applications (like PowerPoint, or Flash) that allow the construction of hypermedia, provide a wide range of cinematic 'effects' (such as dissolve, fade, zoom-in/out, etc.), without necessarily leading to the construction of 'cinematic hypermedia'. These features can effectively be used to produce attractive and entertaining interactive presentations. Those presentations, however, are not any less literary or any more cinematic just because the features that embellish them are borrowed from the cinematic practice. As Miles points out, the extent to which a hypermedia is 'literary' or 'cinematic' depends on the extent to which it is dominated by the linguistic and grammatical order of the *word*, or by the visual and rhetorical order of the *image*[1].

However, this reduction of the cinematic in a literary hypertext is not so surprising, if we consider that cinema itself has undergone a major literary reduction during the evolution of its own language - both in practice and in theory (Jost, 1987; Gaudreault, 1989). What Bordwell (1987) describes as Classical Hollywood cinema is based on transparent narrative models aiming at the representation of logical cause-effect sequences of events in coherent space-time worlds. Such representation relies on rhetorical patterns whose role is to facilitate the interpretation of the images passing by on the screen through an unambiguously ordered narration. It is not by chance that, in developing a narrative theory of cinema, narratology has provided a very useful framework (Metz, 1968/74).

Cinematic avant-garde movements (such as the Russian avant-garde, the Frnech Surrealism, the Nouvelle Vague, etc.) in different periods sought repeatedly to show how this is not the only way cinematic language might have developed, but such conceptions of the medium never entered the mainstream production and always had a relatively short life. However they gave cinema a chance to push its linguistic and expressive forms much further than the mainstream cinematic industry ever felt the need to push them, and to re-open the moving image to its primordial polysemy (Biro, 1982). And it is during one of these avant-garde experiences that cinema came as close to hypertext as it possibly could.

For Miles (1999) hypertext is cinema's revenge on the word. In fact, I would add that cinema started to take its revenge on the word already in the 1960s, during cinematic movements like the French Nouvelle Vague, and with cinematic authors like Alain Resnais. Not only did these artists deconstruct the conventional rhetoric of mainstream cinema by breaking up the linearity of classical narration and leaving the viewer to find and choose all the possible connections between discourse fragments. They also had their scripts written by authors from the literary Nouveau Romans (like Marguerite Duras and Alain Robbe-Grillet), whose narrative structures became more and more fragmented, and whose literary style became more and more 'pictorial' as they went on writing for those cinematic authors.

At the time, though, neither the cinematic authors of the Nouvelle Vague nor the literary authors of the Nouveau Romans possessed a medium capable of sustaining what they were trying to achieve: freeing the polysemy of the cinematic or literary image from the semantic constraints of linear editing and writing, viewing and reading. They were working with media that were technically linear, and could only push them to a limited extent before polysemy became unintelligibility (Ropars-Wuilleumier, 1970). To go further and definitely break through the narrative linearity, they would have needed a medium with the same technical characteristics that hypertext has, a medium that was capable of reifying interactive viewing and reading paths, allowing viewer and reader to give discourse fragments alternative arrangements in a sensitive discourse space.

In other words, I would suggest that it is in this off-stream European avant-garde cinema of the 1960s and '70s that the genesis of 'cinematic hypertext' writing can be traced. In this cinema, script-writers work side by side with directors, the cinematic image generates directly from their word and their word is born as image already (whether it is for the screen or for the book). In this cinema, connections that refuse to establish a univocal continuity of action, time and space in the fictional world reveal the presence of a previously hidden 'writing machine'. It is in this cinema that the "*allure of the cinematic*" (p.218) immanent to hypertext (Miles, 1999) expresses itself most fully. Therefore, it is in looking at this cinema that one understands why hypertext theory needs to look at cinematic theory and practice in order to grasp fundamental aspects of hypertext as a medium.

The focus of this connection between cinema and hypertext is the equivalence between the *cinematic edit* and the *hypertext link*. In particular, Miles looks at them as moments of transitions from one discourse unit to the other (Miles, 1999; Miles, 2001), from what is known (the discourse unit being displayed) to what is unknown (the discourse unit that is to come). Like the edit, a link is a 'risky promise' to get somewhere further on a coherent path, to get to something connectable to (that is, that coheres with) what has already come. And like with the edit, the hypertext reader gives this promise great credit: "*If this link has taken me to this node, this node must be somehow connected with the node that I come from...and I will find out how.*", or "*There is a link here, it must take me to something related to this node or words...what will it be? How am I going to connect it to what I have got here?*"[2].

For Miles this moment of suspension, experienced by the hypertext reader with trust ("*this must take me to something relevant*") and anxiety ("*what will I find and will it make sense?*") at the same time, would be emblematically expressed in cinema by the figure of the *dissolve*. Most of the time, the edit makes itself as invisible as possible to minimise the disruption to the continuity of the fictional representation. With the dissolve, though, the edit acquires duration and corporeality, which gives substance to the performance of the transition, and materialises the 'joints' of the cinematic discourse at the expense of the narration's transparency.

Giving the cinematic transition duration and corporeality, however, is not the only way of making the edit perceivable. The edit does not only perform the syntactic transition from one shot to the other, it also connects "*separations*" (Miles, 1999), that is, it establishes a semantic connection between originally separated fragments. This connection takes the form of the juxtaposition between two shots, that is, between two units of meaningful content. To ensure the continuity of the representation and the fluidity of the narration, in the praxis of classical cinema the juxtaposition of shots is regulated by a number of formal criteria. These criteria are relatively flexible, but their violation is tolerable only to an extent, beyond which any sense of continuity, fluidity, and therefore transparency gets lost. At that point, the flowing becomes jumping and the game of juxtapositions becomes self-evident, liberating the force of the juxtaposition act itself. This is what happens with the cinema of Resnais and Godard, and this is what utterly characterises the hypertext experience, where the juxtaposition act is arranged by the author, but is accomplished by the reader himself (Mancini, 2000; Mancini and Buckingham Shum, 2001; Mancini, 2003; Mancini and Buckingham Shum, 2004).

2. Cinematic Language and Cinematic Coherence

Cinematic signification is based on the juxtaposition of shots, by which the film's discourse is generated. The shot is the cinematic minimal linguistic unit (the frame being the minimal technical unit), which, in semiotic terms, is the equivalent of a linguistic enunciation (i.e. the simplest shot is already a rich semantic unit). By *juxtaposition*, such 'self standing fragments' generate the film discourse before the viewer's eyes: a series of related shots constitutes the sequence, a series of related sequences constitutes the macro-sequence, and a series of related macro-sequences constitutes the film. Relations between shots, sequences and macro-sequences are to be established at different levels and in multiple ways. The practice of reading cinematic text precisely consists of establishing connections between shots, and the ability to read consists of being able to establish coherent connections[3].

This 'cinematic literacy' is acquired over time through exposure, and consists of becoming acquainted with the representational conventions and patterns that regulate the cognitive connection of shots. The most basic of these conventions and patterns progressively developed through a process of 'cultural selection' that took half a century of cinematic practice since the birth of the medium. All along they have been guiding the viewer's interpretation of the shot chain, allowing him to construct a coherent cognitive representation of the film's discourse. Due to the iconic and indexical nature of the medium and the semantic complexity of its minimal linguistic units, though, these conventions and patterns do not constitute a grammar, they constitute a rhetoric. That is, in contrast to natural language, which responds to grammatical rules as well as to rhetorical conventions, cinematic language only responds to rhetorical conventions, that is, cinematic language has no grammar. And this is due to the nature of the cinematic signifier.

The minimal linguistic unit of natural language is the phoneme, a non-signifying differential element, whose combination generates morphemes (words) successively articulated to generate the enunciation (De Saussure, 1922). However, while the phoneme is a *symbolic* abstract element, the *shot* is an *iconic* and *indexical* semantically rich element (Peirce, 1931-35), which, in semiotic terms, is the equivalent of a linguistic enunciation (Metz, 1974). In natural language the association between the signifier and the signified is *non-motivated*, that is, the correspondence between them is generally convention-based[4]. This means that in natural language abstract concepts can be explicitly expressed, while the user refers to a mental representation of the concrete experiences that have lead to the development of that abstract concept in the first place[5].

In contrast, because the cinematic sign is produced through the technical mediation of the pro-filmic reality (Metz, 1974), in cinematic language the association between the signifier and the signified is *motivated*, that is, the correspondence between them is much less convention-based. And this means that cinematic language expresses abstract concepts in a more implicit way, through the re-presentation of concrete elements (situations and events), leaving the viewer to construct additional layers of meaning by interpreting what is displayed on the screen[6].

As we have seen (Chapter 2), in natural language the connections between enunciations (which are the equivalent of the cinematic linguistic unit) can be signalled by morphemes, that is, cue phrases. Cue phrases express abstract concepts in themselves, that is, they express the concept corresponding to the specific relation that they signify. For instance, the cue phrase "*because*" between the enunciations "*I missed the bus*" and "*I left home late*" expresses a concept of causality, that is, the coherence relation holding between the two spans of text[7]. Obviously, the relation would hold and the concept of causality could still be inferred even if the construction was paratactic, that is, even if the cue phrase "*because*" was not there. However, the point is that natural language is capable of directly indicating an abstract concept like causality, entirely independently from the content of the related text spans.

In cinema, however, connective and cohesive devices like cue phrases do not exist, for the reasons that we have explained above. In cinema there are no formal elements that indicate a specific abstract concept, and especially the abstract concept of a discourse connection. This means that cinematic connections are fundamentally always paratactic and they are established not on the basis of a grammatical sign, but on the basis of a number of contextual elements. That is, to know that a connection is meant to hold between two shots, I need to see a whole sequence (or at least a good section of it) before I am able to get a global picture of whatever is represented and identify the relations that hold between the different shots. For instance, if a shot shows a character's eyes and the following shot shows a green landscape, then the user interprets the second shot as the character's view; but if in a third shot, a camera zoom out from his eyes shows the character to be in a snowy landscape, then the user realizes that there is a conflict between the two views, and must seek another plausible interpretation for that edit.

In other words, in cinema linguistic elements do not have a univocal and specific meaning; meaning must be defined contextually, which is why cinematic language cannot be considered a grammar, but has to be considered a rhetoric (Metz, 1974). As a consequence, in principle, any cinematic connection tends to be seen as potentially coherent, as viewers seek constantly to make sense of transitions. From this it also follows that a connection is not in principle right or wrong, but good or bad, effectual or ineffectual, as the cinematic sequence has to be deciphered as a structural whole (Miles, 1999).

Interestingly, something similar happens in text whenever there is paratactic construction. That is, when connectives are not used to indicate the relation holding between two text spans and two discourse fragments are simply juxtaposed, the reader is left the responsibility to make a decision about the relation holding between them, which opens the possibility that more than one relation might hold. As we have seen, this is supported by experimental evidence that shows that it takes longer for the reader to identify a relation that is not signalled by a connective (Sanders an Spooren, 2001). It is plausible that the extra time that the text reader takes to decide which relation holds between two juxtaposed text spans is mirrored into the moment of indecision and anxiety that Miles characterises as the experience of both the film viewer and the hypertext reader during the transition between shots and between nodes.

The next section discusses how cinematic viewers are enabled to interpret shot connections in order to recognise discourse structure. First, it describes the cinematic formal apparatus that authors can use to shape discourse connections, and therefore structure recognisable discourse patterns. Discourse structure being focused on, it then describes a set of cinematic rhetorical patterns, developed through the medium's evolution and referred to in classical cinema. Finally, it talks about the norms according to which cinematic codes need to be used within such rhetorical patterns in order for them to be perceived as unambiguous and readily interpretable.

3. Cinematic Coherence and Cinematic Cohesion Devices

Although cinematic discourse relations are not explicitly expressed by specific linguistic devices, a number of formal elements are used by the audience to cognitively connect and group the shots of a film in ways that facilitate the construction of a coherent representation of the film's contents. Given the complexity of the cinematic medium and therefore of the cinematic signifier, these formal elements result from the articulation of several linguistic parameters. Casetti and Di Chio (1992) group them under five main categories (shown in Table 4.1).

CLASSES AND SUBCLASSES OF CINEMATIC CODES				
Basic Technological Codes	*Medium's Codes*	sensitivity	more or less sensitive film	
			more or less film granularity	
		format	super8 (more realistic effect)	
			35/70mm (more detailed, spectacular image)	
	Sliding Codes	rate	18 frames per sec.	
			24 frames per sec. (today)	
		direction	forward	
			backward	
	Screen Codes	surface	reflecting	
			transparent	
		luminosity	canvas (based on)	
			plaster (based on)	
Visual Codes	*Iconic Denomination And Recognition Codes*	(allow us to isolate, identify and recognise distinct objects)		
	Iconic Transcription Codes	rendering		
		distortion		
	Iconic Composition Codes	figuration		
		plasticity		
	Iconographic Codes	(determine the organization of complex figures)		
	Stylistic Codes	(reveal the personality and idiosyncrasy of the author)		
	Photographic Codes	perspective organization (determine distribution of objects in space with respect to a point)		
		screen edges (determine space-in and space-off)		
		shooting modalities	scale of shots	very long shot
				long shot
				medium shot
				total
				whole figure
				american shot
				half figure
				close up
				very close up
				detail
			angle degrees	frontal
				plongée
				contre-plongée
			inclination degrees	normal inclination
				oblique inclination
				vertical inclination
		illumination		neutral
				marked
		colouring		black&white
				colour
	Movements Codes	pro-filmic movements (in the reality in front of the camera)		
		real camera movements		Panoramic
				Dolly
		apparent camera movements		Zoom-in
				Zoom-out

Graphic Codes (visual appearance of text)	captions		
	subtitles		
	titles		
	writing form		
Sound Codes	nature and origin	voice	character
			narrator
		noises (diegetic)	
		music (diegetic and commentary)	
	location of the sound	in (diegetic from within the visual field)	
		off (diegetic from outside the visual field)	
		over (extra-diegetic from outside the represented world)	
Syntactic Codes (montage codes)	association by identity (an element of the image is in both or all the connected shots)		
	association by analogy and contrast (two shots' content is similar or contrasting)		
	association by proximity (two shots show contiguous elements in the diegetic world)		
	association by transitiveness (one shot's content is the continuation of other shot's)		
	association by combination (two shots are juxtaposed without connecting element)		

Table 4.1. Casetti and Di Chio's classification of cinematic codes' categories and subcategories (this is a re-elaboration of a table in Casetti and Di Chio, 1992, pp.66-67).

Basic technological codes, concern the physical composition of the cinematic message. Among them are *medium codes*, like *sensitivity* to light (films that are more sensitive also have a coarser grain creating different visual effects) and *format* of the film (Super8 gives a more natural and realistic effect, but 35mm and 70 mm give a more detailed and spectacular image, and allow faster camera movements). Also, among basic technological codes are *sliding codes*, like *rate* (at the beginning it used to be 18 frames/sec, but nowadays it is 24 frames/sec, with different visual effects) and *direction* (which can be the same as the direction of the shooting or contrary). Finally, there are *screen codes*, like *surface* (which can be reflecting or transparent), *luminosity* (which depends on whether the material is canvas or plaster), and *width* (screens can be very small or very big, and obviously the effect on the viewer is very different).

The second large group Casetti and Di Chio account for is constituted by *visual codes*, determining the modalities of representation and the perception of what appears on the screen. They include *iconic denomination and recognition codes* (thanks to which we can isolate, identify and recognise distinct objects within the shot), *iconic transcription codes* (which determine the graphic representation of any object according to cultural conventions and stereotypes), *iconic composition codes* (that determine the composition of the visual space within the shot, in terms of grouping objects and putting them in perspective), *iconographic codes* (that determine the organisation of complex figures), and *stylistic codes* (those aspects of the image that reveal the personality and idiosyncrasy of the author). Visual codes also include *photographic codes*, like *perspective organisation* (that determine the distribution of objects in space with respect to a point), *screen edges* (which discriminate a space-in and a space-off), *shooting modalities* (determining the *scale of shots – very long shot, long shot, medium shot, total, whole figure, American shot, half figure, close up, very close up, detail*; the *angle degrees – frontal, plongée, contre-plongée*; and the *inclination degrees – normal inclination, oblique inclination* and *vertical inclination*), *illumination* (it makes a difference whether it is neutral or marked) and *colouring* (which can be black&white or colour). Finally, visual codes include *movement codes*, like *pro-filmic movement* (when it is the object and the reality in front of the shooting camera that are moving[8]), *real camera movements* (which may consist of *panoramic* and *dolly*) and *apparent camera movement* (that is, the *zoom in* or *out*).

Another major group of parameters described by Casetti and Di Chio includes *graphic codes*, like *captions'*, *subtitles'*, *titles'* and *writings' form*, determining the appearance of text on the screen, its visual form.

Sound codes, concern the *nature and origin* of any sound, like the *voice* of a character or the voice over of a narrator, *noises* originating in the represented world, and *music* originating within the represented world as well as commentary music. Among the sound codes there is also the *location of the sound's source*, which can be *in* (coming from within the space visible in the shot), *off* (coming from outside the space visible in the shot, but still belonging to the represented world, that is, the *diegetic* world[9]) and *over* (coming from outside the represented world and having the role of narrative commentary).

Finally and very important is Casetti and Di Chio's fifth category of codes: *syntactic codes*, or montage codes, determining the criteria of association between shots. Shots can be associated (edited) by *identity* (when an element of the image is present in both or all the connected shots), by *analogy and contrast* (when the content of one shot is similar or equivalent to the content of the other shot; when the content of one shot contrasts with the content of the other shot), by *proximity* (when two shots show elements that are meant to be contiguous in the diegetic world), by *transitiveness* (when the situation presented in the first shot finds its continuation and conclusion in the second shot) and by simple *combination* (when two shots are simply juxtaposed without presenting any connecting element, as it happens for instance in the conjunction between the last shot of a sequence and the first shot of the following sequence, with no other elements of connection provided).

All of these codes determine the form of each shot and each sequence in the film, and a good praxis of cinema requires the ability to handle the interaction between them, while an intelligible film requires them to be handled according to certain rhetorical conventions and linguistic norms. Theoreticians like Burch (1969), Metz (1974), Chatman (1978; 1990) and Branigan (1992) have described and categorised these conventions and norms: the conventions concerning the different modalities in which space, time and events can be represented; the norms concerning linguistically appropriate or effective ways of reifying those modalities.

The next subsection describes a categorisation of rhetorical patterns that can be shaped through the cinematic codes just described. Although the use of such codes determines in first instance the internal organisation of shots, in the economy of this work the aspect of shot composition is not discussed[10]. That aspect is here taken for granted to focus on the next level of cinematic composition: the organisation of sequences (however, we will touch on the aspect of shot organisation when discussing cinematic compositional and transitional norms using filmic examples).

3.1. Cinematic Rhetorical Patterns

The first systematic categorisation of cinematic rhetorical patterns is the one proposed by Metz: *La Grande Syntagmatique* ("*the great syntactic system*", 1974). At the highest level, Metz divides cinematic syntagmas into three major groups: *autonomous shots*, *a-chronological syntagmas* and *chronological syntagmas*. A syntagma is a large and articulated relatively independent discourse unit representing the whole of a scene, which is a narrative section defined by unity of action, time, or space, depending on its narrative function (Metz's classification of syntagmas is shown in Table 4.2.).

CLASSES AND SUBCLASSES OF CINEMATIC RHETORICAL PATTERNS				
Autonomous Shots	*sequence-shot*			
	Autonomous Inserts	*non-diegetic*		
		subjective		
		shifted diegetic		
		explicative		
A-Chronological Syntagmas	*parallel syntagma*			
	brace syntagma			
Chronological Syntagmas	*descriptive syntagma*			
	Narrative Syntagmas	*alternate syntagma*		
		Linear Syntagmas	*scene*	
			sequence	*ordinary*
				episode

Table 4.2. Metz's Grande Syntagmatique: a categorisation of cinematic sequence types (this table is from Metz, 1974).

Among the *autonomous shots* are *sequence-shot* and *autonomous insert.* In the sequence-shot syntagma, a whole scene is shown from beginning to end in a single shot without any edit cuts, which means that whatever is represented is characterised by unity of time, space and action. With respect to the pro-filmic, the camera is placed in a position from which the development of the whole action - for instance a dialogue around the dinner table - can be followed. Linguistically close to the very origins of cinema, this is the syntagma preferred by the directors of the Italian Neo-Realist cinema - as in films like *Roma, Cittá Aperta* (Roberto Rossellini, 1945) or *Ladri di Biciclette* (Vittorio De Sica, 1948) - whose mission was the truthful and least mediated representation of war and post-war reality.

In the *autonomous insert*, a detail that is 'external' to a scene is brought into that scene by one short shot. The autonomous insert can be *non-diegetic*[11], when a detail taken from another world or situation is brought in as term of comparison with the represented world or situation. For instance, in *La notte di San Lorenzo* (Taviani brothers Paolo and Vittorio, 1982), a battle between partisans and fascists takes place in a field, where a character who loves Homer's epic poetry is hit by a fascist weapon: by inserting a shot showing him in a Greek armour being pierced by lances, he is compared to a dying hero in a Homeric epic.

In the *subjective* autonomous insert, what is inserted in a single shot is a flash from a character's memory or fantasy, obviously external to the reality in which he is being represented. For instance, in a room a character sees the photo of someone who is dead and a shot picturing that person alive appears.

In the *shifted diegetic* autonomous insert, a one-shot flash back or forward appears in the middle of a scene. This syntagma is similar to the subjective insert, with the difference that in this case it is not the memory or fantasy of a character to motivate the insertion of the shot, rather it is the 'memory' or 'projection' of the film itself. Its function is to make the viewer 'read' the present situation in the light of something preceding or following it. And since its 'motivation' is external to the represented world, the use of such a rhetorical solution may end up making the narration 'opaque' (as opposed to transparent), depending on how its insertion is handled (if the duration is too short, if the editing is not smooth enough, etc.).

Finally, in the *explicative* autonomous insert, a detail is inserted into a scene to explain and make more understandable a situation. For instance, the detail of a letter's text - enlarged to the point where the viewer can read the bad news written in it - inserted into a scene showing a young woman in the act of crying while she reads the letter.

In the group of the a-chronological syntagmas there is the *parallel* and the *bracket* syntagma. In the *parallel* syntagma a double or triple series of shots alternate representing different actions taking place. These actions, though, are never converging, running parallel to one another till the end of the sequence, being connected by some sort of comparison or contrast but not by any temporal or even spatial relation. For instance, a sequence representing the day of a poor man and the day of a rich man in the big city would contrast the different conditions in which they live, the different ways in which they work, eat, and face the difficulties of life.

In the *bracket* syntagma, a number of shots are grouped together not necessarily with temporal or spatial relations, or continuity of action. They simply evoke and put together situations that have something in common in some respect, by gathering 'samples' from those situations. For instance, to represent the horrors of the war, images of dead, injured, fighting, crying, wandering, and fleeing people can be put together in one syntagma to be read as a unit.

In the group of the chronological syntagmas there is the *descriptive* and the *narrative* syntagma. In the descriptive syntagma, the shots that find themselves connected illustrate different aspects or elements of the same place, environment or situation. In this pattern the dimension of time is suspended, because despite the time it necessarily takes for the shots to display on the screen, they are meant to be read as simultaneous. In addition, there is unity of space because the represented elements are meant to physically coexist. For instance, to describe a forest, a number of shots respectively showing an open field, a few trees, animals running around, a landscape, flowers, and so on, could be put together.

Narrative syntagmas can be of different types. In the *alternate* syntagma two series of alternating shots respectively represent the development of two actions. This pattern is similar to the parallel syntagma, with the fundamental difference that in this case at the end of the sequence the two actions converge. This means that between the two series of shots there is meant to be simultaneity, and that the consecutiveness of the shots within each series is meaningful from the narrative point of view. For instance, in Charlie Chaplin's films, the scenes where the police run after Charlie are often represented with this linguistic solution: shots showing the running policeman alternate with shots showing the running Charlot, until the two come together in the same shot and Charlot is caught. This syntagma was an early and fundamental conquest for cinema, because it freed its language from the constraints of linearity imposed by the medium[12].

In contrast to the alternate syntagma, in the *linear* syntagma the shots are all to be read consecutively, as illustrating the development of a single action. When the action is meant to be continuous, that is, when there is unity of time, we have a proper *scene*. When the action is represented in a discontinuous way, we have a proper *sequence*. The scene is used for short actions whose parts are all relevant and worth seeing, like for instance in a dialogue. Instead, the sequence is used for longer actions in which only some parts are narratively relevant and therefore worth representing. For instance, it would be impossible and irrelevant to represent a battle as a scene, since most likely representing only a few parts would be enough to give the viewer the information he needs in the economy of the narration.

Finally, the sequence can be of two types. When it represents the parts of an action that is extended but is still to be considered as a unit, we have an *ordinary* sequence. When it represents distinct episodes that are part of separated actions but need to be considered to belong to a particular situation or event, we have the *episode* sequence. This is the case if, for instance, instead of just representing a single battle, a sequence puts one after the other a number of little scenes representing the different battles that a character has been through, or that have happened in a war.

3.2. Cinematic Compositional and Transitional Norms

Metz's syntagmas described above, are abstract models of cinematic rhetorical patterns, and in the praxis of cinema they have many exceptions, as Metz himself admits. However, they can be identified in films frequently enough to have become established analysis tools for theoreticians and practical rules for film-makers to follow (as in Classical cinema) – or to break (as in Modern cinema). The implementation of these narrative patterns undergoes a number of norms, the most important of which concern the editing between shots: it is on the way in which the different shots of a film connect that the effectiveness of rhetorical patterns depends. The function of these norms is to make it easy for the viewer to perceive shots as connected to one another, and as connected in a certain way, making up specific patterns (Burch, 1969).

Essentially these norms place requirements or constraints on the articulation of the technological, visual, graphic, sound and syntactic codes described above, within each shot and between different shots. They pertain to the way the formal elements of the cinematic medium and their interaction across the film are to be handled. That is, they prescribe criteria for the formal organisation of the whole film, for its parts and their interaction. The foremost of these criteria is *consistency*: certain choices need to be maintained throughout the entire film if the use of the formal elements that they involve is to be meaningful or acceptable at all. When formal elements are used with consistency, this creates regularities, and determines the establishment of local codes that will guide or condition the viewer's interpretation of the film.

A film's language is based on networks of regularities working across the film itself: some characterise the cinematic language in general and come from the cinematic practice; others characterise a single film and depend on the particular choices made by the film makers. In fact, this is a fundamental aspect of cinematic language. Since, as we have seen, the meaning of a cinematic sign is not intrinsic but is established contextually, the practice of setting contexts through the consistent and regular use of formal elements is the key to deciphering the meaning of any cinematic sign.

For instance, if I choose a black-and-white film, the scale of greys will set the viewer's perception, and he will interpret whatever is represented in the movie on the basis of that zero degree. If then I insert a coloured element or an entire coloured shot, the viewer will perceive that insertion as meaningful. This is what happens with the red flag hoisted on the ship in *Bronenosets Potyomkin* (*Battleship Potemkin*, Sergei Eisenstein, 1926) (Eisenstein, 1964) and with the little girl's red coat in *Schindler's List* (Steven Spielberg, 1995): because everything is in greyscale, the symbol of the communist revolution represented by the flag screams out even more because it is the only element to have a colour; similarly, the little girl becomes an individual, a unique human being because her figure stands out from the grey mass of the crowd that surrounds her (yet she moves around unnoticed by the people around them, as the Holocaust's bloodshed went unnoticed by the world).

In some films, particular lighting is used in certain scenes, while another type of lighting is used in other types of scenes. In *Deserto Rosso* (*Red Desert*, Michelangelo Antonioni, 1964) red lighting is used to express the unquietness of the main character's inner world (Cuccu, 1990). This meaning is established by the fact that the shots in which she appears or the shots that are meant to represent what she sees have that lighting. Other films or cinematic schools use visual (iconic, photographic and movement) codes in a very characteristic way. For instance, in Expressionist cinema, lights produce very strong contrasts, the actors act in a very dramatic way and wear very strong make up, the *mise-en-scene* is full of angles, diagonal lines, and so on - as in films like *Faust* (Friedrich Murnau, 1926) or *Metropolis* (Fritz Lang, 1927).

Apart from consistency, another main criterion determining the use of formal elements within and between shots is *continuity*. Continuity is important at the formal level, to provide integrity to the film as a discourse and as a work of art, but it is also critical as far as the representation of diegetic space, time and events are concerned. Practically all the rules of montage have the purpose of establishing continuity between the different parts of a film, which is the base for the organic unity and fluidity of its narrative. The most important of these rules concern the linking between shots that are to be read as parts of one sequence.

For instance, whenever two shots in which the camera is moving are edited, a sense of continuity will be produced if the movement of the camera is on the same axis in both shots. If a sequence represents the bus journey of a child to school showing from his point of view the streets that the bus drives across, the camera will be moving sidewise in one direction; if the shots are linked on the same camera movement, this gives the sense of the continuity of the journey itself, from the point of departure to the point of arrival. If a director wants to show the same journey setting the point of view outside the bus in the street, he might have the bus entering a shot from one side and exiting from the other. To maintain continuity in the linking of the various shots, if the bus exits the previous shot from the right side of the visual field, typically it will enter the following shot from the left.

One way of representing a dialogue is to alternate a series of shots respectively showing the characters engaged in the dialogue. To give continuity and cohesion to the editing, one of the characters will always be looking towards the right side of the visual field, while the other character will always be looking towards the left side. This way, it will seem that they are looking at each other, which gives a sense of continuity to the physical space in which they find themselves and to their action. If, instead, the dialogue is represented from an external point of view and the characters are both visible in the same shots, then their relative position in the visual field should stay unvaried from one shot to the other, to give a sense of stability to the representation of the space and continuity to the action.

Continuity of action often also requires continuity of space, which means that, to represent in more than one shot an action that is meant to start and end on the same spot or in one circumscribed place, the scenario of the different shots should remain the same. If however I want the action to stretch from one place to the other, I have to let the discontinuity of place show in the connection between the two shots. If I wanted to show the action of a character moving from one place to another place, while it would be appropriate that I established the connection based on the direction of his motion, it would be less appropriate if I did so on the exact continuation of his motion: from the first to the second shot, the scenario would be different, and it would be impossible that a motion started in one shot could exactly continue in the following shot, without giving the viewer the feeling of an artificial connection. However, if it did, and the use of other formal elements was consistent with that, then it might be meaningful. For instance, in *Hiroshima mon amour* (Alain Resnais, 1959), the main protagonist is recounting how her mother punished her (for having slept with a German soldier) by locking her in the cellar of the house. She says that the mother "threw" her in the cellar, and when she says that, a shot shows her in her room (on an upper floor) being grabbed by the mother and violently pushed off the visual field on the right side. In the next shot, she comes in from the left side, with exactly the same speed and her movement being exactly continuous (which in reality is obviously impossible, since the cellar is a separate place located two floors below her room). However unrealistic, the function of that linking is to emphasise the concept of "being thrown" into the cellar expressed in the dialogue and to underline the hostility of her family.

The list of examples showing how the criteria of consistency and continuity are interlaced and constitute basic principles of cinematic language is obviously endless. Some film schools and film-makers rigorously follow them within the tradition of classical cinema; other schools and film makers follow them in dialectic with classical conventions. However, the two criteria of consistency and continuity have to be followed, as they create the conditions for the intelligibility of any film. In fact, the use of cinematic formal elements according to the criteria of consistency and continuity makes the filmic discourse units identifiable and their articulation perceivable. In other words, the consistent and continuous use of formal elements provide cohesion to the film's discourse, and this allows the viewer to construct a coherent cognitive representation of the film's content.

4. From Cinematic Coherence to Hypertext Coherence

The thesis of this book is that the way cinematic language works, through the use of its formal elements according to a number of principles that lead to the activation of certain discourse patterns, is very relevant to hypertext, especially as far as the problem of discourse coherence is concerned (Mancini, 2000; Mancini and Buckingham Shum, 2001; Mancini, 2003; Mancini and Buckingham Shum, 2004). The fact that cinematic language is sequential and based on images, whereas - scholarly - hypertext is interactive and mainly based on text, constitutes a technical but not necessarily a linguistic difference, as far as the discourse construction dictated by the medium is concerned.

As we have seen, the great 'openness' of the cinematic shot to multiple connections comes from its very semantic richness, as well as from the absence of abstract connectives. And for the same reason that the cinematic shot is such a semantically rich discourse unit, this openness is also a necessity. That is, the semantic richness of the shot is due to its iconicity and indexicality, which bind the denotative dimension of the cinematic sign to the act of *monstration* (Gardies, 1981; 1993), the *here and now* of the camera mediation. In other words, because what generates the cinematic sign is the mechanical mediation of the *pro-filmic* reality, the cinematic shot can only show what was there when the mediation took place. Categories of space and time, as well as all abstract concepts, have to be represented from there, through the articulation of "here-and-now fragments".

It takes two text sentences, one after the other, to say: "*That Winter was incredibly harsh, and hardly any of the animals in the forest made it to the Spring*". In principle, it may take a dozen shots to express the same idea through a cinematic sequence, and they will have to be read not necessarily as a sequence, but according to patterns like for instance the alternate or the descriptive syntagma[13]. At the same time, while expressing that concept, the dozen of shots making the sequence will be expressing many other concepts. The very consequence of all this is that, despite cinema being, technically speaking, a linear medium, cognitively speaking it is much less linear than natural language is, and this makes cinematic discourse much closer to hypertext discourse than linear, paper based, text could possibly be[14].

Furthermore, we have seen how text cohesion is established through connective devices - cue phrases - which give formal expression to the relations holding between discourse parts by indicating them at different levels of specificity[15] and facilitate their understanding, while remaining external to the related text spans themselves. We have also seen how, due to the iconic and indexical nature of the cinematic sign, in cinema this cohesive function is not exercised by denotative devices that explicitly express the relation holding between shots. Instead, this function is achieved at a connotative level, through the concurrent and contextual use of formal elements, according to principles of consistency and continuity. In this respect too, cinema is closer to hypertext than text is: although in hypertext the use of cue phrases or labels is possible, its effectiveness is at least questionable, not to say highly problematic. And in fact, they tend not to be used, which contribute to making hypertext nodes the autonomous discourse units that they are: self standing cores of contents potentially connectable to many other autonomous discourse units - just like cinematic shots.

Also, despite scholarly hypertext's strong reliance on text, and the fact that hypertext discourse is often made of text nodes (probably "*embellished*" with images and graphics), hypertext itself remains a visual medium (see Chapter 1). In fact, any text based discourse unit perceivable on the surface of the electronic screen is, before being anything else, a luminous visual object in a visual field, the final product of a stratification of codes at the base of which is a series of zeros and ones. Each hypertext node can have the same textual content, and yet be visually shaped in many different ways according to a number of formal parameters: font, font size, font style, window shape, window size, window background, absolute and relative position on the screen, and so on. As in cinema, each of these formal parameters holds linguistic potential at the connotative level, and like in cinema this potential can be exploited by their concurrent and contextual use.

Miles makes explicit reference to Metz as he demonstrated how, even if individual shots are rich discourse units already, it is only when they are articulated in (and are perceived as) autonomous sequences that they form distinct narrative units (Miles, 2000). Similarly, he also refers to Bernstein and Rosenberg's work on hypertext *patterns* (Bernstein, 1999) and *episodes* (Rosenberg, 2001), whose recognition and interpretation as autonomous segments of discourse is crucial to the intelligibility of structure in hypertext. In other words, like in cinema, fictional and non-fictional hypertext narration is about developing syntactic series. From the same perspective, this work suggests that the "*sequence formed by a series of links*" (Miles, 2000, *Link Meta-structures* node) that Miles talks about could be represented as a pattern through the use of formal elements. These formal elements should connote the connection between nodes rather than the content of the nodes itself, and this should be achieved through their concurrent and contextual use, according to principles of *consistency* and *continuity*.

As Miles proposes, rather than imitating the syntagmatic structures that cinema has developed over half a century of evolution and that are specific to that particular medium, *cinematic* hypertext should investigate the design of recognisable syntagmatic structures 'native' to hypertext's technical properties. Furthermore, the use of cohesive elements is fundamental in the recognition of these semantic structures, as they constitute these structures' formal expression, facilitating the cognitive representation of hypertext discourse relations. Just as in cinema, it is not the relationship established by a single edit that is meaningful, but the network of relationships that can be discerned within the whole structure.

The next chapter defines the cinematic syntagmas described here in terms of the cognitive coherence relations derived from text analysis, and analyses two examples of cinematic sequences to show how the way in which cinematic features lead the viewer to interpret discourse connections can be traced back to CCR. In other words, we will see how, being *cognitive categories*, CCR can be applied to other media, and in particular to cinema.

Notes

[1] What it's meant by visual and rhetorical order of the image will become clear later on.

[2] These are my words, as in the sentences reported in brackets two lines below.

[3] Since the meaning of any single shot changes depending on how it is connected to the others, this is a crucial aspect of the reading practice. Kuleshov's experiments (which re-sequenced the same set of shots to tell different stories) are famous for providing evidence of this phenomenon in cinema (Kuleshov, 1974).

[4] For instance, the word "dog" has nothing in common with its meaning, that is, with the concept (mental representation) of the animal to which it refers.

[5] For instance, the concept of love is associated in my mind to a series of concrete experiences and situations in which that abstract concept manifests itself and that have allowed me to develop that cognitive category. However, natural language enables me to explicitly express that abstract concept, without having to explicitly refer to all those experiences and situations that I associate with it.

[6] For instance, the concept of love would be expressed by showing the actions of two people in situations that provide evidence of the fact that they love each other, and that therefore what exists between them is love.

[7] To be precise, the concept expressed consists of a positive, backward, causal relation (see Chapter 2).

[8] Pro-filmic being the reality that is in front of the camera and that is being shot.

[9] Diegetic refers to the fictional world represented in the film, and diegetic is any element that is part of that represented world.

[10] Simolarly the aspect of text spans composition was not discussed, when we talked about text coherence.

[11] Non-diegetic being an element that is (comes from) outside the fictional world. In *La notte di San Lorenzo,* set in an Italian village at the time of World War II, the allegory of the Homeric hero constitutes a non-diegetic insertion.

[12] The first examples of this discovery are already from the beginning of the 1910s, and can be found in Griffin's films.

[13] For space and spatiality issues in cinema see Gardies (1993), and for time and temporality see Bettetini (1979).

[14] Interestingly enough, parataxis and fragmentation typically characterise the style of Nouveau Romans writers, with the consequence that often those novels are very difficult to read as pieces of literature, but much easier to "see" as if they were describing cinematic sequences.

[15] For instance, the connective *and* can simply indicate conjunction ("*I had some pasta and I tried the pudding*"), but it can also loosely indicate causality ("*I left late and I missed the bus*"), or even contrast ("*I like savoury food and she likes sweets*"). This is because *and* is a very generic connective, it is very high in the hierarchy of connectives, and it can therefore be used to indicate different types of relations. However, for each of them, there will be better indicators (*because* and *but*), in that they are more specific than *and* is (Knott, 1996). We could then say that connectives like *and* express connections that are midway between paratactic and specifically cued connection.

Cinematic Hypertext
C. Mancini
IOS Press, 2005

5. Applying Discourse Coherence Relations to Cinema

If coherence relations are a cognitive phenomenon, they should constitute a principle of discourse coherence not just in text, but in other media too, at least in those in which discourse is generated through the connection of discrete discourse units, as happens in cinema. Moving from this assumption, in this chapter the same cinematic patterns previously described are analysed in terms of Cognitive Coherence Relations (mirroring the analysis in chapter 3 with link taxonomies). Following this, two cinematic sequences are taken as examples to be analysed in terms of coherence relations, interpreting the shot connections that the sequence's visual elements lead the viewer to make. The purpose of this exercise is to motivate the idea that hypertext discourse could be shaped in the same way as cinematic discourse is shaped, because transitions in both media can be described using coherence relations.

1. Cognitive Coherence Relations and their Applicability to a Visual Medium

What makes the CCR theory so interesting with respect to other coherence relations theories is that CCR do not just account for text coherence alone, they claim to account for cognitive coherence. As previously discussed (Chapter 2) the psycholinguistic approach to text analysis considers coherence a cognitive phenomenon, that is, coherence would not be a property of text itself, but a property of the *cognitive representation* of it that the reader constructs while reading. The understanding of a text would then depend on the coherence of this representation (Sanders and Noordman, 2000).

From this perspective, all linguistic markers of coherence relations - cohesive devices - constitute superficial representations of underlying cognitive connections, which - in principle - can be established by the reader no matter whether they are marked or not in the text. Although cue phrases are there to signal what underlying cognitive connection is meant to hold between two text spans, paratactic connections are frequent in text and – depending on the context - they can be still intelligible despite the fact that there are no indices there to alert the reader (Sanders and Noordman, 2000).

If coherence relations are a cognitive phenomenon, determining the cognitive representation of text, then they should also constitute a principle of discourse coherence in other media that are capable of conveying abstract conceptual categories without necessarily being text-based, at least in those media in which discourse is generated through the connection of complex discrete semantic units, like in text and in hypertext. And since cinema presents these characteristics, the connections holding between cinematic discourse units (linguistic equivalents of text spans), as well as the connections holding between hypertext nodes (linguistic equivalents of cinematic shots), as well as the connections holding between text spans, should be readable in terms of cognitive coherence relations, at one or more than one discourse level. At the same time, in cinema as in text, it should be possible to signal coherence relations in ways that are consistent with the specific characteristics of the medium in question – unless they were not represented at all and the connections between conceptual units are paratactic. If this is true, then, CCR could constitute a new analytic tool for cinematic discourse, and also provide insights into new ways of handling the problem of discourse coherence in hypertext.

To show the applicability of CCR to cinematic discourse, two CCR-based analyses of non-prose narrative media are presented here. Firstly, the most popular set of cinematic rhetorical patterns - Christian Metz's *Grande Syntagmatique* (Metz, 1968 - Chapter 4, § 3.1.) - is analysed in terms of CCR, and the meaning of cinematic transitions is explained in those terms. Secondly, a detailed analysis of two filmic examples is presented: a sequence from *Rear Window*, and a sequence from *2001: A space Odyssey*. The relevance and validity of these applications for the purposes of this investigation are determined first of all by the fact that these analysis are performed on discourse structures that, given the characteristics of the cinematic medium, either present no equivalent to linguistic cue phrases, or make occasional use of formal elements whose semantic value is relative and not absolute - that is, their meaning is determined "locally" by their consistent use within a single act of discourse (in this case, the film). Secondly, although technically speaking cinematic discourse is linear, cognitively speaking cinema is one of the least linear of all media (see Chapter 4, § 4.).

2. Cognitive Coherence Relations and Cinema: la Grande Syntagmatique

As previously detailed, Christian Metz identified and described a number of cinematic rhetorical patterns and conventions (referred to as *syntagmas*), that emerged in a process of gradual "natural selection" among all the possible linguistic structures that the cinematic medium was allowing, and that reached their more sophisticated stage of development within what was defined as Classical cinema[1]. The Grande Syntagmatique having already been systematically described (Chapter 4, § 3.1.), this section redefines one by one its various syntagmas in terms of CCR. The purpose of the mapping is not to produce a univocal interpretation of conventional cinematic syntagmas, but to show that interpreting cinematic patterns through CCR is possible. The fact that there can be more than one way of interpreting each syntagma in terms of CCR partly depends on the semantic complexity and polysemy of the cinematic sign with respect to the written word. Plus, being cinematic syntagmas rhetorical patterns, each of them can be used to express infinitely varied contents, and therefore different sets of relations depending to the narrative content. Finally, the same narrative content itself can be interpreted in different ways at different levels.

It could generally be expected that in a-chronological patterns, like *parallel syntagma* and *brace syntagmas,* a-chronological relations, like conjunctiveness and disjunctiveness, as well as similarity and contrast, would mainly tend to hold between the shots. These relations, though, could be expected in the chronological *descriptive syntagmas* too, because the *DS* is meant to express simultaneity. For all the other chronological patterns, like *alternate syntagma*, *linear syntagma*, *scene properly called*, *ordinary sequence* and *episodes sequence*, chronological relations, like sequentiality and causality, could also be expected to prevailingly hold between the shots. Finally, autonomous inserts, *sequence shot* and *insert*, could be expected to hold different relations with either the rest of the sequence in which they are embedded (as in the case of the *insert*), or with the other sequences (as in the case of the *sequence-shot*). Below is a more detailed analysis of each syntagma.

The *parallel syntagma* represents, through alternating shots, different actions taking place simultaneously but in different diegetic spaces and without ever converging. This usually means that the actions represented find themselves in disjunction with each other, that is, the respective shots alternating from each series hold a disjunctive relation with each other. At times, though, the parallel actions, although not converging, are meant to be considered as complementary and equivalent, non-subordinated, parts of a larger picture or whole, in which case they find themselves in conjunction rather than in disjunction. Obviously, though, the parallel syntagma represents the development of the alternating actions, which means that the chronological dimension is represented as well, in this pattern, and therefore, that somewhere sequential relations are also holding between shots[2]. They would hold within and between the shots composing each single series, that is, representing each single action.

In the *brace syntagma*, instead, the temporal dimension is irrelevant, as irrelevant as the spatial dimension, after all. In fact, this pattern has an evocative function, that is, it constructs the picture of a narrative situation or diegetic reality through 'samples' that can be completely disconnected, incoherent, from the temporal and spatial point of view. Since the different shots are meant to evoke a situation or fictional reality, they are meant to be considered as the complementary parts of an organic whole, whose coherence is to be found more at an enunciation level than at a diegetic level. Therefore, the relations that could be expected to hold between the shots of a brace syntagma are mainly conjunctive.

The *descriptive syntagma* representing a situation or environment, and implying simultaneity, the main relation to be expected to hold between the sequence shots is definitely conjunctiveness, because the elements represented by each shot are meant to constitute the coexisting and complementary non-subordinated parts of an organic whole.

With *narrative syntagmas*, however, sequential and causal relations start to play a very significant role, since what is represented through these narrative patterns is action developing in time and according to a cause-effect chain.

The *alternate syntagma* is similar to the a-chronological parallel syntagma, except that it represents converging actions instead of simply parallel ones. In fact, the convergence of the two (or more) action threads creates in the sequence a dramatic focus around which every element presented in the sequence is organised. This has three consequences: the action threads relate to each other definitely more in a conjunctive way than in a disjunctive way, as they constitute the two sides of a broader unique action; the sequentiality is accentuated by the converging process, since the end-goal exerts a 'pulling' effect on what comes before, that is, it sets up a vector along which the action can develop to reach its meant accomplishment; finally, the convergence towards a final goal creates the space for causality, that is, a causality relation holds between the developing action and the final result, the achieving of the final goal or status.

Linear syntagmas are, from a CCR perspective, quite similar, in that they represent a single action thread, which normally implies sequential and/or causal relations holding between the component shots. The main difference is that a syntagma like the *scene properly called* represents an action with continuity of time and space, that is, the representation has the same duration and compactness that the action would have in real life, whereas the *ordinary sequence* is a sort of summary, representing only the parts of the action that are considered to be dramatically effective or functional (the rest is cut off and simply taken for granted or inferred).

The *episodes sequence* may be slightly different, gathering along a single action thread units that are relatively accomplished and therefore independent from each other. In this case, as we would expect, sequentiality becomes a looser connective, while causality may not connect the different episodes at all. However, in this case, conjunctiveness (or its negative) remains a valid connective, since the episodes of the sequence, although relatively independent, still constitute the complementary non-subordinated components of a whole.

All these relations may be found both as connectives between the shots composing a single sequence, and as connectives between sequences. This is fundamental when looking at *autonomous shots*, as they do not have internal articulation (in terms of editing) and relate directly to the sequence or sequences within or between which they find themselves. The *sequence shot* is the most complex of all, as it represents a complete action with its own temporality and spatiality. It can relate to other sequences by conjunctiveness (if coexistence is to be inferred, but not temporality), sequentiality (if also temporality is to be inferred, but not causality) or causality (if also causality is to be inferred).

The *insert* is a relatively simpler linguistic unit, but it may play many different roles and therefore relate to the hosting sequence in many different ways. If it is *non-diegetic*, its typical function is to establish a comparison between elements of the hosting sequence and elements of itself, a comparison that is therefore describable with similarity or contrast relations.

If it is *subjective*, its function is to bring memories or fantasies of a character into the present situation of the diegetic world, and its relation with the situation is often describable as causal, since typically something occurring in the diegetic world triggers the character's thinking.

If it is *dislocated diegetic*, it constitutes either a *flash back* or a *flash forward*, which may typically relate to the hosting sequence by sequentiality, causality, similarity, or the three of them at the same time (as in the case of analogical montage).

Finally, if the insert is *explicative*, it brings in a speculative *detail* that refers to the present situation or environment, but that constitutes a deeper elaboration of what has been already represented.

In general, it could be said that certain categories of shots tend to have different functions, but mainly they connect to the rest either as elaborations, or as background. For instance, not only the explicative insert, but any *detail* or *close-up* shot has an elaborative function, as they explore further or more deeply something that has been represented already[3]. On the other hand, comprehensive shot types lend themselves to play the role of background for something that has been represented already or that is to be represented yet, as in an *establishing* or *master shot*.

Metz's Grande Syntagmatique is described in terms of CCR also in Table 5.1., following which the applicability of CCR to the interpretation of cinematic discourse is demonstrated in the analysis of two famous cinematic examples.

CINEMATIC RHETORICAL SYNTAGMAS				**CCR HOLDING BETWEEN SHOTS**
Autonomous Shots	*sequence-shot*			With other syntagmas' shots: usually conjunctive, sequential or even causal.
	Autonomous Inserts	*Non-diegetic*		With the shots of the embedding syntagma: usually comparison or contrast (enunciation level).
		Subjective		With the shots of the embedding syntagma: typically causal (diegetic level) and elaboration (enunciation level).
		Shifted diegetic		With the shots of the embedding syntagma: typically sequential or causal (diegetic level), maybe similarity or elaboratin (enunciation level).
		Explicative		With the shots of the embedding syntagma: typically elaboration.
A-Chronological Syntagmas	*parallel syntagma*			Between the syntagma's two shot series: prevailingly disjunctive, possibly conjunctive (diegetic level). Within each of the syntagma's two shot series: possibly sequential or causal (diegetic level). With other syntagmas: possibly sequential, causal (diegetic level), elaboration or background (enunciation level).
	brace syntagma			Within the syntagma's shots: usually conjunctive (enunciation level only). With other syntagmas: usually elaboration or background (enunciation level).
Chronological Syntagmas	*descriptive syntagma*			Within the syntagma's shots: usually conjunctive (diegetic level). With other syntagmas: usually elaboration or background (enunciation level).
	Narrative Syntagmas	*Alternate syntagma*		Between the syntagma's two shot series: prevailingly conjunctive (diegetic level). Within each of the syntagma's two shot series: usually sequential or causal (diegetic level). With other syntagmas: usually sequential, causal (diegetic level).
		Linear syntagmas	*Scene*	Within the ssyntagma's shots: usually sequential and causal (diegetic level). With other ssyntagmas: usually sequential, causal (diegetic level), maybe elaboration or background (enunciation level).
			Sequence	Within the syntagma's shots: usually sequential and causal (diegetic level). With other syntagmas: usually sequential, causal (diegetic level), maybe elaboration or background (enunciation level).
			Episode sequence	Within the syntagma's shots: usually conjunctive, sequential and maybe causal. With other syntagmas: usually sequential, causal (diegetic level), maybe elaboration or background (enunciation level).

Table 5.1. Metz's cinematic syntagmas (1974) interpreted in terms of CCR.

3. Cognitive Coherence Relations and Cinema: Two Cinematic Sequences

The analyses reported here are performed on two sequences taken from two different movies. The first one, *Rear Window*, directed by Alfred Hitchcock in 1954, belongs to the tradition of the best Classical cinema and constitutes a highest expression of it. The second film, *2001: A Space Odyssey*, directed by Stanley Kubrick in 1968, constitutes a 'classical' of Modern cinema, whose language constantly pushes the edges of the Classical tradition to the limits of a 'comfortable' readability.

3.1. From Alfred Hitchcock's Rear Window

Jefferies is a photographer, confined to a wheelchair for six weeks, his broken leg in a cast. Bored to death, and obsessive voyeur, spends his days looking with his binoculars through the rear window into neighbours' houses. He soon becomes suspicious that the man living in one of the flats on the other side of the rear court has killed his wife. Not believed by the police, he and his girlfriend Lisa try to gather evidence of the neighbour's guilt. Sneaking into his apartment, Lisa manages to get hold of his wife's wedding ring, but is discovered by the neighbour who realises that he is being spied upon. After the police take Lisa away, and while Jefferies' housekeeper rushes to the police station to get her back, the neighbour comes to his apartment to recover the ring.

When the murderer enters Jefferies' apartment in the middle of the night, the photographer is waiting for him in the wheelchair, the lights off, armed with his camera. Not being able to move, he uses the flash as a weapon to temporarily blind the intruder and buy some time before the women can return with the police. He "shoots" the aggressor several times, and each time he manages to delay him a bit. When is about to get caught, Jefferies screams out of the window, and Lisa comes to his rescue with the police, just in time.

Sequence X

1. *Close-Up*: The door opens, the assassin enters the room and closes it behind himself. Everything is dark, although his eyes are visible. Silence.
2. *Long Shot*: Counter shot: Jefferies is sitting still in his wheelchair, his left leg in the cast. The rear window is open behind him. All is dark and silent.
3. *Long Shot*: Counter shot: The assassin stands at the door, in the dark: "What do you want from me?".
4. *Long Shot*: Counter shot: Jefferies sits still on his wheelchair. Silence.
5. *Long Shot*: Counter shot: The assassin stands at the door, in the dark: "Your friend, the girl, she could have turned me in. Why didn't she?".
6. *Long Shot*: Counter shot: Jefferies sits still on his wheelchair. Silence.
7. *Long Shot*: Counter shot: The assassin stands at the door, in the dark: "What is that you want from me? You want money? I don't have any money".
8. *Long Shot*: Counter shot: Jefferies sits still on his wheelchair. Silence.
9. *Long Shot*: Counter shot: The assassin stands at the door, in the dark: "Say something!"
10. *Long Shot*: Counter shot: Jefferies sits still on his wheelchair. Silence.
11. *Long Shot*: Counter shot: The assassin stands at the door, in the dark: "Say something, tell me what you want!".
12. *Long Shot*: Counter shot: Jefferies sits still on his wheelchair. Silence.
13. *Long Shot*: Counter shot: The assassin stands at the door, in the dark: "Can you get me that ring back?".
14. *Long Shot*: Counter shot: Jefferies moves his hand on his lap towards the camera: "No". The assassin off: "Tell her to bring it back!". Jeffries: "I can't, the police have it by now".

15. *Long Shot*: Counter shot: The assassin starts to advance towards Jefferies (that is, towards the camera).
16. *Medium Close Shot*: Counter shot: Jefferies takes the camera from his lap, covers his eyes with one hand and "shoots" the guy with the other hand.
17. *Long Shot*: Counter shot: While advancing, the assassin gets 'hit' by the flash and stops.
18. *Close-Up*: He brings his hands to his glasses adjusting them, while squeezing his eyes.
19. *Long Shot*: Counter shot: A circle of orange light expands through the visual field, blurring the image of the journalist, who in the meanwhile recharges the camera with a new flash.
20. *Close-Up*: Counter shot: The assassin re-opens his eyes and starts moving forward again.
21. *Medium Close Shot*: Counter shot: Jefferies completes the recharge of the camera, looks backward out the window, turns to his front again, covers his eyes with one hand, and "shoots" with the other hand.
22. *Long Shot*: Counter shot: While advancing, the assassin gets hit by the flash and stops.
23. *Close-Up*: He brings his hands to his glasses adjusting them, while squeezing his eyes.
24. *Long Shot*: Counter shot: A circle of orange light expands through the visual field, blurring the image of the journalist, who in the meanwhile recharges the camera with a new flash.
25. *Close-Up*: Counter shot: The assassin re-opens his eyes and starts moving forward again.
26. *Medium Close Shot*: Counter shot: Jefferies completes the recharge of the camera, looks backward out the window, turns to his front again, covers his eyes with one hand, and "shoots" with the other hand.
27. *Long Shot*: Counter shot: While advancing, the assassin gets hit by the flash light and stops.
28. *Close-Up*: He brings his hands to his glasses adjusting them, while squeezing his eyes.
29. *Long Shot*: Counter shot: A circle of orange light expands through the visual field, blurring the image of the journalist, who in the meanwhile recharges the camera with a new flash.
30. *Close-Up*: Counter shot: The assassin re-opens his eyes and starts moving forward again.
31. *Medium Close Shot*: Counter shot: Jefferies completes the recharge of the camera, looks backward out the window, turns to his front again, covers his eyes with one hand, and "shoots" with the other hand.
32. *Long Shot*: Counter shot: While advancing, the assassin gets hit by the flash light and stops.
33. *Close-Up*: He brings his hands to his glasses adjusting them, while squeezing his eyes.
34. *Long Shot*: Counter shot: A circle of orange light expands through the visual field, blurring the image of the journalist, who in the meanwhile recharges the camera with a new flash.
35. *Close-Up*: Counter shot: The assassin re-opens his eyes and starts moving forward again.
36. *Medium Close Shot*: Counter shot: Jefferies completes the recharge of the camera, looks backward out the window, turns to his front again, covers his eyes with one hand, and "shoots" with the other hand.
37. *Close-Up*: Jefferies turns around once more to look out the window.
38. *Very Long Shot*: Through the rear court, through a window of the rear building, Lisa and a few police men are visible. Jefferies off camera: "Lisa!".
39. *American Shot*: Counter shot: The assassin is now quite close, and keeps advancing towards Jefferies, who keeps screaming.
40. *Close-Up*: The assassin is now on the journalist, and the two start fighting...
41. on...

The sequence would continue for quite a number of shots as a *scene properly called*. Up to this point, though, technically speaking, this is an *alternate* syntagma, that is, a narrative syntagma structured to express simultaneity between a two or more series of facts or events happening at the same time. Since Griffin's times, this has constituted the solution to the representation of simultaneity in a linear, visual medium: showing two or more series of shots referring to two or more developing actions, alternating the shots of each series. The difference with the parallel syntagma, though, is that there has to be at least one shot showing the convergence between the different simultaneous actions, as evidence of the fact that they are actually convergent. In this respect, the construction of this (part of the) sequence is also a very "classical" one.

From a CCR perspective, like the descriptive syntagma, by definition, the *alternate* syntagma expresses conjunctive relations holding between the respective shots of the converging actions (despite the sequentiality of the presentation). In contrast to the parallel syntagma, where the parallel actions never converge to a common focus or solution, and where therefore there is a disjunction between the distinct actions going on simultaneously, in principle the alternate syntagma presents the elements of a larger picture made up of simultaneous elements. So, we can assume a *conjunctive* relation holding between the various sequence's shot/counter-shots representing the action of the aggressor, on the one hand, and the action of the victim, on the other (1-2, 3-4, 5-6, 7-8, 9-10, etc.).

In some cases, though, the development of one action thread will affect the development of the other action thread, so the relation between two shots belonging to different series will be connected by *causality*. It is the action that Jefferies makes with the flash of his camera that causes the assassin to slow down: the orange light that we see spread across the scene's field represents the vision the assassin has of the room after having been "shot" with the flash, and it is directly caused by the flash manipulated by Jeffries. This is the case, for instance, with shot 16 towards shot 17, 18, 19...but not 20. In fact, in that shot, "despite" having been momentarily blinded by Jeffries' action, the aggressor starts to move forward again: the relation, in this case is of *negative causality*.

At the same time, since the sequence represents a double action developing in time, obviously the shots representing the respective actions will hold *sequential* relations with each other. For instance, all the shots representing the moving of the assassin towards Jeffries hold sequential relations with each other one.

Finally, *causality* comes back again in the last shot of the analysed sequence (shot 40), where the assassin grabs Jefferies' neck. This is the last shot of the sequence, where respectively the assassin and Jefferies' actions converge, which represent the final result, the consequence of all that has come before. That is, the assassin had walked into the room to attack Jefferies, which is what he ends up doing (from Jefferies' point of view, of course, this is a case of negative causality, because he has failed to stop the attacker).

3.2. From Stanley Kubrick's 2001: A Space Odyssey

A monolith mysteriously appears on the Earth at a time when man is not yet man, and still competes with other herbivores to survive, sleeping in groups in the ground for shelter. The megalith is huge and scares the apes, when they discover it, at their awakening. Its sharp, perfect, regular shape contrasts with the shapeless waste landscape where they live. What is it? What is it bringing?

The day progresses. In one part of the desert, littered with bones, under the harsh sun a group of big black apes is foraging in the ground, looking for something. Eventually, one of them comes across a big bone and starts to play with it. She starts to bang it around against other bones, lightly at first, and then harder and harder, until she raises her arm in the air, and begins to violently beat the skull of a dead animal, which breaks under the blows.

Shortly afterwards, she is on top of a hill, eating a big piece of meat.

Sequence X-1

n. *Close-Up*: Low angle: The megalith, parallel to the camera, is filling the scene. Its upper profile looks like a horizon, from behind the centre of which the sun is just rising. A newly waxing moon is still up in the sky, aligned above the sun. A deafening shrill sound is pervading the environment. Cut.

Sequence X

1. *Establishing Shot*: A vast, rather flat desert extends between cloudy shadows and midday sun. Complete silence.
2. *Long Shot*: Rocks and sand are filling the field. Silence.
3. *Long Shot*: Sharp rocks and sand. Silence.
4. *Establishing/Master Shot*: A number of big black apes are silently and solitarily foraging in the ground, which is covered in bones, picking up little things to eat.
5. *Medium Shot*: One ape is foraging and eating alone, her head down. At certain points, she raises her head and glances to look at something immediately in front of her.
6. *Close-Up*: Low angle: "Flash back" autonomous insert, diegetic but displaced from the previous sequence, with speculative function: the megalith, parallel to the camera, is filling the scene. Its upper profile looks like a horizon, from behind the centre of which the sun is just rising. A newly waxing moon is still up in the sky, aligned above the sun. No sound, this time.
7. *Medium Shot*: The ape sees a big long bone in front of her and picks it up, looking at it with inquisitive interest. The overture of Strauss' *Also sprach Zarathustra* starts over. She starts banging it against the other bones with increasing energy and violence, in increasingly exasperated gestures, in time to *Zarathustra*'s allure.
8. *Detail*: The ape's arm rises against the sky (presented in slow motion, the fist holding the bone as a weapon, and comes down again. The music comments accordingly and in synchrony.
9. *Single Shot*: The big bone falls back onto the ground, onto the other bones. The ape keeps beating them with her weapon, and they keep breaking under the blows, amongst the rising dust. One more time the ape arises her weapon and comes down onto the other bones. Commentary music.
10. *Close-Up*: "Flash forward" autonomous insert, dislocated from a hypothetical future sequence, with speculative value, in this case also substitutive of a sequence that will be never shown: an animal, one of the herbivores that shares the apes' territory, crashes to the ground in slow motion, hitting its head. Commentary music.
11. *Close-Up*: The face of the ape, her mouth wide open in a scream, the eyes full of anger. Commentary music.
12. *Detail*: Again, the arm of the ape, raised against the sky, the fist holding the big bone like a weapon, goes down to hit the other bones on the ground. Commentary music.
13. *Detail*: Complementary: The big bone strikes the ground, just next to a skull, missed by little. Commentary music.
14. *Detail*: Again, the arm of the ape, raised against the sky, the fist holding the big bone like a weapon, goes down to hit the other bones on the ground. Commentary music.
15. *Detail*: Complementary: The big bone strikes the ground, this time hitting the skull that breaks under the blow. Commentary music.
16. *Detail*: The big bone strikes the ground again, hitting the skull and other bones that keep disintegrating under the blows. Commentary music.
17. *Detail*: The big bone strikes the ground again, hitting the skull and other bones that keep disintegrating under the blows. Commentary music.
18. *Detail*: The big bone arrives down to the ground again, hitting the skull and other bones that keep disintegrating under the blows. Commentary music.
19. *Detail*: Bones keep disintegrating under the blows. Commentary music.
20. *Detail*: Bones keep disintegrating under the blows. Commentary music.
21. *Detail*: Bones keep disintegrating under the blows. Commentary music.
22. *Close-Up*: Another "flash forward" autonomous insert, dislocated from the same hypothetical future sequence, with speculative value, substitutive of a sequence that will never be shown: the body of the same animal falls on the ground. Commentary music: *Zarathustra*'s overture, about to reach the final climax.
23. *Single Shot*: After dealing the last blow, the ape throws her arms in the air, and brings them down again, bending her body, in a sign of rest and release. She grabs what remains of some of the bones that she has crushed, and then drops them. The symphony's overture comes to his climax and conclusion.

Sequence X+1

1. *Establishing/Single Shot*: The ape enters the desert landscape from the left, walks across the field and turns around. She is carrying a big piece of meat. She looks around herself, stops, and starts to voraciously chew on it.

Cinematically speaking, this is a *scene properly called*, because the representation of the action that is taking place in it presents unity of space and time, and the narrative time is the same as the diegetic time during which the action is supposed to develop and accomplish. With respect to the content organisation, the scene presents a "classical" structure, which consists of the initial description, or exploration, of the diegetic space that will host the imminent action, or of the situation that will constitute its context, followed by the representation of the action itself. Typically, the description of the diegetic space is made up of *panoramics* and *long shots*, whereas the description of the action is given through *single shots*, *close-ups* and *details*. All consistently accompanied, from the action's start to its final climax, by the commentary music.

From a CCR driven analysis of the syntagma, at the level of the relation between sequences, the first thing that one could say is that there is a *sequential* relation between the three sequences, since they represent facts that happen one after the other. However, the formal elements of the signifier suggest that the relation between them is actually a stronger one, it is a *causal* relation, since what happens in the first sequence causes what happens in the second one, which causes what happens in the third one. That is, the montage and the construction of the different shots suggest that the appearing of the megalith causes the ape to discover the use of tools or weapons, which causes the ape to be able to advance on the evolutionary ladder. Concerning the relation between sequence x-1 and sequence x, causality is conveyed by the fact that the discovery of the ape (sequence x) immediately follows the appearance of the megalith (sequence x-1), and by the fact that the same shot from sequence x-1 is inserted into sequence x (shot 6) just before the ape gets "enlightened" and starts using the bone like a weapon, while the commentary music starts over (shot 7). Concerning the relation between sequence x and sequence x+1, causality is conveyed by the fact that what is shown immediately after the ape has finished striking the bones on the ground (sequence x) is her eating a piece of meat (sequence x+1), as it is conveyed by the repeated insertion of a shot showing a falling animal (shots 10 and 22) while the ape is striking the bones (shots 9, 11, 12, and 21, 23).

At the level of relations within sequence x itself, the shots from 1 to 5 can be categorised as *descriptive* (although this is not an entirely descriptive syntagma, the first three describing the landscape and the following two describing the habitual way in which apes look for food). They all can be related as *conjunctive*, since they all contribute to the rendering of a situation: an unforgiving, primitive desert environment where apes have to forage among animal carcases to be able to feed themselves. In this context, the *autonomous insert* of the megalith (shot 6) has no logical connection to the rest but being an anaphoric connection to the arrival of the megalith on earth, that is, the appearance of intelligence and knowledge among the apes, which also makes the sequence an *elaboration* of sequence x-1: knowledge arrives amongst pre-human beings; knowledge expresses itself as the ability to use a weapon to kill other animals and gain supremacy over them. At the same time, though, the *autonomous insert* holds by definition a *disjunctive* relation with the shots that precede and follow, since it is dislocated with respect to the narrative space and time.

After the *autonomous insert* of the megalith (shot 6), action develops. The content of the insert itself holds a *causal* relation with the series of shots that comes immediately afterwards, in that it is there to connect the arrival of the megalith to the discovery about to be made by the ape: the presence of the megalith makes the ape look at a longer bone with new eyes. The following shots (7 to 23) show the consequence of such enlightenment. They hold with each other a series of sequential relations, illustrating the developing of action and its consequences. That is, because what is being described is an action, having therefore a temporal development, the relations holding between the shots are *sequential*. Among the shots bound by sequential relations, though, the majority are *details* or *close-ups*, focusing on particular aspects of the action taking place and exploring it more in depth (8 and 11 to 21): they constitute *elaborations* on the main actions. On the contrary, the few whole/medium-figure shots (7, 9 and 23) put in context the more detailed shots, providing a general *background* picture in which those details have to be referred to. At the same time, the shots are related in pairs by *causality*, where the first shot shows the start of an action and the second shows its consequence: the rising and falling of the arm holding the weapon, and the breaking of the bones on the dusty ground, as with shots 12-13, and 14-15. Shot 16, 17, and 18 show the repetition of the ape's arm reaching the ground and breaking bones, which binds them in a *conjunctive* (and not just *sequential*) manner. Equally, shot 19, 20 and 21 hold a *conjunctive* (apart from *sequential*) relation with each other, in that they show the repetition of the effects of the continuous banging: the bone breaking.

Finally, the *autonomous inserts* of the falling animals (shot 10 and 22), located at climax points of the action (especially shot 22), hold a *disjunctive* relation with the shots of the present action, in that, through analogy, they supposedly refer to a dislocated action expected to take place in the near future, after the ape has learnt to use big bones as effective hunting weapons. At the same time they are connected by *causality* to the shots that show the present action, in that they show the immediate consequences of that action: the killing of other species. Finally, this *causal* concept is expressed through the establishing of an analogy that holds between the beaten bones and the falling animal, while the following shot, showing the ape eating a piece of meat, substantiates the assumption, by displaying the final consequence and conclusion of the whole action.

Now, the fact that three different relations appear to hold between the shots of the falling animal and the shots of the beaten bones can be explained in terms of different levels of the cinematic enunciation.

3.3. Analogy, Subjectivity and Pragmatic Relations at Cinema

In linguistic terms (Benveniste, 1974), *enunciation* is the act of enunciating, through which the speaker, the *enunciator*[4], establishes his subjectivity. The formal apparatus of the enunciation is constituted by certain linguistic signals (personal pronouns, verbal forms, space-temporal signals) whose function is to position the *enunciated* with respect to the enunciation act and to the enunciator himself. Although the enunciation is always a subjective act, its subjectivity may be more or less expressed in the enunciated. While in the enunciated "*Today your pack arrived at my home address*" the enunciator manifests itself through the use of the pronoun '*my*' and addresses its interlocutor through the pronoun '*your*', in the sentence "*Mail leaves the post office every day at 8am*" the enunciator 'disappears' behind the apparent objectivity of the enunciated.

The iconicity and indexicality of the cinematic linguistic sign gives the cinematic enunciation an appearance of objectivity: the cinematic signification process is based on the *monstration* (Gardies, 1993) of audio-visual chunks whose only space-temporal dimension is 'here and now'. We have seen (Chapter 4, § 3.1-4.) how, through the observation of practical norms and the use of rhetorical patterns, the cinematic enunciation aims at generating the illusion of self-represented worlds driven by their own space-temporal laws (Metz, 1968; 1972; Burch, 69; Chatman, 1978; 1990;). However, despite its apparent objectivity, the cinematic enunciated can display marks of the enunciation act, through elements that in a way or another refer to it: when elements of the scene 'frame' the action or restrict the visual field; when a character looks into the camera; when the film shows the shooting or the projecting of a movie; when the voice over is used; when unusual shooting angles and camera movements are used without apparent justification in the diegetic world; when the editing produces inconsistencies or discontinuities in the space-temporal dimension of the diegetic world; when stylistic aspects are so accentuated that they compete with the realism of the representation; etc. (Metz, 1991). In Modern cinema, these marks are often purposely multiplied and the violation of classical representational norms and conventions makes it all the more obvious that the film is the product of an enunciation act.

In narratological terms (Genette, 1972), the filmic enunciated corresponds to the *recount*, the narrative discourse through which the film's diegetic events are accounted and the diegetic world is represented. The film's diegetic events and world, in turn, constitute what in narratological terms is the *story*. The point of view from which the story is accounted, the information that is provided on the diegetic world, the order in which events are presented depend on the narrative strategy followed by the recount. The narrative strategies of the cinematic recount determine what to show, how to show it and in what order; what to emphasise and what to leave implicit; how to shoot and construct each scene; how to represent characters and environments; etc.

In the light of these considerations, we can now see how the relations between the shots of the bones and the autonomous inserts of the animal, in the scene described above, hold at different levels. The disjunction relation holds at the diegetic level, because at that level, there is nothing that justifies the connection of the two shots: the continuity of the action is simply broken by the insertion of an element that is not part of it in any way. In order to understand the connection between the shots, its function is to be considered at the narrative level: the insertion is a narrative solution to express the relation of causality that exists between the action of beating performed by the ape and the death of the animal, somewhere down the line. Finally, the analogical relation is to be explained at the enunciation level: the autonomous inserts described above, constitute an example of how the enunciation act can show through the texture of the cinematic enunciated.

Generally speaking, non-diegetic or dislocated autonomous inserts have the power of breaking the diegetic flow and therefore the continuity and the realism of the narration, in particular when, like in this case, they hold an analogical relation (functioning as a *similarity* relation) with the previous and following shots. Eisenstein used to call this analogical editing *intellectual montage* (Glenny and Taylor, 1991): the viewer has to make an intellectual connection, whether poetic or rhetoric in general (in this case, as often, it is a metaphorical connection), in order to understand the edit. And such 'intellectual' reflection functions as a commentary that comes from outside the diegetic world, from the enunciating instance.

A very famous example of analogical montage, conveyed by the substitution of an element of diegetic realism with a metaphorical image inserted as dislocated autonomous shot, is provided in *Strike* (Sergei Eisenstein, 1917). To express the idea that striking workers are treated like animals by the police of the regime, a few shots representing cows taken to the slaughter-house and actually slaughtered are inserted in the flow of the main action, as an assumption about the conclusion of what is brutally being carried out by the police towards the strikers. A comparison is made between the workers and the cows, that is, a similarity relation is established between the two, which works as a comment about a regime that treats men like animals.

In CCR terms, this sort of commentary editing corresponds to *pragmatic causal* relations: the autonomous inserts of the falling animal, which obviously does not belong to the present action, can be interpreted as a claim, whereas the shots of the bone beating can be interpreted as the argument of the claim. That is, since the ape has discovered the use of weapons and is now beating those bones (argument), she will soon kill real animals with her new weapon (claim): assumption based on the metaphorical substitution of the real animal with the bones. Similarly, in *Strike*, a claim is being expressed by the shots showing the cows, and the argument to support that claim is being expressed by the shots showing the workers being taken away by the police.

Interestingly enough, the scalar approach to discourse relations' source of coherence (Pander Maat and Degand, 2001 - Chapter 2, note 10) corresponds to the idea that these commentary passages constitute moments in which the enunciation act and the enunciating instance become apparent. Pander Maat and Degand propose that whether a relation is semantic or pragmatic depends on the degree of implicit involvement of the speaker in the construction of the relation, the pattern argument-claim implying more involvement than the pattern cause-consequence[5]. The first one requires a subjective positioning with respect to the relation that is predicated to hold between the two discourse parts, whereas the second one simply consists of objectively reporting a relation that holds between two events in the real world. So, we can say that, in CCR terms, in *2001* and in *Strike*, the enunciating instance's involvement into the construction of the relation manifests itself in a way that it does not manifest itself in more classical narrative regimes. The same can more or less be said of much cinema, especially, but not only, Modern cinema.

3.4. Conditionality at Cinema

Finally, a relation that was not encountered in the analysed examples is *conditionality*. In both sequences it was easy to identify, among the logical ones, additive, sequential and causal semantic or pragmatic relations. However, generally speaking, conditional (that is, causal hypothetical) relations, are more difficult to find expressed in cinema. This is due to the fact that (as seen above) cinematic language is based on the act of *monstration* and, because of its iconic and indexical nature, cannot rely on the use of abstract connectives to suggest logical relations. As we have seen (Chapter 4), cinematic linguistic techniques can represent time and space, in so doing expressing sequential, additive and causal relations. However, expressing something like conditionality is more complicated, because through *monstration* it is more difficult to express hypotheses than it is to express facts. In order to express conditionality, cinema has to show both what happens if the required condition does not hold, and what happens if that condition does hold, otherwise the relation between condition and consequent effect is simply interpreted as causal.

A cinematic example of conditionality is expressed by *Smoking, No Smoking* (Alain Resnais, 1993). The film is constructed on the description of the chain of causes and effects triggered by the main character's choice of smoking or not smoking. The story follows one main thread for a short while, until the protagonist finds herself in front of a pack of cigarettes and has to make a decision: shall she smoke or shall she not smoke? Here the story comes to a turning point: the following part of the film shows what happens if the protagonist chooses to smoke, then the film goes back to the turning point and the rest shows what happens if the protagonist chooses not to smoke. With a very hyper-textual move, the film expresses not only *conditionality*, but *alternative* as well, and it is exactly the existence of an alternative that makes it possible to interpret each story line as respectively conditioned by two different choices.

The same thing happens in *Sliding Doors* (Peter Howitt, 1998), where the story line splits in two different routes as a consequence of the protagonist catching or not catching an underground train before it leaves the station. The structural difference here is that the film montage is based on the continuous alternation of scenes respectively representing the different effects derived from the two different alternatives.

Connections may be accounted for between the shots that constitute a single syntagma or between the sequences that constitute a film. In general, shot connections hold together cinematic discourse parts. These discourse connections can be interpreted, at the diegetic level, as accounting for the relations between the events that develop within the represented world. However, at the enunciation level, they can be interpreted as accounting for the relations between the parts of a discourse that develops about the represented world.

4. Cognitive Coherence Relations and Cinema: a Conclusion

The analyses performed above show how cognitive coherence relations can account for discourse connections in a medium like cinema, whose discourse is constituted by the articulation of discrete, rich semantic units. It emerges how it is possible to use cognitive coherence relations both to analyse cinematic discourse patterns in general, and to analyse specific film sequences, which reveals relevant correspondences between text coherence and cinematic theory. In fact, this even suggests that - because of the iconicity and indexicality of the cinematic sign - it is in cinematic language that the expression of the most primitive relations can be detected in their essential form, which would make cinematic language a very interesting test bed for the study of cognitive coherence relations in general.

For the purposes of this work, what we have observed above provides important insights into the way hypertext discourse can be looked at and ultimately represented, based on fundamental similarities between cinema and hypertext (Chapter 4) and on the fact that cinematic language is able to suggest discourse coherence relations through formal non-textual features. The next chapters shows how this could work in hypertext.

Notes

[1] In fact, in the practice of Classical cinema these rhetorical patterns are used with more exceptions than regularities, as Metz (1964) himself acknowledges and Branigan (1992) shows more in detail, but they still work as effective analysis tools. See Chapter 4.

[2] Which is not the case for instance in the descriptive syntagma.

[3] However, since it is a matter of relations, and therefore of relativeness, if a detail or a close-up are shown, before a more general picture of the situation or action is provided by the sequence, then, when broader shots appear to provide this more general picture, these broader shots tend to set themselves as background to the details and close-ups already shown.

[4] While in spoken discourse the figure of the enunciator corresponds to the figure of the speaker, in literature and in cinema the enunciator is not identifiable with any real person (like the author/s) or any individual figure (like a narrator), rather it is an instance that is intrinsic to the text/film discourse itself, and that is responsible for delivering all information concerning the represented world, 'dosing' it according to specific narrative strategies (Gardies, 1993).

[5] The fact that the involvement of the speaker is what determines the relation's source of coherence is a generally accepted concept in psycholinguistics (see also Pander Maat and Sanders, 2001). However, the scalar approach accounts for the fact that, given the iconicity and indexicality of the language, in cinema the degrees in which the enunciating instance reveals itself are potentially infinite.

Cinematic Hypertext
C. Mancini
IOS Press, 2005

6. Visual Languages to Render Coherence Relations

The previous chapters tackled the issue of coherence in text and in a visual medium (cinema) that has many similarities to hypertext. In this chapter the connections between text discourse processing and visual discourse processing are presented and analysed. It is shown how certain principles of text cohesion have an equivalent in the principles of visual cohesion long established by Gestalt Theory. Therefore, it should be possible to 'translate' cohesive aspects or elements of textual coherence into graphic terms. With the objective of producing in hypertext a cohesive visual representation of coherence relations, this chapter also presents elements from semiology of graphics, which are then subsequently applied to designing discourse relations in hypertext.

1. Text Discourse and Visual Discourse Processing

We have previously seen (Chapter 5) how cognitive coherence relations can be used to analyse the connections between cinematic discourse units (that is, cinematic shots). We also have seen that the interpretation of cinematic discourse connections is determined by and through visual features. The viewer connects shots and sequences with one another on the basis of visual elements that establish the continuity of diegetic time and space according to certain linguistic conventions typically expressed in the classical cinematic syntagmas.

Here it is proposed that, beyond the parallel between cinema and hypertext, the consistent expression of discourse connections through visual features constitutes the lesson that cinema can offer to hypertext. Cinema covers numerous genres (like musical, horror, thriller, comedy, drama, etc.) and schools (like Expressionism, Surrealism, New Realism, Nouvelle Vague, etc.): each one may make use of very different conventions and linguistic forms, and even within a single genre or school, film styles may vary considerably. However, as far as connectivity is concerned, certain basic patterns recur, which are always consistently represented within any specific genre, or at least within any specific film (that is, within any specific act of discourse).

For instance, if a dissolve is used in a particular film to indicate a flash-back (whether sequentiality or causality or similarity are expressed through it), then throughout the film the dissolve will consistently be used to indicate flash-backs, so that the viewer can rely on the meaning of that sign to produce a coherent interpretation of the sequences where that sign appears. Although that same feature could be used to introduce the thoughts of a character (expressing the passage from one to another discourse level[1]), it would not be used with that function in the same film - unless the director wanted to create an effect of ambiguity between the past as recounted by the enunciator and a character's thoughts (like in *L'anée dernière á Marienbad*, Alain Resnais, 1961).

The fact that in cinema the meaning of each linguistic sign is not absolute, but relative to its use and to the use of the other linguistic signs in context, is as relevant as the fact that each of the classical rhetorical patterns can express multiple sets of coherence relations. Based on what we have previously discussed, firstly about the possibility of using cognitive coherence relations to define discourse connections in hypertext argumentation (Chapters 2, § 2.3.; and 3, § 3.3), secondly about the parallels between hypertext and cinema and the applicability of cognitive coherence relations to cinematic discourse (Chapters 4, § 4.4; and 5, § 5.4), this observation leads us to a proposal. Since, on the one hand, CCR can be used to identify and define hypertext discourse connections, on the other hand, visual features could be used to represent those same relations, once they have been defined.

In this perspective, the representation of the connections between hypertext nodes, textual or otherwise, would be delegated to the visual dimension. The advantage of this approach is that, since - in contrast to text - visual features are not capable of representing abstract concepts themselves, the definition of the connections would remain implicit, leaving the reader to decide what they want to read into those features (the pedagogical potential of this approach are discussed in the concluding chapter). Instead, what would result visibly and recognisably as a consequence of a concurrent and consistent use of visual features would be the presence of an overall shape perceivable in the form of local discourse patterns. Just as in cinema, it would not be indicated explicitly what logical relations exist between different shots, but it would be left to the viewer to reflect on, recognise, learn and internalise the discourse structure from the formal elements that he perceives, that is, to understand how the different shots could or should be connected with one another.

In this respect, the main function of coherence relations as a base for the definition of hypertext links is to make sure that visual features are used consistently and that their use is based on basic, primitive (hence widely applicable) relational concepts, which would be reflected in the consistency and clarity of the discourse's visual structure. Of course, just as the specialisation of basic cognitive coherence relations into finer grained argumentation links is possible (see Chapter 3, § 1), so is the use of visual features, although obviously the more complex the visual structure the less incisive and recognisable the discourse structure can be. For instance, in SchoIOnto's (Buckingham Shum et al. 2000) link taxonomy, quite a number of link types can be classified as variations of causality relations, each of which could in theory be represented by a specific combination of visual features. In this respect, a trade-off between specificity of the relations and readability of their visualisation should be found for any specific taxonomy, according to the functions that the final representation has to serve.

However, independent from the specific choices of representation and their granularity, the underlining idea is to use cognitive coherence relations as a base for the definition of more or less articulated sets of link types, and to express the corresponding relations through a number of visual features. These will have no meaning in themselves, but that, if used consistently and in combination with one another, constitute the base for the creation of a visual language directly defined by the context of use of its visual components. In other words, what is proposed here could be defined as coherence relation visual design.

2. Parallels between Textual and Visual Processing

In 1995, Campbell published *Coherence, Continuity and Cohesion - Theoretical foundations for Document Design,* in which she established a parallel between textual and visual organisation, by comparing principles that pertain to the perception of discourse unity and principles that pertain to the perception of visual unity (Grice, 1975). Initially, she examines the concept of text unity and describes it in terms of *coherence* (contextual unity, involving connections between the discourse and the context in which it occurs) and *cohesion* (co-textual unity, involving connections within the discourse itself). She then analyses Grice's cooperative principle, which states that, in order to perceive discourse as unitary, the interlocutor expects it to have certain characteristics. The parameters describing these characteristics from the recipient's perspective are: *relation*, according to which a discourse part is expected to be relevant to a previous part of the discourse; *quantity*, according to which a discourse part is expected to provide the right amount of information (not too little, not too much); *manner*, according to which a discourse part is expected to be clear enough; *quality*, according to which a discourse part is expected to be accurate and correct.

Subsequently she analyses the concept of unity described by Gestalt Theory (Wertheimer, 1938) and compares its principles of visual design with Grice's principles of discourse coherence. Gestalt design principles are: *continuity*, according to which the viewer expects the elements of a configuration to extend along a continuous line; *figure-ground*, according to which the viewer expects a configuration to be made of a single figure against a single background; *closure*, according to which the viewer compensates the incompleteness of visual information by interpreting a partial figure as a complete whole; and *constancy*, according to which the viewer expects objects to maintain constant physical properties across different contexts.

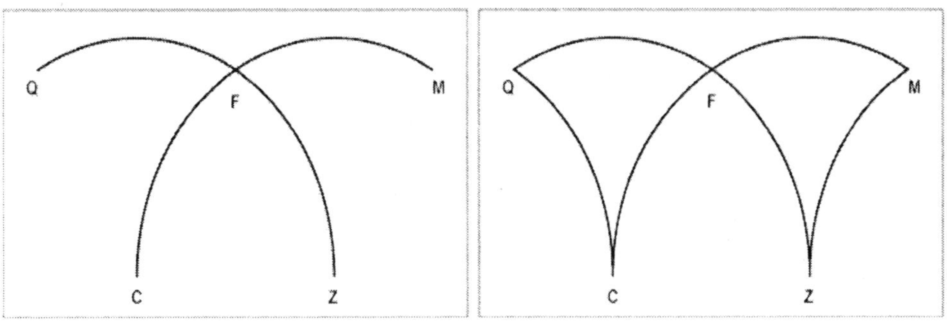

Figure 6.1. a. Illustration of Gestalt principle of continuity, according to which two elements of an incomplete figure are perceived as coherently connected if one appears to be the continuation of the other: the four converging segments are perceived as two crossing lines. **b.** Illustrates how, if new elements are added to the configuration, another form of continuity is perceived in the new configuration: now two tangent fan-shaped objects are perceived instead of the two crossing lines.

She finds a correlation between Grice's principle of *relation* and Gestalt's principle of *continuity*, observing that just as in discourse two spans of text are perceived as coherent if the content of the second span appears to be relevant to the content of the first span, likewise in visual configurations, two elements of an incomplete figure are perceived as coherently connected if one appears to be the continuation of the other. For example, between the sentences "*The bus was late. I didn't make it in time for the meeting.*" and "*The bus was late. The apple tree was blossoming.*"[2] the first pair is perceived as more coherent, since the situation described in the second span of text seems the natural continuation of the situation described in the first span. Instead, perceiving a coherent connection between the situation described in the first span and the situation described in the second span is much less immediate[3].

Likewise, in Figure 6.1.a., the most immediate way of interpreting its elements, is to assume that the configuration is created by the intersection in F of the curved lines QZ and CM, rather that by the tangency of the angular lines QFC and ZFM, since the first interpretation allows one to assume the continuity of the elements composing the configuration[4].

Relation and continuity are the only principles between which Campbell sees a correspondence, and she concludes that the additional three principles proposed by Grice (manner, quantity and quality) seem to have no analogues in Gestalt theory. However, the full correspondence between Grice's principles and Gestalt's principles is resolved by Riley and Parker (1998), who observe that the reason why Campbell could not find complete correspondence between the two sets of principles is that the two sets were expressed in terms that are too specific and therefore hardly comparable. Riley and Parker claim that it is possible to find the correspondence at a more abstract definition level, and produce themselves a set of principles "interfacing" Grice's and Gestalt's principles (see Table 6.1).

VISUAL PRINICIPLE (GESTALT)	**← META-PRINCIPLES →**	**TEXTUAL PRINCIPLE (GRICE)**
CONTINUITY: Expecting elements to extend along a continuous line.	COHESION: Interpreting a stimulus in the way that requires the least effort.	RELATION: Expecting items in a discourse to be related.
FIGURE/GROUND: Expecting a single figure against a single background.	CLARITY: Imposing a single interpretation on a stimulus.	MANNER: Expecting discourse to be unambiguous.
CLOSURE: Interpreting a spatial figure as a whole.	COMPLETENESS: Interpreting a stimulus as whole.	QUANTITY: Expecting discourse not to contain too much/little information.
CONSTANCY: Expecting objects to remain stable across different contexts.	CORRECTNESS: Interpreting a stimulus at face value.	QUALITY: Expecting discourse to be truthful, not misleading.

Table 6.1. Riley and Parker's (1998) meta-principles accounting for both Gestalt principles of perception and Grice's principles of text interpretation.

In this more abstract set, *cohesion* corresponds to Grice's *relation* on the one hand and to Gestalt's *continuity* on the other hand. According to this principle the perceiver will interpret a stimulus in the way that requires the least effort. In the sentence "*The woman reported that she had been experiencing headaches*", say the authors, the interpretation that requires the least effort and offers the least resistance is that the woman is the same person who had been experiencing headaches, which means that in order to understand the meaning of the sentence I don't have to enlarge the context of my representation to any other element (in this case, another subject). It is the same principle that in cinema leads me to assume that a shot showing a hand holding a pistol, followed by a shot showing a pair of walking legs, and a following shot showing a corpse on the floor, are connected to one another, and that the hand belongs to the owner of the walking legs. That is, I assume that conjunctiveness, sequentiality and causality relations hold between the three shots.

For the authors, *clarity* corresponds to *manner* on the one hand and to *figure-ground* on the other. And according to this principle the perceiver will impose a single interpretation on a stimulus, as they show in their examples. In ambiguous figures, like Rubin's famous face/vase (Figure 6.2), one can only perceive either the faces or the vase, that is, one can successively focus on either, but not on both at the same time. In the sentence "*Jane hid the letter from Dan*", say the authors, one can assume either that Jane did not want Dan to see the letter, or that she did not want the letter that she had received from Dan to be seen. In any case, one interpretation excludes the other. The same thing may happen in cinema, for instance, when certain *autonomous inserts* introduce information that could be either attributed to a character's thoughts or to events of the diegesis, but the lack of clear formal elements makes it difficult for the viewer to decide how to interpret the shot and what relations (elaboration, sequence, cause, etc.) to establish between that shot and the other shots. *L'Année Dernière á Marienbad* is all constructed on such destabilizing ambiguity, which makes the viewer unable to reply on his acquired knowledge of the represented world.

→ ***"Jane hid the letter from Dan"***

Figure 6.2. Edgar Rubin's face/vase (1921) illustrates Gestalt's principle of *figure-background* and sentence exemplifying Grice's maxim of *manner*, both corresponding to Riley and Parker's principle of *clarity* (1998).

Riley and Parker argue furthermore, that *completeness* would correspond to *quantity* on the one hand and to *closure* on the other, and according to it the perceiver will interpret a stimulus as whole, whenever possible. In the example "*John likes football more than Gloria does*", one would be able to complete the sentence ("*more than Gloria does like football*"), whereas in the example "*John likes football more than Gloria*", say the authors, one would not have enough there to *bridge* the gap of information and decide whether John likes football more than Gloria does, or whether John likes football more than he likes Gloria. A famous 'bridgeable' picture referred to by the authors is Kanizsa's triangle (Figure 6.4). In cinema this principle can be seen in action whenever a partial representation of a place or a character is recognised and taken for the whole thing, since the information that it contains is sufficient to bridge the gaps, that is, to provide a realistic and consistent, or simply recognisable, enough representation.

→ ***"John likes football more than Gloria does"***

Figure 6.3. Gaetano Kanizsa's Triangle (1955), example of bridgeable figure illustrating Gestalt's principle of *closure* and sentence exemplifying Grice's maxim of *quantity*, both corresponding to Riley and Parker's principle of *completeness* (1998).

For instance, in the representation of a character's daily life, certain stereotypical elements may constitute the equivalent of the vertexes of Kanizsa's triangle: if I see the area around the vertexes, I can bridge the gap between them by imagining the sides. Likewise, if I see a shot showing the character having breakfast alone at home, a shot showing him silently sitting at his desk in the office, a shot showing him at a restaurant's table alone, I can hypothesise that the character has a lonely life. That is, I infer that the three shots are related by conjunctiveness as parts of a whole, and once I have inferred that the elements that I see are part of a broader reality, I can create in my mind a representation of the city as a whole, imagining also what I cannot see on the screen. In fact, one of the most used cinematic syntagmas depends on the bridging ability of the viewer. In Metz's *ordinary sequence*, an action is represented through its critical or essential moments, skipping what is not crucial to its understanding, counting on the fact that the viewer will fill the gaps himself, interpreting the constituent shots as connected by sequentiality as well as by conjunctiveness. In general, as previously seen (chapter 4), cinematic language is based on creating, or better, suggesting, diegetic worlds through partial representations, and the principle of completeness underlies all cinematic techniques.

Finally, Riley and Parker argue that *correctness* would correspond to Griece's *quality* on the one hand and to Gestalt's *constancy* on the other. And according to this principle the perceiver will interpret a stimulus at face value. The authors report the example "*The horse raced past the barn fell*", where, used to the noun-verb sequence, one assumes that the horse is the agent of raced, until one gets to the end of the phrase and realises that the phrase needs to be reinterpreted and the horse needs to become the agent of fell: "*The horse that raced past the barn fell*". The example of the horse is then compared to that type of 'impossible figures' that we know from Escher and also from Magritte, which purposely and playfully violate the gestalt principle of constancy (Figure 6.4).

→ ***"The horse raced past the barn fell"***

Figure 6.4. Lionel and Roger Penrose's Triangle (1958), example of impossible figure illustrating Gestalt's principle of *constancy* and sentence exemplifying Grice's maxim of *quality*, both corresponding to Riley and Parker's principle of *correctness* (1998).

A cinematic example of this type of violation is provided by the representation of space and time in *Marienbad*, where the viewer is constantly forced to go back and forth to figure out the connections between all the space-temporal fragments. One of the several examples of *Marienbad*'s 'impossible figures', is provided by a scene, where the main characters are walking along the corridors of a palace: a short series of long-shots shows them coming towards the foreground; from one shot to the other, the environment changes, as if they where walking across different corridors, while their motion is perfectly continuous, which is 'impossible' from the point of view of the diegetic reality - since the characters' motion should have been consistent with the discontinuity of the space where it is taking place. That is, shots that according to the action taking place appear to be connected by conjunctiveness, on the one hand, and on the other hand, appear to be disjunct as far as the diegetic space is concerned.

With *Marienbad*, like with so much contemporary cinema, there is no solution to the puzzle posed by the film, which is a cause of frustration and at the same time fascination. However, this is the way cinematic language normally works: like in Riley and Parker's example of the horse, the viewer has to constantly go back to the previous shots to check whether the connections that he had assumed to hold between elements actually hold, and at any time his interpretation may have to change. For instance, if I see a close-up showing the face of a man in the act of looking ahead, and then I see the shot showing a landscape with a lake in the summer, I assume that the man finds himself in front of the lake in the act of contemplating it. If, however, the next long-shot back to the man shows me that he actually finds himself immersed in a winter mountain landscape, I have to reinterpret what I have seen so far: I have to make a new assumption on the connections between the different shots…till the next shot to come will make my set of assumptions change again.

The fact that Campbell, Riley and Parker's were able to establish parallels between visual and textual processing - based on the assumption of higher-level innate cognitive capabilities of the human species - is consistent with the psycholinguistic approach to text coherence and with the conception of cognitive relational primitives as principles of coherence in discourse (Chapter 2)[5]. This grounds the hypothesis that visual elements can be used to express textual cognitive coherence. From here, the subsequent step is the discussion of the notion of visual meta-discourse, according to which the cognitive organization of text documents can be visually represented.

3. Visual Languages and Document Design

In text, the concept of meta-discourse (discourse about the discourse) refers to that type of information that does not concern the propositional content itself, but the organisation of the discourse and the position of the enunciator towards the discourse content (Vande Kopple, 1988). Textual meta-discourse is expressed through cues and indicators that help the writer to influence the reader's interpretation of the propositional content, and allow the reader to move through the text with a clearer understanding of the discourse structure. In other words, meta-discourse and its devices are expressions of the text's coherence and fundamental elements of its cohesion.

3.1. Visual Meta-Discourse

Vande Kopple's (1988) classification of meta-discourse vocabulary consists of seven categories, classified as *textual* and *interpersonal*. Textual categories include *connectives*, revealing discourse organisation and inter-textuality, and *code glosses*, parenthetical definitions within sentences. Interpersonal categories include *illocution markers*, identifying discourse acts; *validity markers*, assessing the probability of truth of the propositional content (and including in turn *hedges*, *emphatics* and *attributors*); *narrators*, letting the reader know who said what; *attitude markers*, revealing attitudes of the writer towards the propositional content; *commentary*, directly commenting to the reader (Table 6.2).

CLASSES	CATEGORIES	FUNCTION
Textual Metadiscourse	*Connectives*	Reveal discourse organization and intertextuality.
	Code Glosses	Parenthetical definitions within sentences.
Interpersonal Metadiscourse	*Illocutionary Markers*	Identify discourse acts.
	Validity Markers	Assess probability of truth of the propositional content.
	Narrators	Let the reader know who said what.
	Attitude Markers	Reveal writer's attitudes towards propositional content.
	Commentary	Directly comment to the reader.

Table 6.2. Vande Kopple's (1988) classification of textual meta-discourse markers in written text.

CATEGORIES	EXPRESSION	EFFECT
FIRST IMPRESSION	General look of the document.	Genre recognition.
HEFT	Bulkiness of the document.	Willingness to read.
CONVENTION	Expected appearance for the type of document.	General perception.
CHUNKING	Document organization in sections and subsections.	Facilitated browsing.
EXTERNAL SKELETON	Formatting elements of the document.	Structure recognition.
CONSISTENCY	Constancy of the document's style.	Stable visual reference.
EXPENSE	Economical and aesthetic aspects of the document.	General reception.
ATTRACTION	Visual standard of the document.	Attention maintaining.
INTERPRETATION	Iconic codification of information in the document.	Text complementing.
STYLE	Visual form of the document's text.	Text embellishment.

Table 6.3. Kumpf's (2002) categorisation of visual meta-discourse parameters for document design.

Kumpf (2000) extended the concept of meta-discourse from the textual realm to the visual realm, putting forward the notion of *visual meta-discourse*, and he suggests the use of ten categories according to which meta-discourse could be visually represented (Table 6.3).

Kumpf's ten categories of visual meta-discourse aim at expressing the meta-discourse of text through its graphical elements. *First impression* concerns the general look of a document in terms of conventional formats, which helps the reader to immediately recognise its genre. *Heft* concerns the bulkiness of a document, which influences the perception of a document and the willingness to use it depending on the contexts. *Convention* describes what readers expect from the appearance of a document in relation to what they actually have before their eyes, which influences their perception of it. *Chunking* concerns the arrangement of text into discrete visual parts, such as paragraphs, which help the reader to go through it. *External skeleton* concerns elements of the format like page numbers, headings, indentations, headers or footers, etc., which quickly show the reader how the document is assembled. *Consistency* concerns the constancy of style that provides the reader with a stable visual reference against which to organise and view the information provided by the text. *Expense* concerns the economical and aesthetic aspects of a document, which depend on the context of its use and affect the reader's reception of the document. *Attraction* concerns the setting and maintaining of a visual standard to capture and keep the attention of the reader through the document to its end. *Interpretation* concerns the use of tables, graphs and photos in the document, which reformulate information that is already in the text, or provide further information, using visual codes. Finally, with *style* Kumpf describes the visual form that text can take in a document, through font, font style, size, etc., which embellish the text[6].

The parameters described above constitute the various visual dimensions of a document according to which the text's meta-discourse can be shaped through the use of graphic features. In good document design, these dimensions concurrently contribute to provide a general sense of cohesion and coherent structure, which in turn reinforces the discourse's structure. In order for this to happen, in each of Kumpf's dimensions, the use of graphic features needs to follow certain principles, which underpin document design in general. These Gestalt principles (Campbell, 1995) guide the use of graphic elements in creating a visual representation of the cohesion and coherence expressed through the contents of written documents. The first of this principles is *similarity*: formal similarity is capable of creating a sense of visual cohesiveness resulting in the perception of continuity and unity, which allows the viewer to connect certain elements and to keep certain other elements separated. However accentuated, similarity is more strongly perceived when similar elements of configurations are also close to one another: *proximity* (spatial and temporal) is another fundamental Gestalt principle of cohesion, and it crucially co-operates with the principle of similarity to produce a sense of continuity.

In fact, both similarity and proximity can work together to reinforce the perception of unity and continuity between the elements of a configuration, or they can work in opposition to ambiguate the relation between elements that would otherwise be perceived as united and continuous (Figure 6.5). Similarity and proximity can also create a sense of discontinuity when they are used with a foregrounding function, that is, when a dissimilar element finds itself surrounded by a large number of similar elements (Figure 6.6). In general, when these two principles work consistently in association, the *intensity* with which similarity and proximity between the elements of a configuration appear has an impact on the sense of unity and continuity: the more accentuated the similarity and proximity between two elements, the stronger the sense of unity and continuity between them.

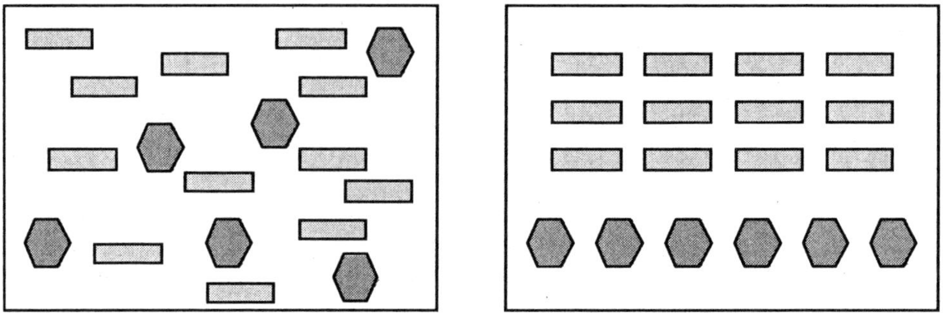

Figure 6.5. Illustration of the Gestalt principles of *similarity* and *proximity* and the effect that they produce on the perception of the elements of a configuration. When they work together, as in the configuration of the right, they produce an effect of unity and continuity. When they work in opposition, like in the configuration on the left, they produce and effect of ambiguity and discontinuity (Campbell, 1995).

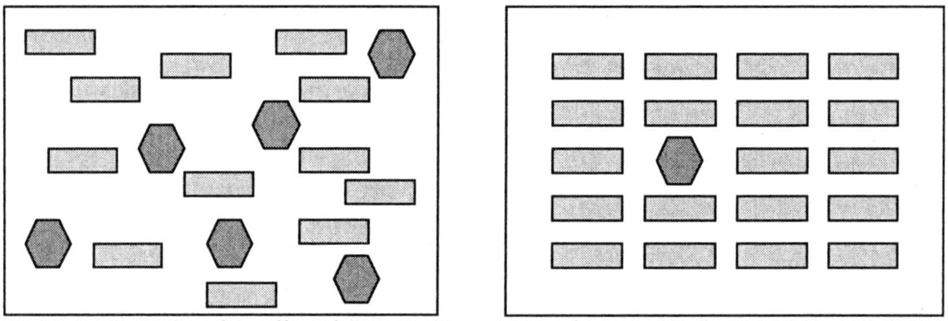

Figure 6.6. Illustration of the effect of discontinuity used with a foregrounding function. When a dissimilar element is surrounded by a large number of similar elements, the dissimilar element is brought to the foreground, as in the configuration on the right (Campbell, 1995).

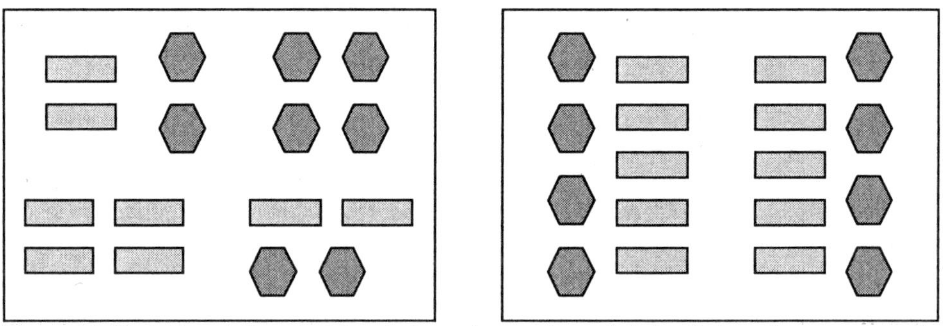

Figure 6.7. Illustration of the principles of size and symmetry and their effect on the perception of a configuration. People tend to group the elements of a configuration in large and symmetrical units, as in the configuration on the right, rather than in small and asymmetrical units, as in the configuration on the left (Campbell, 1995)

Finally, *size* and *symmetry* constitute another pair of parameters determining the level of unity and continuity perceivable between the elements of a configuration. There seems to be a natural tendency to group the elements of a configuration to create large, symmetrical units rather than small, asymmetrical ones, which means that there is a tendency on the part of the reader/viewer to visually organise any configuration in compact and balanced parts as far as possible (Figure 6.7).

The principles of similarity and proximity, size and symmetry, all can be observed in document design, to express the document's visual meta-discourse as described in Kumpf (2000). Likewise, they could constitute principles of hypertext design, to express the visual meta-discourse of the electronic interactive document. These principles could guide the use of the graphic elements that characterise the visual dimension of the electronic medium (as opposed to the visual dimension that characterise the paper-based medium) and could constitute the building blocks of electronic documents' visual meta-discourse. In this respect, founded in the seminal work of Jaques Bertin (1967/83/; 1977/81), certain semiologic studies on paper-based graphics, and subsequently on electronic graphics, have isolated a number of linguistic variables that could be fruitfully used to design visual meta-discourse configurations.

3.2. The Language of Graphics

In the 1960s and '70s, Bertin developed the first systematic semiotic theory of graphics, which he proposed as the basis for the scientific use of the graphic sign to represent information (in particular, cartographic information). He was building on a tradition that already existed before the Second World War, cultivated in movements like Bauhaus: in 1944, Kepes, a former member of the German school, proposed the graphic and visual categories of position, size, value, colour, shape, texture, and so on (Knoch, 2000-2001). In contrast, Bertin develops a systematic approach to the use of visual categories, conceiving graphics as a system that is capable of representing data with mathematical precision. The linguistic dimensions of this "mathematics" constitute a system of variables re-elaborated over the years by Bertin as well as by other semioticians of graphics building on his theories, with the aim of extending them from the realm of paper based cartography to the realm of multimedia cartography.

Unlike graphic design – a free and subjective art that acts according to its own rules – "*graphics is a tool that obeys universal laws that are unavoidable and undisputable but can be learned and taught*" says Bertin (2000-2001). Graphics rigorously processes pre-defined data sets to represent relationships between previously defined concepts, by using the properties of the visual image to make relationships of *difference/similarity*, *order* or *proportion* appear among data. "*The image is a meaningful form that is perceived instantaneously and is created within the three dimensions X, Y, Z.*", so "*it can transmit the relationships between three independent data sets*" (Bertin, 2001). This transmission takes place through a specific graphic sign system, and it is based on specific criteria, in order to extract and represent in a non-subjective way the information that is potentially contained in a set of data, and to make it immediately accessible and understandable to the reader.

Bertin's graphic sign system is constituted by two groups of variables, called *variable of the image* and *differential variables*. The first group of variables includes the two dimensions of the Cartesian plane (X and Y), that is, the distribution of graphic objects in the visual field; the size of graphic objects; the value of graphic objects, that is, their degree of luminosity. Size has the ability to show ratios, and in any combination of variables size and value define order (by variation of light energy) prior to the other variables, which are perceived along the Cartesian spatial dimension Z (in depth, that is). These variables are said by Bertin to be dissociative, because they signify different concepts and can be effectively used at the same time to establish relationships. The group of differential variables includes texture; colour; orientation; and shape. These are said to be associative variables, because their use can be associated with the use of the other variables. They do not interfere with the action of the other variables, as they merely have a differential function, that is, they are used to separate elementary images, but they cannot be used at the same time without generating confusion and inconsistency (Bertin, 2001) (Table 6.4).

For instance, two objects having the same shape, size and value find themselves on the plane, they suggest a relation of similarity and equivalence. If one of them has a lighter value, this difference of value suggests an order along the Cartesian dimension Z, which produces an effect of subordination of one object with respect to the other. If the two objects are distributed on the plane next to each other, whether they are related by similarity or by subordination, their relation is emphasized. If they are distributed far apart, their relation is less perceivable. If two objects have the same shape and value, but different size, the difference in size suggests a quantitative difference. If the two objects also have different values, the difference in value suggests a difference in depth, that is, an order along the dimension Z, emphasized by the difference in size.

Now, as mentioned above, if one complements the use of the dissociative variables with the use of the associative variables, they must be used one at a time, to make it possible for the reader to relate to one another the objects on the plane. For instance, if one uses shape to differentiate two objects (eg. icons of different trees on a topographic plan, to identify various kinds of vegetation in an area), the orientation of their shape should be the same (the trees should all be oriented in the same direction), to facilitate their recognition and comparison. Likewise, if texture is used to differentiate two objects, using colour may be superfluous and may end up being confusing. At times, the combination of the dissociative variables with the associative variables requires attention, as it may be problematic. For instance, value can be used to suggest order between two objects having the same shape and different size, but then the two objects need to have the same colour, because variations of value are difficult to perceive between different colours.

GROUP	PROPERTY	CATEGORY	FUNCTION
VARIABLES OF THE IMAGE	*Dissociative* : signify different concepts and can be effectively used at the same time	*DISTRIBUTION*	Emphasises relations.
		SIZE	Shows ratio and order.
		VALUE	Shows order.
DIFFERENTIAL VARIABLES	*Associative* : do not interfere with the action of the other variables, but generate confusion if used at the same time	*TEXTURE*	Differential variables: separate elementary images.
		COLOUR	
		ORIENTATION	
		SHAPE	

Table 6.4. Bertain's (1967-2001) graphic sign system, it's variables and their properties.

In subsequent years, Bertin's variables have been further articulated or extended with other variables, like background and foreground (Brewer, 1992); and transparency

(MacEachren, 2000-2001). Koch (2000-2001) proposed a system of variables for multimedia environments, including visual, sound and tactile variables. In this system the visual variable can be *2D static*, like size, value/shading, texture, colour, orientation, shape and arrangement (Bertin, 1983; Kraak, 1990; Dransch, 1995; Buziek, 1995); *2D dynamic*, like speed, viewpoint and distance (Krigier, 1994); or *3D dynamic*, like perspective and overlapping (Vasconcellos, 1993). The sound variables are location, loudness, pitch, register, timbre, duration, rate of change, order and attack/decay. Finally, the tactile variables of Koch's system are volume, size, value, texture/grain, form, orientation and elevation (Table 6.5).

CATEGORY	VARIABLE
VISUAL	2D Static → *size, value/shading, texture, colour, orientation, shape, arrangement*
	2D Dynamic → *speed, viewpoint, distance, other...*
	3D Dynamic → *perspective, overlapping*
SOUND	*location, loudness, pitch, register, timbre, duration, change of rate, order, attack/decay*
TACTILE	*volume, size, value, texture/grain, form, orientation, elevation*

Table 6.5. Koch's (2000-2001) graphic system of variables for multimedia environments.

4. Visual Languages and Cognitive Coherence Relations

In this chapter we have seen how it is possible to establish a parallel between textual and visual processing, and how textual documents themselves normally express a visual meta-discourse conveyed by a number of graphic features. These visual features can be used to produce a sense of continuity and cohesion between the different parts of the document, which are achieved through the observation of criteria like proximity and similarity, size and symmetry. These criteria can regulate the use of visual linguistic elements, graphic dissociative and associative variables that constitute the building blocks of any visual meta-discourse, whether it is paper-based or electronic.

Based on what was previously discussed, the concept of visual meta-discourse could be extended to hypertext document design, and the document design principles described above could regulate the use of graphic variables, in order to express hypertext discourse structure. In order to do so, since the goal is to represent hypertext discourse structure based on the visual expression discourse connections, graphical effects of similarity and difference; order and proportion; proximity, size and symmetry; should be used to express relational primitives like cognitive coherence relations. Observing these principles in the use of a number of electronic graphic variables, the next chapter proposes the design of a set of coherence relations, selected to produce a first study to test the interpretability of such basic relational concepts when they are expressed through visual dynamic features.

In doing so, though, a fundamental aspect should be taken into account. As we have seen, the Gestalt principles and the graphic variables described above can be used to produce weaker or stronger relations of continuity and cohesion, similarity and difference, foreground and background, order and ratio, between the objects that are distributed on the plane (the visual field). In the electronic environment, these relations become dynamic and therefore more complex, since dynamic variables can represent visual transformations and, in so doing, express temporality. However, although these relations may produce both static and dynamic visual coherence in the most sophisticated ways, they still do not automatically have a correspondence with the cognitive relational primitives on which discourse coherence is based. That is, the conceptual order expressed by visual coherence and the conceptual order expressed by discourse coherence do not necessarily coincide for all of the cognitive relational primitives that are at work in discourse coherence. In other words, if similarity or sequential visual relations in the electronic environment seem to have a perfect correspondence with similarity and sequential relations in textual discourse, for causal or conditional relations this correspondence does not seem to be as straightforward: the conceptual complexity expressed by causality and conditionality requires a sophisticated approach to the use of graphic variables. On the other hand, as we have seen, using as many variables as one can have in electronic environment, requires particular attention and selectiveness, if relations are to be expressed in a consistent and congruent way. This means that, although Gestalt and graphics principles can guide the expression of visual relations, and ultimately basic discourse relations, there is always an element of design involved, leaving room for the creation of ever new codifications. The next chapter proposes one such scheme.

Notes

[1] That is, from the discourse level of the film itself (the enunciation), to the meta-discourse level of the character's thinking.

[2] In fact, as an example of a sentence in which the two spans are not coherently related, Campbell uses the sentence "*The haystack was important. The cloth had ripped.*", which I wouldn't use, since the interpretation of its first span alone is already problematic (what does it mean that "*the haystack is important*" when it stands alone?) without the lack of a clarifying context (for instance "*the haystack was important as a feature of the English countryside landscape, till the end of the nineteenth century*"). This fact must have an effect on the interpretation of the whole sentence, and therefore on the interpretation of the connection between the two spans. Since it is on the connection between the two spans of text that we are focusing at the moment, I prefer to use a different pair of sentences.

[3] For the second sentence, one has to resort to a weakly motivated conjunctive relation between two spans of text that would hypothetically be part of a larger picture, assuming that the enunciator of the sentence is describing a given situation at a given time - where, for instance, someone is waiting for the bus in a spring day. The connection is possible if the sentence is assumed to be 'open', susceptible to completion, which requires an effort of imagination to find coherence in the sentence. On the contrary, the first sentence requires very little imaginative effort: the two spans are easily related through causality, which makes their connection strongly motivated, making the two spans stick together as well as more independent from any external context, therefore 'closed'. The same can be observed in cinema, (as described in Chapter 5), between Classical cinema (ex. *Rear window*) and Modern cinema (ex. *L'Année Dernière á Marienbad*).

[4] However, (referring back to what was said in note 6) also in this case, if more elements of the context are provided, the interpretation of the configuration as composed by the angular lines QFC and ZFM may make more sense than the interpretation of the configuration as composed by the intersection in F of the straight lines QM and CZ, as it is shown in Figure 6.1.b.

[5] The assumption of underlying cognitive functions is also supported, for instance, by the influential work of cognitive scientists as Chomsky (1957) or Pinker (1994).

[6] In contrast to textual meta-discourse categories, the visual meta-discourse categories proposed by Kumpf express simultaneously both textual and interpersonal features, that is, the visual elements that express the cohesion and coherence of text find themselves expressing its rhetorical features at the same time. This is probably due to the fact that text is based on symbolic codes that have the ability to denote abstract concepts in an analytic way, whereas graphics are based on iconic codes whose power of abstraction is bound to connotative aspects, and whose modality of signification is more synthetic than analytic.

Cinematic Hypertext
C. Mancini
IOS Press, 2005

7. Rendering Discourse Relations with Graphics and Animation

In this chapter the principles of visual perception and the variables of graphics presented in the previous chapter guide the design process of rendering cognitive coherence relational concepts through animated visualisations, for experimental purposes. A set of eight more basic and commonly acknowledged relations is selected to be graphically rendered, and its selection is motivated. The set comprises: causality, conditionality, conjunctiveness, disjunctiveness, similarity, contrast, elaboration and background relations. To render these relations, a minimum number of graphic variables is used, in order to keep any visual 'noise' as low as possible and to enhance the distinctiveness of the resulting representations: eight animated relational patterns.

1. Rendering Cognitive Coherence Relations in Hypertext

Chapter 2 of this book discusses how, according to the psycholinguistic approach to text analysis, coherence is a cognitive phenomenon that is achieved through the inference of relational concepts holding together discourse parts, and how these concepts are signalled through a number of cohesive devices that guide the reader's interpretation. Chapters 3 and 5 try to show how these relational concepts, deriving from a small set of primitives, can be used to account for coherence in hypertext and in cinema, as well as in text. Chapter 4 and 5 show how in cinematic discourse, which cannot rely on connective devices comparable to the ones that operate in text, coherence relations can be inferred from the way in which the language's formal - mainly visual - features are used. Finally, Chapter 6 discusses how formal features can be used in document design to produce a visual meta-discourse, how in fact parallels can be drawn between textual and visual processing, and how graphic elements can constitute the variables of a visual language capable of expressing abstract relational concepts like similarity, difference, order, ratio, etc. Now, this chapter presents a set of relational graphic renderings that were designed to verify the main hypothesis investigated in this work.

Based on the elements laid out thus far, we had hypothesised that it should be possible to implement a visual language capable of expressing abstract relational concepts, the relational concepts being the cognitive primitives that determine coherence in discourse construction and interpretation. More precisely, the hypothesis was that both static and dynamic graphic variables could be used to express visual relationships between objects - hypertext nodes - and signify cognitive relational primitives. To verify this hypothesis, we set up an empirical study in which people were asked to evaluate a set of cognitive relations that had been graphically designed. The preparation of the relations' renderings to be tested involved three steps. The first step consisted of selecting a subset of cognitive coherence relations, among the ones identified in previous hypertext and cinematic analyses, with the purpose of rendering them graphically. The second step consisted of selecting a subset of static and dynamic graphical variables that were used according to Gestalt principles and graphic norms to visually render the cognitive coherence relations of the selected subset. The third step consisted of implementing, for each selected cognitive relation, a small animation in which the relation holding between text chunks was rendered through the visual pattern that had been designed to express that particular relation.

The next section of this chapter describes the rationale for selecting the set of cognitive coherence relations to be used in the empirical test. Then, the following section, describes the rationale for the selection of some of the graphic variables and the design principles followed to visually render the traversal of the relations, and it presents the resulting implemented animations. Chapter 8 is devoted to the description of the experiment's preparation and execution, and to the discussion of its results.

2. Selecting an Experimental Set of Relations

For the purposes of the study, the relational sub-set needed to be as representative as possible of the different relation types identified in the previous hypertext and cinematic analyses, that is, to express the most frequently encountered or relevant relations. At the same time, however, it was important to restrict the size of the set, to make sure that the respective renderings could be as different as possible from one another: the fewer relations the greater the distinction between their visual representations. Furthermore, it was desirable that the subset be based on those coherence relations that have high agreement amongst theoreticians, that is, those that are more understood and solidly established in the study of discourse coherence (for instance, causality). Finally, the relations needed to be as close as possible to fundamental primitives, that is, to be as far as possible in their basic form (for instance, semantic rather than pragmatic and in basic rather than non-basic order). As a result of all these considerations, the set of eight relations described below was selected. Table 7.1. shows them organised according to the parameters that define them: causal/additive, positive/negative, actual/hypothetical, conjunctive/comparative. The next section of this chapter shows that it is based on these parameters that the relations were associated to graphical variables to produce their visual rendering for experimental purposes.

Causality. Holding between the propositional content A of a discourse part (text span or cinematic shot) and the propositional content B of another discourse part (text span or cinematic shot), when A is presented as causing B (Sanders et al., 1993; Louwerse, 2001).

Conditionality. The hypothetical form of causality - holding between A and B, when A is presented as causing B, but only if A holds in the first place (Sanders et al., 1993; Louwerse, 2001), or in the case that A is relevant enough (Meyer, 2000).

Conjunctiveness. Holding between the propositional content A of a discourse part and the propositional content B of another discourse part, when A is presented as simply coexisting with B (Sanders et al., 1993), or also being equivalent to B (Pander Maat, 1999; Louwerse, 2001).

Disjunctiveness. The negative of conjunctiveness, holding between A and B, when A is presented as being alternative to B (Sanders et al, 1993; Louwerse, 2001).

Similarity. Holding between the propositional content A of a discourse part and the propositional content B of another discourse part, when A is presented as being similar or equivalent to B in some relevant respect (Knott, 1998; Pander Maat, 1999, Louwerse, 2001).

Contrast. The negative of similarity, holding between A and B, when A is presented as being opposed or unequal to B in some relevant respect (Louwerse, 2001).

Elaboration. Holding between the propositional content A of a discourse part and the propositional content B of another discourse part, when B is presented as elaborating, expanding, explaining A (Mann and Thompson, 1988).

Background. Holding between the propositional content A of a discourse part and the propositional content B of another discourse part, when B is presented as the explanatory context in which A exists or occurs (Mann and Thompson, 1988).

SOURCE OF COHERENCE	BASIC OPERATION	POLARITY	HYPOTHETI-CALITY	COMPARATI-VENESS	RELATIONS
semantic	additive	positive	n/a	non-comp.	*conjunctiveness*
			n/a	comparative	*similarity*
		negative	n/a	non-comp.	*disjunctiveness*
			n/a	comparative	*contrast*
	causal	positive	actual	n/a	*causality*
			hypothetical	n/a	*conditionality*
pragmatic	additive	positive	actual	n/a	*elaboration*
	causal	positive	hypothetical	n/a	*background*

Table 7.1. Sub-set of cognitive coherence relations chosen to be visually rendered and empirically tested. They are here organised according to the relational parameters that define them and that were used to define their visual rendering.

Apart from the general criteria mentioned at the beginning of this section, the choice of each relation was also based on additional criteria. First of all, a major distinction in the various classifications of coherence relations previously described (Chapter 2) was made between two types of basic operation: *causality* and *additiveness* (Sanders et al., 1993). This distinction is a fundamental one and it was the first one to be considered when selecting the corpus of relations to experiment with. Another important distinction concerns the nature of additive relations (Pander Maat, 1999): an additive relation can indicate a coexistence consisting of a complementarity with respect to a whole - in which case it is a conjunctive relation - or it can indicate the equivalence of two entities with respect to some elements or parameters - in which case it is a similarity relation. This distinction is also an important one and merited coverage in the set, so *comparativeness* constituted another criterion of selection (Knott, 1998).

Another fundamental and generally acknowledged distinction concerns the *polarity* of relations, which can be positive or negative (Sanders et al., 1993): negative polarity relations were accounted for as far as additive relations are concerned, and disjunction (negative of conjunction) and contrast (negative of similarity) were included in the experimental corpus. As far as causality is concerned, its hypothetical form, conditionality, was included in the corpus to see what would happen when a complicating factor like *hypotheticality* was added (Sanders et al., 1993).

The relations described thus far are all semantic ones, they are generally acknowledged and least controversial among the theoreticians, and constitute very basic and more robustly defined relational concepts. Despite being acknowledged, the distinction between semantic and pragmatic relations is more controversial, but it was important to include in the set also two *pragmatic* relations, because they recurred so often in the previous hypertext and cinematic analyses. They are elaboration and background (Mann and Thompson, 1988).

The pair also seemed interesting because the two relations seem to express opposite discourse motions. Elaboration holds between a piece of information and added extra information that expands and develops the piece of information already provided. Going in the opposite direction, background holds between a piece of information and another piece of information (pre-existing in conceptual, spatial or temporal terms) on which the first piece of information is based and by which it is contextualised. In the first case extra information is provided to develop a richer and more in-depth picture about a subject. In the second case, basic information is provided to make it possible for the reader to understand a subject, on the basis of what comes before.

3. Designing the Selected Set of Cognitive Coherence Relations

As anticipated in the previous section, the graphic rendering of the selected relations involved the use of text, that is, the text spans of long sentences, originally held together through connectives, were chunked and distributed in different text boxes, which constituted graphic objects. These objects were attributed graphic features and animated in order to visually render the conceptual connection that was originally holding between the text chunks now contained in the objects. The design challenge was to reify the connection between two objects, as expressed by each coherence relation, in as compelling a manner possible, within certain visual and animation constraints, in order to maximise their expressive effectiveness. As in cinematic projection and in hypertext navigation, each representation had to be dynamic, that is, it had to have a temporality. And for each relation, the transition between one representational stage to the other had to be meaningful itself, not only the final state.

To reify the relation renderings, we used examples of argumentative passages from a history of science text, which was selected because it was conceptually not too complex, because its literary style was very accessible, and also because its contents were, ideologically speaking, neutral or at least non controversial, since the subject matter concerned facts of the distant past[1]. This was to make sure that the interpretation of the text's conceptual content and logical connections would not present any difficulty or raise any ambiguity.[2] Out of all the material provided by the book, we selected a particular subject (theories about the orbiting of planets in the solar system), so that all the relations would be reified in the text within the same conceptual context. From the relevant sections, we then isolated short passages of text, each passage consisting of a pair or a triple of sentences. The sentences of each pair or group held with each other one of the eight selected cognitive coherence relations (examples are given below for each relation). Finally, each pair or triple of related sentences was represented on screen respectively within a pair or triple of related text windows, and those windows were attributed certain graphic properties expressing the relation holding between the content of one sentence and the content of the other. The variables used to design the text boxes, so that their composition would generate visual patterns expressing the text's relational patterns, are shown in Table 7.2.

CATEGORY	VARIABLE		USE	MOTIVATION AND FUNCTION
Visual	*2d Static*	*size*	no	Expresses ratio, that is, relationships of quantity (between objects of the same shape), which was not being focussed on.
		value	yes	Expresses order. So gradual change of value was used to express directionality and progress in a chain of events (causality and conditionality) or in discourse progress (background). Radical change of value, however, was not used to express order, but to achieve an effect of similarity (when the value of an object changes to the value of the other) or contrast (when the value of an object changes to the opposite of the value of the other) in comparative relations.
		arrangement	yes	In general, it facilitates comparison and emphasises relationships through proximity. The final positioning along a vertical axis was used to express the order of events in the reality (causality, conditionality – partially also in elaboration), and the final positioning along a horizontal axis was used to express order in discourse (conjunction, disjunction, similarity, contrast – partly also elaboration and background).
		colour	no	Can be used to differentiate elementary images, but reduces comparability of objects that are meant to be equivalent and makes it difficult to use the variable of value. To maximise comparability between objects, they were given the same colour: greyscale only was used.
		orientation	no	Can be used to differentiate elementary images, but may reduce comparability. Plus, being the objects text boxes the only possible orientation is the one that allows comfortable reading.
		texture	no	Can be used to differentiate elementary images, but may reduce comparability. In this case, it would have interfered with the readability of text.
		shape	yes	Can be used to differentiate elementary images, but it may reduce comparability. It was generally determined by the quantity of text and by the imposed length of the objects sides (which needed to be comparable with the sides of other objects). It was used as an expressive variable with conditionality and background (to create an effect of enclosure of one object within another behind it) and with elaboration (to create an effect of differentiation).
	2d Dynamic *(2d*	*speed*	no	The speed at which objects entered the visual field and positioned themselves in relation to others, could have been used to express the strength of the relation (for instance, causal vs additive). However, it was kept as a constant to avoid 'noise' effects.

(Visual Cont/D)	*Dynamic Cont/D)*	*viewpoint*	no	Could be used to express the degree of the writer's involvement in discourse, but was kept as a constant to avoid 'noise' effects.
		distance	no	Could be used to express the degree of the writer's involvement in discourse, but was kept as a constant to avoid 'noise' effects.
		trajectory (added to Koch's list as 'others…')	yes	The trajectory of objects placing themselves to position was used to express the provenance of events (causality and conditionality) or concepts (similarity and contrast).
	3d Dynamic	*perspective*	no	All objects were treated as if they were moving on the plane and as if they were flat, to maintain the representations simple and close to the 'writing plane'.
		overlapping	yes	Was used to express the sense of enclosure of one object within one behind it (conditionality and background), and to express a sense of difference in discourse level (elaboration and background).
Sound	*location, loudness, pitch, register, timbre, duration, change of rate, order, attack/decay*		no	n/a. no sound effect was used for this experimental rendering, in order to reduce the complexity of each representation.
Tactual	*volume, size, value, texture/grain, form, orientation, elevation*		no	n/a.

Table 7.2. Koch's (2000/2001) graphic variables, with the indication of which ones were used to design the text windows for the experiment in order to visually render the subset of cognitive coherence relations. They refer to the design of the boxes alone.

As in Kumpf (2000) and Campbell (1995), the use of these graphical properties would constitute the visual meta-discourse of the selected text, but unlike in Kumpf and Campbell, this meta-discourse would especially and only take into account the expression of the logical discourse's connections. To this end, all cue phrases connecting one sentence with the other in the original text were removed, and all sentences where made grammatically and conceptually independent, in order to let visual clues play the connective role instead – as often happens in hypertext.

In order to be as differentiated as possible (and therefore recognisable by the people involved in the experiment), each representation also had to be kept as minimalist as possible, making use of no more formal elements than strictly necessary. Out of all the graphical variables mentioned above, from Koch's static variables (2000/2001) only *value* and *arrangement* were used, which correspond to two of Bertin's dissociative variables of the image. *Size* was not used as a variable, but came as a consequence of the quantity of text making up each sentence, whose format was a constant. *Shape* (one of Bertin's associative variables – 2000/2001), was only used in the representation of two relations, *elaboration* and *background*; for the other relations, the shape of the windows also came as a consequence of the quantity of text contained in each one. Only *overlapping* was among the 3D-dynamic ones. Instead, the appearance and placement of each text window on screen, which does not seem to be counted as graphical variable by Koch, had discriminating value in the representations designed for the experiment. Table 7.2 shows which variable of Koch's categories were used to design the boxes and with what function, which ones were not used and for what reason.

All these variables were applied exclusively to the boxes containing the sentences, but the text itself was not attributed visual variables. Normally, font, size, style and colour of text were treated as constants, except in one case, where the colour had to invert from the very light grey used by default to a very dark grey, in order to be readable on a much lighter background. That is, even the change of colour, in the one case when it occurred, came as a consequence of other changes and its aim was to maintain the constancy of text readability.

PARAMETER	VALUE	RENDERING OF PARAMETER'S VALUE
Source Of Coherence	Semantic	Positioning of the objects one next to the other. Equal length of the objects' sides that find themselves next to each other.
	Pragmatic	Overlapping of objects on one of the sides (elaboration) or completely (background).
Basic Operation	Additive	Alignment of objects along the horizontal axis (except in elaboration). Use of the same value throughout or at the initial stage (except in similarity, contrast, elaboration). Appearing of the second object next to the first object (except in similarity and contrast) or overlapped to it (elaboration).
	Causal	Alignment along the vertical axis (except in background). Gradual intensification of value from one state of events to the other. Sliding down of the second/third object from behind the first/second object (except in background).
Polarity	Positive	Intensification or stability of value, from the appearance of one object to the appearance of the other (except in elaboration).
	Negative	Change of the value of the object that was first in the visual field to a value that contrasts the value of the object that appears second.
Hypotheticality	Hypothetical	Complete or partial enclosure of an object (containing the text that refers to the consequence) within the object behind it (containing the text that refers to the pre-existing condition).
	Non-Hypoth.	-
Comparativeness	Comparative	Radical change of value of the object that is already in the visual field to contrast or match the value of the object coming into the visual field second. Entering of the second object from the side of the visual field opposite to where the first object is; sliding of the second object towards the first and positioning next to it.
	Non-Comp.	-

Table 7.3. Parameters defining the experimental subset of relations and graphical choices that were made to render them visually.

The specific use of the preselected graphical variables to represent each relation was driven by the previous analysis of the logical content and conceptual implications of the relation itself, and ultimately by their parametrical definition - as illustrated in Table 7.3. and 7.4.

RELATION	SOURCE OF COHERENCE	BASIC OPERATION	POLARITY	HYPOTHETI-CALITY	COMPARATI-VENESS
conjunctiveness	semantic	additive	positive	no	no
similarity	semantic	additive	positive	no	yes
disjunctiveness	semantic	additive	negative	no	no
contrast	semantic	additive	negative	no	yes
causality	semantic	causal	positive	no	no
conditionality	semantic	causal	positive	yes	no
elaboration	pragmatic	additive	positive	no	no
background	pragmatic	causal	positive	yes	no

Table 7.4. Parametrical attributes of each relation: these conceptual attributes were rendered in graphical terms and therefore each of them contributed to shape the relations that they define.

Conjunctiveness. The presence or appearance of two entities or phenomena at the same time in the same space denotes a conjunctive relation. That is, whenever two entities or phenomena are recorded in such circumstances, they are connected by conjunction. Conjunction only says that the two entities or phenomena coexist in the same place at the same time, without saying anything about the reasons behind or the modalities of their co-presence. As far as the specific context of their occurrence is concerned, they play an equivalent and complementary role in constituting a whole. In this respect, as Pander Maat (1999) discussed, they are also similar in terms of the role that they play, that is, of the importance that they have in the general picture.

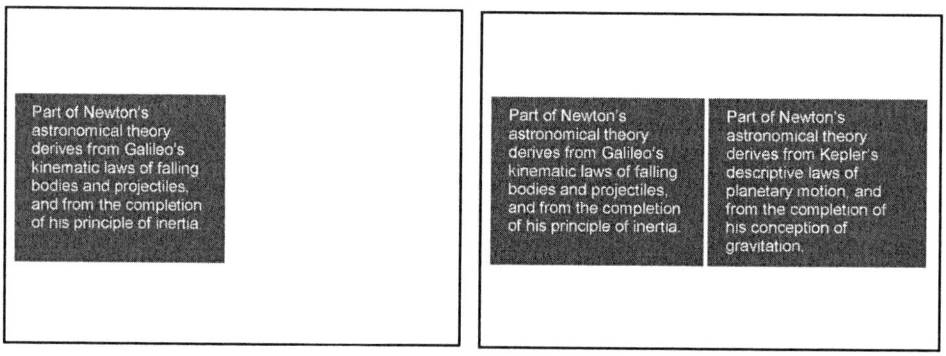

Figure 7.1. Two screen shots from the animated graphic rendering of *conjunctiveness*.

In this specific case, the additive relation was reified by the text spans:

A. *Part of Newton's astronomical theory derives from Galileo's kinematic laws of falling bodies and projectiles, and from the completion of his principle of inertia.*

B. *Part of Newton's astronomical theory derives from Kepler's descriptive laws of planetary motion, and from the completion of his conception of gravitation.*

They were rendered as shown in Figure 7.1. The two respective text windows are given the same value and their vertical sides are given the same length; they appear on the screen next to each other, one at a time, the window containing the first text span appearing on the left and the window containing the second text span appearing on the right after 2 seconds. Firstly, the concept of *addition* is rendered by the windows appearing next to each other, with the order of appearance following the direction of reading familiar in the Western world[3]. Secondly, the concept of *equivalence*, and *similarity* in the sense of Pander Maat (1999), is rendered by the value of the windows' areas, and is reinforced by the fact that their sides are of identical length, and they appear next to each other and not, say, one under the other. The way the windows positioned themselves was the simplest possible one, to render the fact that the two entities are simply related as complementary components of a whole.

Disjunction. The negative of a conjunctive relation is a relation that fails to meet the expectation of conjunction, or else defies the rule set by the positive conjunctive relation (to use Knott and Dale's words, 1996). Two entities or phenomena do not coexist in a space-time interval, but are *alternative* to one another, that is, exclude each other. The relation obviously implies their actual existence, but it also implies that this can only be at different times, in different places, or in different circumstances.

Figure 7.2. Two screen shots from the animated graphic rendering of *disjunctiveness*.

The text spans selected to reify alternative are:

A. *In Galileo's times, one could have embraced the heliocentric theory incurring the consequence of being considered a heretic by the Catholic Church.*

B. *In Galileo's times, one could have rejected the heliocentric theory and still have the chance of being considered a good Catholic.*

They were rendered as shown in Figure 7.2. The text windows are given the same appearance as those used to represent the additive relation, with the difference that when the second window appears on the right 2 seconds after, the window on the left has the value of its background changed to a very light grey, which makes it difficult to read the text. In other words, the concept of alternative, of reciprocal exclusion of the two situations, the defeat of the expectation of additiveness expressed by this negative relation, are rendered through the fact that as the second span of text appears, the first one becomes unreadable.

Causality. On the other side of the spectrum with respect to additiveness, *causality* is the strongest logic relation between two entities or phenomena. The causal relation implies additiveness, in that the two entities or phenomena connected are part of the same picture, context, or situation. It implies sequentiality, that is, order, in that one entity or phenomenon necessarily follows the entity or phenomenon that has caused it (Louwerse, 2001). It implies conditionality, as discussed by Meyer (2000), in that the appearance of one entity or phenomenon necessarily conditions the appearance of the other. However, that bound of conditionality is so relevant (to use Meyer's term), the connection is so specific, that in fact the first entity or phenomenon is directly producing the second.

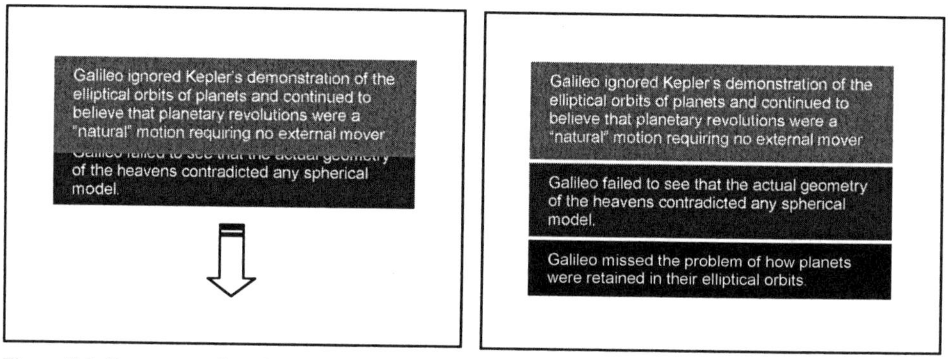

Figure 7.3. Two screen shots from the animated graphic rendering of *causality*. The arrow visible in the left shot (representing the initial phase of the animation) is only illustrative and it is used here (on paper) to signify the box's movement.

The text spans, three this time, selected to reify causality are:

A. *Galileo ignored Kepler's demonstration of the elliptical orbits of planets and continued to believe that planetary revolutions were a "natural" motion requiring no external mover.*

B. *Galileo failed to see that the actual geometry of the heavens contradicted any spherical model.*

C. *Galileo missed the problem of how planets were retained in their elliptical orbits.*

They were rendered as shown in Figure 7.3. The three windows respectively containing the three text spans are arranged one under the other, the second sliding down from behind the first as soon as the first has appeared, and the third sliding down from behind the second as soon as it has reached its position. They all share the same width, while the height of each is determined by the quantity of text contained in each window. The value of the windows' background becomes increasingly darker from the first to the third, and the ratio of increment is the same from the first to the second and from the second to the third, that is, they are equidistant, as far as the value is concerned (as prescribed by Bertin, 2000/2001). In this configuration, the order of the events is rendered by the arrangement of the text windows, while the fact that the second and the third windows appear by sliding down from the previous one renders the fact that the second and the third events follow, and are brought about, respectively by the first and the second event. At the same time, the darkening of the background renders the idea of progression in the forging of a logical chain. Finally, the cohesion between the three events is reinforced by the fact that the three windows have the same width.

Similarity. *Similarity* establishes a connection between two entities or phenomena that may belong to different semantic worlds and that may not have any logical connection with each other. However, the connection established between them often enlightens their nature, and often reveals certain aspects of one or the other that may have been not as evident before the comparison occurred. This relation does not imply chronological order, and between the connected entities or phenomena there is no hierarchy, but rather equivalence, that is, they are independent objects connected on the grounds of what they happen to have in common.

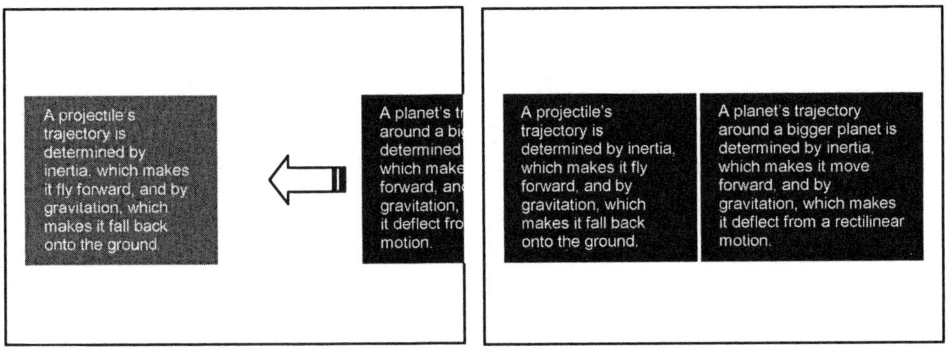

Figure 7.4. Two screen shots from the animated graphic rendering of *similarity*. Here too, the arrow visible in the left shot (representing the initial phase of the animation) is only illustrative and it is used to signify the box's movement.

The text spans selected to reify similarity are:

A. *A projectile's trajectory is determined by inertia, which makes it fly forward, and by gravitation, which makes it fall back onto the ground.*

B. *A planet's trajectory around a bigger planet is determined by inertia, which makes it move forward, and by gravitation, which makes it deflect from a rectilinear motion.*

They were rendered as shown in Figure 7.4. The two corresponding windows are arranged to end up next to each other, with the left-hand one first sliding onto the screen from the centre-left, immediately followed by the second entering the screen from the centre-right and sliding into place next to the first. They have the same height, while their width is determined by the quantity of text contained in each one. The window containing the left text span, the one appearing first, has the default grey background, whereas the window containing the second text span, the one sliding in, has a very dark grey area. However, as soon as the second window reaches the first one, the area of the first one turns into the same very dark grey. In this configuration, the assimilation of the phenomenon described in the first text span to the phenomenon described into the second text span is rendered by the change of background to which the first window is subject. The fact that the second window slides in refers to the "coming together" of different semantic worlds on the basis of a structural analogy between them; while the fact that the second window comes from a side and takes position next to the first window (and not below or above) refers to the fact that the relation is bi-directional (Louwerse, 2001), or multinuclear (Mann and Thompson, 1988). Finally, the cohesion between the two objects is reinforced by their identical height.

Contrast. *Contrast* is the negative of the similarity relation, as it fails to meet the expectation of similarity, or else defies the rule set by the positive similarity relation. That is, a relation that connects two entities or phenomena presuming a possible similarity between them on the basis of certain elements or aspects is finally contradicted on the basis of certain other elements or aspects.

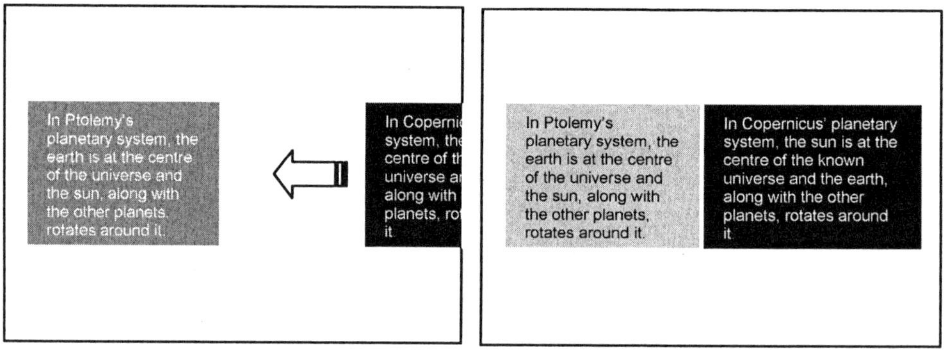

Figure 7. 5. Two screen shots from the animated graphic rendering of *contrast*. Again, the arrow visible in the left shot is only illustrative and it is used to signify the box's movement.

The text spans selected to reify contrast are:

A. *In Ptolemy's planetary system, the earth is at the centre of the universe and the sun, along with the other planets, rotates around it.*

B. *In Copernicus' planetary system, the sun is at the centre of the known universe and the earth, along with the other planets, rotates around it.*

They were rendered as shown in Figure 7.5. The windows containing the two spans of text above are shaped the same way as they are in the similarity relation, with the difference that this time, when the second window reaches the first window already in place, the background of the first one turns into a very light grey, which visually produces a great contrast between the two objects – in this case, and only in this case, the text colour has to change from the standard almost white to almost black. In this configuration, the concept of equivalence and potential comparability between the two phenomena described in the text spans is still rendered by the use of the graphical variables, however the failure of the comparison is rendered by the contrast of the background values.

Elaboration. *Elaboration* connects an element of discourse or a concept to its expansion - in terms of explanation, clarification, or articulation - deeper level of discourse with respect to the expanded element or concept. For some recipients, that expansion may be superfluous to the understanding of the discourse's structure and development, since they already have the knowledge that the elaboration is meant to provide, but for other recipients it may be useful or necessary. In some cases, as we have seen in hypertext discourse (Chapter 3, § 2.1), elaboration may constitute the main connection through which an argument develops and explores its conceptual possibilities.

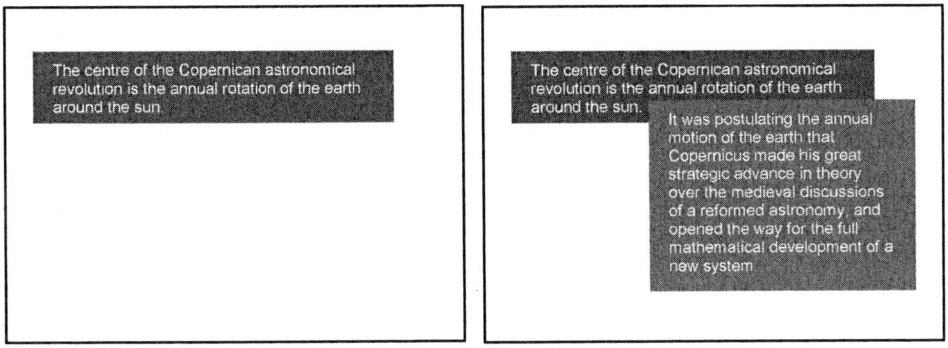

Figure 7.6. Two screen shots from the animated graphic rendering of *elaboration*.

The spans of text selected to reify elaboration are:

A. *The centre of the Copernican astronomical revolution is the annual rotation of the earth around the sun.*

B. *It was in postulating the annual motion of the earth that Copernicus made his great strategic advance in theory over the medieval discussions of a reformed astronomy,. and opened the way for the full mathematical development of a new system.*

They were rendered as shown in Figure 7.6. The two windows containing the spans of text above are this time overlapping, the second one appearing over the first one slightly overlapped to its edges, in a way that the text of the first one can still be read, though. In addition, this time the variable of shape is used, that is, neither the horizontal or the vertical sides of the two windows have the same length. The window containing the first span of text is wider but lower, whereas the window containing the second span of text is about one third narrower and about two thirds taller. In addition, none of the sides of the two windows are aligned, but the right edge of the second window is more to the right than the right edge of the first window. The background of the second window is slightly lighter than that of the first one. In this configuration, the fact that the two discourse units do not belong to the same discourse level is rendered by the differences of shape, background and alignment, as well as by the overlapping of the two objects, which suggests the existence of different layers in the visual field, reinforced by the difference of background. Finally, both arrangement and shape suggest that the second window constitutes an appendix to the first one, a deviation from the main track.

Background. *Background* relates an element of discourse or a concept to its context – in terms of justification for its occurrence, of background defining its meaning. At the semantic level, one of the related entities or phenomena provides the context in which the other entity or phenomenon gains its meaning. On the pragmatic or speech-act level, the content of the first discourse part provides the information needed to understand the content of the second discourse part. As with elaboration, the information provided as background may be unnecessary to some recipients, but very useful and even fundamental to others, depending on their knowledge about the entities or phenomena in question. We have seen also this relation being used frequently in hypertext discourse construction (Chapter 3).

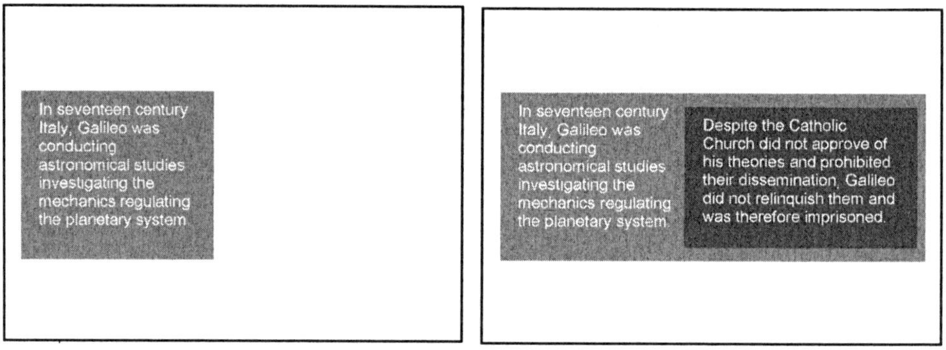

Figure 7.7. Two shots from the animated graphic rendering of *background.*

The spans of text selected to reify background are:

A. *In Seventeenth Century Italy, Galileo was conducting astronomical studies investigating the mechanics regulating the planetary system.*

B. *Despite the fact that the Catholic Church did not approve of his theories and prohibited their dissemination, Galileo did not relinquish them and was therefore imprisoned.*

They were rendered as shown in Figure 7.7. As with *elaboration*, the two windows containing the text spans are differentiated also by shape as well as by area and background intensity. The window containing the first text span has a default grey background, but the window containing the second text span has a darker grey background. This second window appears 'on top' of the first one, or rather, on top of an extension of the first one: as the second window appears to the right of the first, the first is extended so that the second ends up included within the first. This way the second window overlaps the first while all the text of the first one remains readable. In this configuration, the concept of context is rendered by the visual inclusion of one window within the other, and the concept of background is suggested by the layering effect of the overlap, reinforced by the change of value.

Conditionality. *Conditionality* is conceived as sitting between pure causality and background. It is similar to a *causal* relation in that the appearance or occurrence of the second entity or phenomenon involved in the relation depends on the appearance or occurrence of the first entity or phenomenon, although the former does not necessarily directly cause the latter to appear or occur (unless it is a "necessary and sufficient condition"). Conditionality also shares something in common with the *background* relation in that the first entity or phenomenon sets the possibility, the context, in which the second entity or phenomena can exist or hold true. At the semantic level, one of the related entities or phenomena provides the context in which the other entity or phenomenon gains its meaning, while at the pragmatic or speech-act level the content of the first discourse part provides the information for the understanding of the content of the second discourse part. In any case, the two entities or phenomena are not equivalent to each other, and as far as the context in which they exist is concerned, their relation is hierarchical.

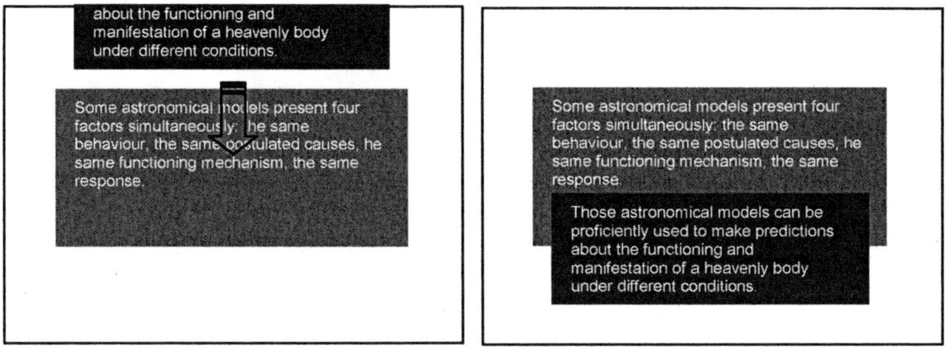

Figure 7.8. Two screen shots from the animated graphic rendering of *conditionality*. Again, the arrow visible in the left shot is only illustrative and it is used to signify the box's movement.

The text spans related by conditionality in this case are:

A. *Some astronomical models present four factors simultaneously: the same behaviour, the same postulated causes, the same functioning mechanism, the same response.*

B. *Those astronomical models can be proficiently used to make predictions about the functioning and manifestation of a heavenly body under different conditions.*

They were rendered as shown in Figure 7.8. According to the conceptual analysis of elaboration, the graphical representation of this relation is something between the visualisation of causality and the visualisation of background. The two windows respectively containing the first and the second text span have different width and area: the first one is wider, taller and lighter, whereas the second one is narrower, shorter and darker. The second is sliding from above, but instead of sliding down behind, it slides down over the first one, and stops when still half overlapping it, as if partly included in it (its text still being fully readable). This configuration renders the idea of context through the difference in shape and the partial overlapping, which suggest inclusion and layering at the same time. However, it also renders the idea of conditionality through the sliding down of the second unit over the first one, and through the darkening of the window's background, as a sign of transformation and development of a situation from one stage to the other.

4. Objectives of the relational renderings

Expectedly, this first attempt to visually design discourse relations has limits and there might be more effective ways of rendering conceptual connections than the patterns presented here. However, what matters above all is that designing conceptual connections following a specific rationale and specific criteria proved to be possible. Although, in designing discourse relations it was apparent that some of them were easier to think of in visual terms than others. That is, relations like causality and conjunction, similarity and contrast, and even elaboration and background, were easier to design than relations like conditionality and disjunction. All this raised a number of issues that needed to be investigated. So, the next step in consisted of evaluating the configurations previously designed, to see whether the rationale motivating their design could be recognised by people who had no explicit access to the design rationale set out above. The central idea of the recognisability of coherence relations rendered using systematic visual design principles could only be evaluated on the basis of empirical data. Specifically, four aspects needed to be investigated:

1. The extent to which the concurrent and consistent use of visual features according to certain perceptual principles and design criteria would determine the expressiveness of the configurations designed to represent the selected set of discourse relations.

2. The possibility that the relation representations that were easier to design would also be the ones that would be more easily recognised.

3. The extent to which the contextual use of the relation representations influences their perception, making each visual configuration recognisable as expressing a particular discourse relation.

4. People's ability to conceive abstract but specific concepts, like cognitive relations, in visual terms, and therefore to discriminate the relational expressiveness of different visual configurations.

The next chapter, shows how these aspects were opeationalised as four experimental hypotheses in an empirical study, describes the experimental elements and procedures, and discusses the study's results.

Notes

[1] In a pilot study, where we used a philosophical hypertext essay (see the analysis of Kolb's hypertext, Chapter 3) or ideologically loaded texts (Greek and Greek, 2000), the content was so hard for subjects to understand or so controversial to accept neutrally that it interfered with the primary effect that was being investigated, namely their perceptions of the animated link transitions.

[2] The experimental sessions were designed to be not more than an hour long in order not to bore or exhaust the volunteer subjects, thus imposing a practical limit on the complexity of the material in order to maximise subjects' attention on the relational transitions of interest in this study. In a learning context, more demanding materials would be used with students.

[3] At least in Western civilizations.

Cinematic Hypertext
C. Mancini
IOS Press, 2005

8. Evaluating 'Cinematic' Discourse Relations: an Empirical Study

This chapter describes and reports the results of the first empirical study designed to evaluate the expressiveness and effectiveness of the relational animated configurations whose design process was presented in the previous chapter. The methodology followed in the study, the experimental materials and the sample of the participants are presented, and the results of the test are analysed - quantitatively and qualitatively - from different perspectives. The limitations of the study are also discussed and possible improvements for future tests are suggested. Overall the results appear to be quite promising and motivate the continuation of this kind of research with further theoretical investigation, new empirical studies, and software support, described in the conclusive chapter.

1. A First Empirical Study

The empirical study constitutes a first verification of the design implications of this work's theoretical contributions: that cognitive coherence relations between textual nodes in an argument can be rendered 'cinematically', using systematic graphical and animation cues, in such a way that viewers with no training are able to interpret them. Other studies could be designed to investigate the implications of this proposal for learning and comprehension, which are discussed in the next chapter. This first study focussed very specifically on a fundamental question: are there stereotypes held by viewers that can be exploited to communicate abstract conceptual relationships between textual nodes in visual ways? If so, then these are prime candidates for rendering coherence relations. As detailed below, the hypothesis of this study was that viewers would consistently choose from several visual renderings the one that was designed to best convey that relation (Chapter 7).

1.1. Motivating the Selection of Alternative Patterns

In order to verify the hypotheses motivated in the previous chapter, we designed and conducted an empirical study asking people to choose, from three different 'cinematic' representations the one that best expressed each relational concept. That is, for each relation, three different representations were presented: the one that had been especially designed to represent that particular relation, plus two alternative representations designed for the purposes of the experiment[1].

In particular, always using the same text:

Causality was given the representation already described and, as alternative options, the representations that had been respectively designed for *conjunction* and *disjunction*. **Conditionality** was given the representation described above and, as alternative options, the representations respectively designed for *elaboration* and *contrast*. **Conjunction** was given the representation described above and, as alternative options, the representations respectively designed for *contrast* and *disjunction*.

Disjunction was given the representation described above and, as alternative options, the representations respectively designed for *background* and *similarity*. **Similarity** was given the representation described above and, as alternative options, the representations respectively designed for *contrast* and *causality*. **Contrast** was given the representation described above and, as alternative options, the representations respectively designed for *conjunction* and *similarity*. **Elaboration** was given the representation described above and, as alternative options, the representations respectively designed for *similarity* and *contrast*. **Background** was given the representation described above and, as alternative options, the representations respectively designed for *contrast* and *similarity*. The associations are summarised in Table 8.1.

TESTED REPRESENTATION	ASSOCIATED REPRESENTATIONS	
causality	conjunction	disjunction
conditionality	elaboration	contrast
conjunction	contrast	disjunction
disjunction	background	similarity
similarity	contrast	causality
contrast	conjunction	similarity
elaboration	similarity	contrast
background	contrast	similarity

Table 8.1. List of the relation renderings to be tested and the alternative options that were associated with them for the experiment.

The rationale for choosing the alternative representations to be presented with each relation was based on the consideration of some of the study's limitations. First of all, this being the first attempt to graphically represent cognitive coherence relations, we could not count on the reliability of our design, that is, on its effectiveness. Therefore it was important that the graphical representations that might have easily been interchangeable be not presented together, because this would have produced an unnecessary dispersion of votes. For instance, if the pattern designed for causality had been presented with the pattern designed for conditionality, this would have competed with the causality pattern and the final result of the experiment would have been less clear. Instead, associating the causality pattern with the conjunction and disjunction patterns was intended to make subjects' sensitivity to the visual expression of abstract relational concepts more evident. So, for each relation, the intended pattern was associated with other two patterns that were distant enough from the intended one. For further studies, though, after having tested the design of each relation's pattern, it will be easier to make more daring associations (see Chapter 9, § 9.2).

It would have been interesting also to see what the results would have been if the alternative representations of each relation had been selected according to a criterion of 'opposite values'. However, not enough relations were being tested this time to rigorously apply this criterion for each relation. For instance, the causality pattern could have been presented with the patterns designed for the additive relation (this being the opposite value of the basic operation parameter), plus the pattern designed for negative causality (this being the opposite value of the polarity parameter), if there was one. However, for causality (as for most of the relations) it was not possible to set up a systematic test of this sort, because the corresponding 'opposite value' relations were not being tested at that stage. The only case in which this was possible was similarity, whose representational pattern is associated with the contrast (negative polarity) and causality (opposite value of the basic operation) patterns, but being an isolated case it could not be considered meaningful (see Chapter 9, § 9.2).

Finally, alternatively to this systematic approach, something that could have been done would have consisted of proposing not just two alternatives for each relation, but as many alternatives as the relations being tested – an 8x8 matrix. This way, each relation would have been given as alternative representation all the representations designed for the other relations (which means seven representations), and it would have not been necessary to make any choice at all. However, this was not possible for practical reasons, because from the pilot studies it had emerged that too many alternatives (and seven turned out to be too many) would have overloaded the subjects and made it difficult for them to perform the experiment to its completion. If all seven possible alternatives had been associated to each relation for the subjects to choose from and sort the representations as they felt it was appropriate, we would have certainly had a more rigorous scenario, but its benefits would have been defeated by the load of the requested performance – at least in the context of the first study (Chapter 9, § 9.2).

1.2. Experimental Materials

All representations were created in Microsoft PowerPoint, within a single file containing 24 animated slides, that is, 8 groups of three slides corresponding to the 8 relations examined. Before each triple of slides, a white slide only reporting the name of the relation represented in the three following slides was inserted. Each slide of every triple contained the animation of a different relation representation, whose order within the triple itself was random: the main representation could find itself in first, second or third position. This way, since the slides were to be visualised sequentially, people would come across the main representation of each relation randomly. Finally, the slide display was controlled by an experiment conductor (and not by individual subjects), to make sure that each pattern would be looked at for the same length of time.

Additional material was prepared on which people could record their choices. It consisted of 8 forms, each one devoted to the analysis of a relation and bound to the others in the same order that the relation representations were given with the PowerPoint slides. All the forms were structured in exactly the same way and consisted of three sections (see Figure 8.1). A section at the very top of the page provided an abstract, succinct, definition of the relation being examined in that form, so that people could have a clear idea of the relational concept that they were being asked to focus on. In the section immediately underneath, the abstract relational concept was expressed by the example used in the animations. In the textual example, however, the cue phrases originally contained in the text spans (but removed in the visual representation), were still in place. Underneath, in the third section of the form, three pairs of thumbnails were provided, respectively referring to the three relation representational options. These were intended as 'aide memoire' for the subjects. For each pair, the thumbnail on the left showed the beginning stage of the corresponding slide animation, while the thumbnail on the right showed its final state. Also, the pairs were ordered from the top to the bottom of the section according to the order of display of the three representational options. Next to each pair of thumbnails, on the right side, there was a letter (A, B, or C) labelling the corresponding representational option, and just below it a space to write notes.

CONDITIONALITY = A is condition for B *(if A, then B)*
Two entities or phenomena are related by the fact that in order for the other to be there or happen the first one must be there.

TEXT EXAMPLE

If some astronomical models present four factors simultaneously: the same behaviour, the same postulated causes, the same functioning mechanism, the same response.
Then those astronomical models can be proficiently used to make predictions about the functioning and manifestation of a heavenly body under different conditions.

VISUAL REPRESENTATION

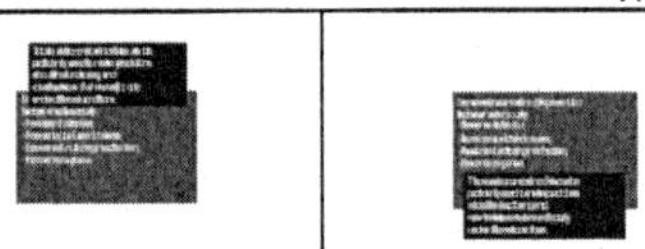

Do you prefer option **A**? (please, circle)
Can you tell why? (please, write below)

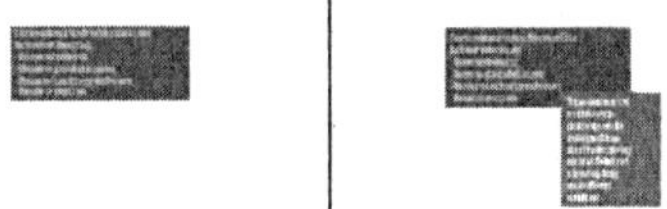

Do you prefer option **B**? (please, circle)
Can you tell why? (please, write below)

Do you prefer option **C**? (please, circle)
Can you tell why? (please, write below)

Figure 8.1. One of the eight forms given to the subjects to gather their votes on the preferred options. At the top is an abstract definition of the relation in question. Underneath a text example is provided that implements the relation, and below it, the three representational options are listed. The thumbnails on the left show two different stages of each animation, as a mnemonic help for the subject. On the right there is room to express a choice and comment on it.

1.3. Subjects

Subjects were recruited on a voluntary basis from the Knowledge Media Institute (KMi), at The Open University[2]. The choice seemed appropriate because KMi is a technology research lab, but only few people (who were not involved in the experiment) are specialised in the study of hypertext. Therefore, their intellectual tools and technical skills were similar to those of a scholar in the future who might use hypertext for the purposes of their research activity, without necessarily being a specialist hypertext researcher. 24 KMi members took part in the experiment, a multiple of 3, the number of the options to choose from for each relation. For practical reasons, they had to work in 5 groups of 6, 6, 5, 3 and 4 subjects each.

1.4. Experimental Procedure

All subjects worked in the same environment - the auditorium of the lab - under the same low lights, in front of the same quality screen and sitting at the same distance from it. They were asked to read through the definition of the relation and the text exemplifying it that was provided on the first form, then watch the three representational options presented one after the other on the screen, and mark on the form the option that they preferred by circling the corresponding letter, and optionally explaining in an adjacent note why that particular option was preferred over the other two. After seeing the representational options and choosing their favourite representation for the first relation, they did the same for the second relation, and so on, through to the eighth. To mark their preferences and write their notes in all the forms, everyone was given and asked to use a green pen.

After the completion of this first round, subjects were asked to repeat the entire process. This was done to give them the option to change decisions made during the first round. They could do so by simply circling a different letter and adding their comments in the appropriate space. To make it possible to track any changes afterwards, the green pens were replaced with red pens, which they were asked to use to make their corrections. People were offered the opportunity to make changes for two reasons. Firstly, so that they would have time to 'get into' what was a novel task and understand what exactly was required of them. Secondly, this was based on the assumption (Hypotheses 3 - next section) that people would need to go through all the relations and all the representational options before they would be able to evaluate the relative expressiveness of each option and decide what relation each option would express most effectively. For instance, one might have initially chosen option B for *conjunction*, only to realise on getting to *background* that they should have chosen B's configuration. In other words, it was expected that people would attribute meaning to each representational option not just in absolute terms, but also in relative terms: it would be within the context of the whole set of renderings that people would be able to rate the best one for each relation[3].

1.5. Experimental Predictions

Given the above method, four issues raised at the end of Chapter 7 translate as four hypotheses. **Hypothesis 1**: subjects will choose the rendering that we had designed to represent the relevant relation. **Hypothesis 2**: the renderings which were easier to design are more likely to be chosen. **Hypothesis 3**: if during the second round subjects change their previous choices, this will be in the direction predicted by Hypothesis 1. **Hypothesis 4**: subjects will find the task meaningful, as evidenced by coherent choices and explanatory notes, even if not the choices predicted by Hypothesis 1.

TESTED RELATION	OPTION A	OPTION B	OPTION C
causality	conjunction	**causality**	alternative
conditionality	**conditionality**	elaboration	contrast
conjunction	contrast	disjunction	**conjunction**
disjunction	**disjunction**	background	similarity
similarity	contrast	**similarity**	causality
contrast	conjunction	similarity	**contrast**
elaboration	similarity	**elaboration**	contrast
background	similarity	contrast	**background**

Table 8.2. List of the tested relations with the three representational options proposed for each of them. The one in bold corresponds to the expected choice, that is, to the representation that was originally designed to express the particular relation being tested. In other words, the table shows which 'preferred' option was predicted for each relation.

1.6. Results

The results of the experiments are reported in Tables 8.3. and 8.4.

G	S	CAUSALITY			CONDITION.			CONJUNCT.			DISJUNCT.			SIMILARITY			CONTRAST			ELABORAT.			BACKGROU.		
1	1	A	B	C	A	B	C	A	B	C	A	B	C	A	B	C	A	B	C	A	B	C	A	B	C
	2	A	B	C	A	B	C	A	B	C	A	B	C	A	B	C	A	B	C	A	B	C	A	B	C
	3	A	B	C	A	B	C	A	B	C	A	B	C	A	B	C	A	B	C	A	B	C	A	B	C
	4	A	B	C	A	B	C	A	B	C	A	B	C	A	B	C	A	B	C	A	B	C	A	B	C
	5	A	B	C	A	B	C	A	B	C	A	B	C	A	B	C	A	B	C	A	B	C	A	B	C
	6	A	B	C	A	B	C	A	B	C	A	B	C	A	B	C	A	B	C	A	B	C	A	B	C
2	7	A	B	C	A	B	C	A	B	C	A	B	C	A	B	C	A	B	C	A	B	C	A	B	C
	8	A	B	C	A	B	C	A	B	C	A	B	C	A	B	C	A	B	C	A	B	C	A	B	C
	9	A	B	C	A	B	C	A	B	C	A	B	C	A	B	C	A	B	C	A	B	C	A	B	C
	10	A	B	C	A	B	C	A	B	C	A	B	C	A	B	C	A	B	C	A	B	C	A	B	C
	11	A	B	C	A	B	C	A	B	C	A	B	C	A	B	C	A	B	C	A	B	C	A	B	C
	12	A	B	C	A	B	C	A	B	C	A	B	C	A	B	C	A	B	C	A	B	C	A	B	C
3	13	A	B	C	A	B	C	A	B	C	A	B	C	A	B	C	A	B	C	A	B	C	A	B	C
	14	A	B	C	A	B	C	A	B	C	A	B	C	A	B	C	A	B	C	A	B	C	A	B	C
	15	A	B	C	A	B	C	A	B	C	A	B	C	A	B	C	A	B	C	A	B	C	A	B	C
	16	A	B	C	A	B	C	A	B	C	A	B	C	A	B	C	A	B	C	A	B	C	A	B	C
	17	A	B	C	A	B	C	A	B	C	A	B	C	A	B	C	A	B	C	A	B	C	A	B	C
4	18	A	B	C	A	B	C	A	B	C	A	B	C	A	B	C	A	B	C	A	B	C	A	B	C
	19	A	B	C	A	B	C	A	B	C	A	B	C	A	B	C	A	B	C	A	B	C	A	B	C
	20	A	B	C	A	B	C	A	B	C	A	B	C	A	B	C	A	B	C	A	B	C	A	B	C
5	21	A	B	C	A	B	C	A	B	C	A	B	C	A	B	C	A	B	C	A	B	C	A	B	C
	22	A	B	C	A	B	C	A	B	C	A	B	C	A	B	C	A	B	C	A	B	C	A	B	C
	23	A	B	C	A	B	C	A	B	C	A	B	C	A	B	C	A	B	C	A	B	C	A	B	C
	24	A	B	C	A	B	C	A	B	C	A	B	C	A	B	C	A	B	C	A	B	C	A	B	C

Table 8.3. Summarisation of the experiment's results. **G** column indicates the different groups of subjects working in one session. **S** column indicates each subject, and the row corresponding to each subject reports the answers that the subjects gave for each relation. The column under each relation's name reports the results obtained by each option with all the subjects. The three options for each relation are indicated with the letters **A**, **B**, **C** (as shown in Table 8.2). The letter in bold indicates the option that was originally designed to represent that particular relation. The votes obtained by an option in the first round are indicated in dark grey. The votes that an option obtained in the second round are indicated in light grey. Any votes in the second round, which migrated from one option to another, are indicated in light grey with white lettering.

- X Votes gained by an option in first round.
- X Votes lost by an option in second round.
- X Votes gained by an option in second round.

CAUSALITY			CONDITION.			CONJUNCT.			DISJUNCT.			SIMILARITY			CONTRAST			ELABORAT.			BACKGROU.		
A	**B**	C	**A**	B	C	A	B	**C**	**A**	B	C	A	**B**	C	A	B	**C**	A	**B**	C	A	B	**C**
4	**19**	1	**10**	5	9	6	0	**18**	**12**	5	7	2	**16**	6	4	0	**20**	1	**21**	2	0	3	**21**
-3	**+4**	-1	**+3**	-1	-5	-3	-0	**+3**	**+1**	-1	-1	-1	**+3**	-2	-0	-0	**+0**	-0	**+0**	-1	-0	-0	**+0**
+1	-1	+0	-0	+2	+1	+0	+0	-0	-1	+1	+1	+0	-1	+1	+0	+0	-0	+2	-1	+0	+0	+0	-0
2	**22**	0	**13**	6	5	3	0	**21**	**12**	5	7	1	**18**	5	4	0	**20**	3	**20**	1	0	3	**21**

Table 8.4. Numeric results from the experiment. The dark grey row shows the votes that each option gathered for each relation in the first round - the votes gathered by the 'expected options' are shown in bold. The first light grey row shows the votes gained by the 'best candidate' options (in bold) and lost by the other options in the second round. The second light grey row shows the votes lost by the 'best candidate' options and gained by the other options. The last row shows the final results.

2. Analysis of the Study's Results

The results are discussed as they relate to each hypothesis.

Hypothesis 1. *That subjects will choose the rendering that had been designed to represent the relevant relation.*

The numbers on the second table seem to largely support the first hypothesis. From the final results, in fact, it is immediately visible that all the options that were predicted to be chosen for each relation in fact were by far the most often selected, gathering far more than one third of the votes. This seems to clearly indicate that people recognised a particular expressiveness in the options that had been designed to express the set of discourse coherence relations. That is, the concurrent and consistent use of graphical elements, to render the set of relational concepts according to specific perceptual principles and the design criteria (described in Chapter 6), produced a set of visual configurations (described in Chapter 7) that people were able to recognise as representing those relations. To verify that these results were not just a coincidence, and that people did not just choose what they were expected them to choose by chance, a *Chi squared* test (Robson, 1973) was carried out. The test's procedure can be summarised by the equation $\chi^2 = \Sigma\,(O - E)^2\ /\ E$, where O = observed frequency (how many people choose an option), E = expected frequency (how many people can be expected to choose an option), χ^2 = significance level of the result (a number over which the result is significant, because the probability of it being random are very low). For two degrees of freedom (as in this case), χ^2 critical values referred to are: 5.99, which means that the probability that a result is random is <0.05 (result has 95% of probability to be significant); 9.21, which means that the probability that a result is random is <0.01 (result has 99% of probability to be significant); 13.82, which means that the probability that a result is random is <0.001 (result has 99.9% of probability to be significant). In this case, the expected frequency of a choice was 8, that is, in average 8 people could be expected to choose each option, since there were 24 subjects and 3 possible choices to make. The observed frequency for each option varied from relation to relation. For instance, for *causality* this frequency was 2 (option A), 22 (option B), 0 (option C). So, from each of these observed frequencies, the expected frequency was subtracted (2-8; 22-8; 0-8) and the square of the result calculated (36; 196; 64), and then divided by the expected frequency (4.5; 24.5; 8). Then, the three results so obtained were summed up (37): the final number was the significance number for the results obtained (see Table 8.5 for an example). When this number exceeded the smallest χ^2 critical number (5.99), the choices made by the subjects were probable to be significant. The subjects' choices were tested for all the relations (the results are shown in Table 8.6).

	RESULTS SIGNIFICANCE FOR CAUSALITY				
	O	E	(O – E)	$(O - E)^2$	$(O - E)^2 / E$
A	2	8	-6	36	4.5
B	22	8	14	196	24.5
C	0	8	-8	64	8
					$\chi^2 = 37\ (p < 0.001)$

Table 8.5. Chi squared results for *causality* (calculated on the final results). For this relation the probability that subjects chose option B by chance are lower than 0.001%.

RELATION	RESULTS FOR THE TESTED REPRESENTATION	PROBABILITY OF SIGNIFICANCE
Causality	22	$\chi^2 = 37$ ($p < 0.001$)
Conditionality	13	$\chi^2 = 4.750$ ($p > 0.05$)
Conjunction	21	$\chi^2 = 32.25$ ($p < 0.001$)
Disjunction	12	$\chi^2 = 3.25$ ($p > 0.05$)
Similarity	18	$\chi^2 = 19.75$ ($p < 0.001$)
Contrast	20	$\chi^2 = 28$ ($p < 0.001$)
Elaboration	20	$\chi^2 = 27.25$ ($p < 0.001$)
Background	21	$\chi^2 = 32.25$ ($p < 0.001$)

Table 8.6. Summarisation of chi squared results for all tested relations (calculated on the final results).

As it appears from the results of the test, for most relations there is significant evidence to say that the choices made by people in the experiment were not just a coincidence, but real preferences. In fact, for six of them $p<0.001$, which means that the result is very significant. This is compounded by the fact that most people motivated their choices, that is, they expressed the rationale that they had followed to chose one option and reject the others: if people could motivate what they chose, it is unlikely that they chose randomly.

Conditionality and *disjunction*, though, did not obtain the strong results obtained by the other relations, which is confirmed by the Chi squared test: for these relations the significance level did not reach $p<0.05$, which means that the chances that the predicted options could have not gathered votes by chance are lower than 95%. There are in fact very good reasons why this could have happened, and the meaning of this result is discussed later on in this section. However, it must be said that the fact that both the options that were respectively predicted for conditionality and disjunction doubled the votes obtained by the other options cannot be easily dismissed.

Now, the levels of significance calculated above refer to the final results, that is, to the votes gathered by the different options after the second round, during which the 'best candidates' gather some more votes. So, those relations whose predicted option exceeded any significance level thanks to the votes of the second round might have not exceeded it with the votes of the first round alone. To verify this, it was enough to calculate the significance level for the relation (apart from conditionality and disjunction) whose predicted option gathered the least votes in the first round. This was *similarity*, whose 'best candidate' option only gathered 16 votes in the first round, datum of which the level of significance was $\chi^2 = 13$ ($p < 0.01$). Since this was already significant, it was apparent that the results obtained for relations whose predicted option gathered more than 16 votes were equally or even more significant.

Hypothesis 2. *That the renderings which were easier to design are more likely to be chosen.*

The data also supported the hypothesis that both the design and the recognition process were grounded in basic perceptual principles. We have noted already that designing graphical elements to render discourse coherence relations was more intuitive for some relations than for others. For instance, it was easier to devise a scheme using arrangement or luminosity to render the concept of *causality* than to render the concept of *conditionality*. The relations whose graphical representation was more straightforward to design were also those where the predicted option received most votes: the predicted options for *causality* and *conjunctiveness*, *elaboration* and *background*, *similarity* and *contrast*, were voted between 18-22 times out of 24, and at the same time they were more straightforward to design than *conditionality* and *disjunctiveness*, whose predicted option was chosen only 13 and 12 times respectively.

Causality and *conjunction*, *similarity* and *contrast*, *elaboration* and *background* do not require this complex time-space projection and variation of the narrative axis, but present different situations as given: *causality* presents two situations one of which follows the other; *conjunction* presents two coexisting situations; *similarity* brings together two analogous situations; *contrast* brings together two opposing situations; *elaboration* presents a situation and its explanation; *background* presents a situation and its premise. The narrative linearity expressed by these relations can explain why it was easier for us to design and for the subjects to recognise their visual pattern.

On the other hand, the fact that for *conditionality* and *conjunctiveness* the predicted option was chosen only by respectively 13 and 12 people could be explained by the fact that *conditionality* and *disjunctiveness* are, from the point of view of the relational content, more complex. *Conditionality* consists of a causality concept in its hypothetical form, and hypotheticality undoubtedly introduces a complicating factor with respect to the primitive form of *causality*. Whereas pure *causality* simply presents a situation and its consequence, *conditionality* hypothesises a situation before the consequence is presented. The complication is exactly mirrored in the projection into a space-time dimension and narrative axis different from the "here and now" before the consequent situation can be presented. This is why in cinematic visual language - based on the *monstration* of the "here and now" space-temporal unit - representing a primitive causal relation is more straightforward than representing a conditional relation[4]. The representation of the latter, in fact, requires some kind of expedient, like a flash-forward showing someone's thoughts or an actual back and forth showing different alternatives in the development of an action. Examples of this kind of solution are provided by *Smoking, No Smoking* or *Sliding Doors* (see Chapter 5, § 3.4.).

In fact, the expedient used by these movies to represent the concept of *conditionality* constitutes at the same time a representation of the concept of *disjunction*. By showing what happens if one decides to smoke (or if one misses the tube), going back in time to the point where the decision of smoking (or the action of missing the tube) was made, and restarting from there to show what happens if one decides not to smoke (or catches the tube), the movie also shows alternative developments of the story. This is because every time that a condition is hypothesised, the alternative to that condition, in which the hypothesised condition does not verify, is automatically set. Both conditionality and disjunction imply the projection into a time-space dimension that is not the "here and now" space-temporal unit, and the cinematic and visual expression of these concepts is correspondingly more complex. Interestingly enough, in our experiment, *disjunction* was the other relation whose predicted option was not chosen as often as the other relations.

***Hypothesis** 3. That if during the second round subjects change their previous choices, this will be in the direction predicted by Hypothesis 1.*

The impact of the second round in leading votes to converge on the predicted option seemed to be supported by experimental data, although more weakly than for other hypotheses. For the first five relations presented, the predicted option did gain votes in the second round: 4 for *causality*, 3 for *conditionality*, 3 for *conjunction*, 1 for *disjunction* and 3 for *similarity*. In contrast, *elaboration* and *background* did not gain any. This could be due to the fact that, after going through a number of relations, people were better able to evaluate the different options provided for one relation in comparison with the options provided for other relations. As a consequence, in the second round, the last three relations gained no votes, while the first five relations did. However, this could also be due to the fact that people needed some time simply to grasp what exactly was required from them, and so the first five relations served to some extent as 'practice trials'. Both hypotheses could be valid, but either way, the relevance of the contextualisation seemed to be plausibly supported, although at that stage and with those numbers nothing more specific could be said (further studies could aim at gathering more evidence in support of this hypothesis).

Interestingly (as Table 8.3 shows), for some relations, for three specific subjects, the predicted options *lost* votes in the second round instead of gaining them: *causality* (S18), *disjunction* (S12), *similarity* (S8) and *elaboration* (S18) lost one vote each.

Although this goes against the predicted trend, the subjects' comments on the reasons for their changes do indeed provide evidence of coherent reasoning. Subject 18 justified their second round change for the *causality* relation, from option **B** to option A with the note "*Colours are better represented here*", (that is, in option A). This is a curious explanation, since option A for *causality* uses the pattern designed to represent *conjunction*, and in this pattern colour is not a variable, which raises the suspicion that the subject was looking at the correspondence between the colours of the patterns shown on the screen and the colours of the patterns printed on paper - since in the case of option **B** the colours on paper and the colour on the screen do not exactly match due to a technical limitation.

For the *elaboration* relation, subject 18 motivated their second round choice, option A (using the pattern designed to represent *similarity*), by saying that it "*shows continuation*". That is, they gave preference to the idea of the *continuity* between the initial concept and its elaboration, rather than to the idea of the *expansion* of the initial content into an additional larger discourse unit, or to the idea of the *passage* from one discourse level to the other.

Subject's 12 reasoning behind the first round choice of option **A** to express *disjunction* matched closely the reasoning behind the design of the predicted option, namely to present a discourse unit, and then fade it when the second discourse unit appears as a sign of alternation. In the second round, the change to option C was motivated by the fact that "*the two segments of information are not presented at the same time*". Now, the two discourse units were not presented at the same time in option **A** either, but it is possible that what the subject gave preference to was the fact that in option C the second discourse unit does not just appear next to the first, but comes in from the side of the screen, that is, *from a distance, from another place.*

Subject 8 did the same as subject 12 but for the *similarity* relation, recording the same rationale that lays behind the design of the predicted option, as a motivation to choose option **B** in the first round: the fact that the two discourse units end up having the same colour seemed to reinforce the idea that they are similar and comparable. In the second round, however, the subject motivated their change by saying that in C the two discourse units looked "*similar*", whereas in B they were in fact looking "*the same*".

In summary, even if though in the second round subjects 12 and 8 changed their choice in favour of a representational option that was not the predicted one, there is evidence that they had 'extracted' (or better, inferred) a very good understanding of the rationale behind the design of the predicted option chosen in the first round. That is, they found the representation chosen in the first round to be meaningful.

Hypothesis 4. *That subjects will find the task meaningful, as evidenced by coherent choices and explanatory notes, even if not the choices predicted by Hypothesis 1.*

The fourth hypothesis seemed to be largely supported by subjects' choices, and above all by the comments that they made to motivate those choices. All 24 subjects completed their task and most of them provided comments: only 2 subjects did not comment on all of the options that they chose; 13 commented on all of the chosen options only; 9 subjects commented on the options that they chose and on some of the options that they had not chosen; and 2 subjects made suggestions for the use of alternative or extra features (such comments had been invited). Of all the comments provided for choosing the expected options, many expressed in more or less detail a rationale that was similar to the rationale that was indeed behind their design (see Chapter 7, § 3), evidencing an understanding of the use of visual elements to render the relational concepts examined.

18 subjects commented on *causality*, 18 subjects also commented on *conjunctiveness*, 16 subjects commented on *contrast*, 14 subjects commented on *elaboration*, 12 subjects commented on *background*, 11 subjects commented on *similarity*, 9 subjects commented on *disjunctiveness*, and 7 subjects commented on *conditionality*. This means that few subjects voted for an option without commenting it or without providing a comment that showed an understanding of its design rationale. This strongly supports Hypothesis 4 that the subjects would be able to think of coherence relations in visual terms and, vice versa, of visual patterns in terms of coherence relations.

In this respect, it is also very interesting to see how subjects have commented on the choices that they made when these choices were not in favour of the expected option. For *causality*, two subjects chose option A (the one that had been designed for *conjunctiveness*, the weaker basic relation): one was subject 18 whom we have discussed already; the other one instead appreciated the sense of linear continuity expressed by that option.

For *conditionality*, six people chose option B (originally designed for *elaboration*) and five people chose option C (originally designed for *contrast*). Most of the subjects who chose option B appreciated the sense of dependence between the first discourse unit and the second discourse unit generated by the overlapping of one over the other, which constitutes a similar, although blander, feature proposed by solution **A** itself. Those who chose option C, made in general less meaningful comments, however one subject appreciated the fact that the box containing the hypothesis becomes lighter once the box containing the conclusion comes in, "*as if it had been consumed*".

For *conjunction*, only three people chose option A (originally designed for *contrast*), and two of them motivated it with the fact that the difference of shading characterising the two units better rendered the sense of their distinction and complementarity at the same time. For *disjunction*, five people chose option B (originally designed for *background*) and seven people chose option C (originally designed for *similarity*). Some subjects in the first group appreciated the fact that the enclosure of the first discourse unit within the second discourse unit established a relation between the two, whereas the difference of shades generated a sense of difference, that is, of alternative. Instead, the people who chose option C generally appreciated the equivalence of the two alternatives represented by the shading, dimensions and alignment of the two discourse units.

For *similarity*, one subject chose option A (originally designed for *contrast*) and five subjects chose option C (originally designed for *causality*). The group that chose option C mostly commented that similarity is better expressed in this pattern because the two discourse units appear to be "*similar*", that is, comparable, but not "*identical*". For *contrast*, only four people chose option A (originally designed for *conjunction*), and they seemed to have generally appreciated the simple animation of this option over the change of colour of the expected option.

For *background*, only three subjects chose option B (originally designed for *contrast*), saying that the difference of shade between a discourse unit and the other was desirable and that the lighter unit looked as if it was in the background when the second unit appeared.

Finally, for *elaboration* three people chose option A (originally designed for *similarity*) and one subject chose option C (originally designed for *contrast*). Those who chose option A seemed to appreciate the sense of continuity that the pattern according to them provided between one discourse unit and the other.

Even these results, then, show that most people were able to express preferences and motivate their choices with a rationales, even when they did not choose the option that they were expected to choose for each particular relation. In general, that subjects showed through their comments to be most sensitive to features such as colour, text box dimensions, overlapping, animation, and to how these features generated a sense of equivalence or a sense of hierarchy. Above all, though, they showed that they tried to interpret the use of visual features in order to match their concept of any particular relation, and that they could be creative in their interpretation. Admittedly, given the task, a rationalisation of the graphic configurations was to be expected anyway: after all, this is a fundamental human 'sense making' drive. What matters, however, is that this tendency is there and that it could be effectively exploited to help people make sense of hypertext discourse structure.

3. Limitations of the Study

The results of this first study were quite encouraging. However, naturally the study itself is subject to a number of limitations. First of all, although the rendering of the relations followed the perceptual principles grounded in Gestalt Theory and design criteria recommended by semiotics of graphics, the process of applying these principles and criteria to create a graphical interpretation of abstract relational concepts is still a creative, subjective process. If one is a good designer, with a natural disposition towards visual processes and good visual language design skills, they have more chances to produce distinctive, expressive renderings that form a coherent set, and increase the probability of the study producing positive results. However not all hypertext writers are necessarily good graphic designers, therefore what they would produce in terms of visual patterns might not be effective at all.

A response to this point is that the relation representations were not the product of an expert design, although having a background in visual arts must have influenced the develop our sensitivity to visual languages. However, our rationale simply made very intuitive choices, dictated by our experience of the physical world and by certain cultural conventions, some of which are arguably shared by human kind in general, and others, at least by Western culture. For instance, gravity is an element that is bound to condition every one's sense of direction as a necessary path: if I drop an object from height X, it will necessarily fall to height Y, and subsequently to height Z, if nothing stops it. In our case, the metaphor of gravity seemed perfect to represent the sense of necessity that exists in the passage from one situation to another in causal relations - which is why we used patterns that develop from top to bottom with text boxes that literally descend from the one above them (coming from behind the previous box in pure *causality*, and coming down over the previous box in *conditionality*).

Another phenomenon - this time of cultural origin - which provides sense of direction is the fact that in the Western World people write and read from left to right. It seemed that this pattern could be used to express a sense of development in relations that are of an additive nature, like *conjunctiveness* and its negative, and *similarity* and its negative. The same intuitive considerations of isomorphism between conceptual components and physical or cultural experience of the world were made for the other features used in designing the relational patterns. The underlying assumption was that if we were sensitive to these stereotypes, also other people would be, and the results of the study seem to show that in fact they are.

These aspects could be studied further from a psychology of perception perspective, to progressively identify as many as possible elements of isomorphism between perceptual phenomena derived from physical and cultural stereotypes and the conceptual content of cognitive discourse relations. Hypertext writers could then progressively refer to these design principles when they create their hypertexts, not in a prescriptive way, but as a resource, in the same way that a writer can refer to certain writing rules to produce quality texts and a graphic designer can refer to design rules to create quality graphics. In other words, relational representation conventions could develop and become a reference point for the hypertext designer and writer. In fact, the point is that, since hypertext is a visual medium as well as a textual medium, to be a good hypertext author being an aware designer is as important as being an aware writer.

A further limitation of this study is the fact that it does not examine all the coherence relations that have been identified and analysed by linguists and psycholinguists. So, we might have selected only the ones that seemed to better lend themselves to support the fundamental hypotheses of this work. The response to this point is that for logistical reasons it would have not been possible to test those hypotheses on all relations. However, linguists and psycholinguists have yet to agree on a common set of relations, and many of them still remain to be studied in a sufficient depth (Chapter 2). From the literature, though, some parameters like *basic operation* and *polarity* are well established, and therefore provided a platform for evaluation.

Besides, when initiating the investigations of a new phenomenon, one is more likely to detect 'major contours' if one starts with simpler objects and circumstances. If the first results are positive and the first acquisition can be established for those simpler cases, one can proceed with investigating more complex objects under more complex circumstances. The concluding chapter proposes that, after a number of initial studies on the possibility of visually representing the most basic cognitive relations, a number of other studies can be conceived to investigate the possibility of representing more complex relations.

Another weakness of this study might be that we used only short fragments of text in a minimal number for each pattern, and that an approach that seems to work under these conditions might not work when applied to larger, more complex hypertext nodes: they would contain at least several sentences connected to one another already in rather complex discourse units, and they would possibly generate larger clusters of nodes interfering with one another on the screen. Again, in starting the observation of a phenomenon it is preferable to look at simplified cases. However, the analysis carried out on David Kolb's hypertext dissertation in terms of coherence relations (Chapter 3, § 2., and Appendix) shows that such a transfer from laboratory environment to real hypertext is possible at least as far as the application of coherence relations to hypertext discourse is concerned - which is theoretically founded on the concept of global coherence (described in Chapter 2, § 2.1.). As far as the graphic design of hypertext relations is concerned, before rendering major scholarly hypertext, which would require many more assumptions about the effectiveness of design decisions, we needed to carry on first a preliminary study on the possibility of representing binary relations.

A further consideration to be made is that the larger and more complex the single nodes of a hypertext are, the less that hypertext exploits the potentiality of the medium and the more it stays close to the paper based paradigm (Chapter1, § 2.). The larger the nodes and the fewer the connections, the more difficult and less beneficial the visual representation of hypertext relations would be. However, the more a hypertext is articulated in small discourse units, richly interconnected in a way that exploits the medium's technical characteristics, the more the use of a languages like the one investigated here would make sense and be beneficial. In other words, the more hypertextual hypertext is[5], the more valuable a hypertext relational visual language becomes.

Finally, the results of this study might have been affected by technical aspects concerning the potentialities of the PowerPoint application that was used for the realisation of the experimental material. For instance, a couple of subjects were disturbed by the speed of the animations, which influenced their choice (to our disadvantage, in terms of confirming the hypotheses, we hasten to say). Also, although every effort was made to recreate the same conditions for the performance of each group, admittedly those conditions were not exactly the same, due to occasional external disturbances. It is possible that this may have influenced the results. However, given their strength, and the care with which the experiment was run, it is not possible to attribute to those technical factors any significant role.

Notes

[1] Obviously, to create the two alternative representations of each relation, we used the same textual content that we had used for the main representation, but giving it a different graphic and animation format.

[2] http://kmi.open.ac.uk

[3] The establishment of a locally coherent language within the context of a film is how cinematic language in general works, and how cinematic sequences are interpreted (see Chapter 4). We hypothesised that this might be the case also with the interpretation of visual configurations designed to represent discourse relations. However, it has to be said that the development of cinematic patterns to express narrative structures was not simply causal: there are objective factors that determined the development of those

particular patterns and not others. These factors have to do with the spatiality and temporality of the cinematic signifier, and ultimately with the iconicity and indexicality of the cinematic sign. For instance, in the alternate syntagma, the way the parallelism of action is represented is partly conventional, but partly it is 'necessary': if I want to follow actions going on at the same time, I have to alternatively pay attention to one and the other, that is, I have to 'move' from one scenario to the other, as I don't have the gift of ubiquity. In classical cinema, the cinematic pattern developed to represent the alternation of action emulates the behaviour of a (super)human point of view and its physicality – this changes in Modern cinema: *Jules et Jim* (François Truffaut, 1962) is an early example.

[4] In this respect, the background relation, which shares aspects with the conditionality relation, is different in that the background situation is not considered as a possibility or as a hypothesis, but is given as a fact.

[5] See Chapter 1, note 11.

Cinematic Hypertext
C. Mancini
IOS Press, 2005

9. The Form of Coherence in Hypertext Discourse: Proposal for a Cinematic Hypertext

This final chapter retraces the steps that this work has taken towards the idea of 'cinematic hypertext', and it summarises the contributions that this work brings to the study of hypertext discourse and of the hypertext medium. It also discusses further steps that could be taken, both in terms of theoretical and empirical work, to advance further to the implementation of an environment for authoring. A functional specification is proposed that describes how a 'cinematic hypertext' system could work, and following that, how it could support the work of both scholars and students in the different situations in which argumentation is involved. Finally, the journey concludes with a reflection on the evolution of the language of visual media and on the possible evolution of hypertext's language.

1. Step by Step Towards the Idea of Cinematic Hypertext

This book opened with the reflection that the hypertext medium has expanded the horizons of written discourse by making new writing forms possible. However, we saw how not all discourse functions seem to be equally well served by the non-linear medium. In fact, Chapter 1 cites a number of researchers who conclude that non-linearity makes hypertext unfit for argumentation, unless discourse order is in some way re-established, for instance, by using navigational patterns, by providing a topography of the contents, or by mirroring the thread of the argument in overview nodes. We have then seen how beyond, and directly connected to, the issue of order in argumentative hypertext is the issue of discourse coherence, which concerns all non-linear discourse, not only argumentation.

Chapter 1 discussed how discourse coherence is largely a matter of discourse shaping and how different scholarly hypertext systems take different approaches to argument representation. It then looked into advantages and disadvantages of the semantic, spatial and page-based hypertext approaches, and suggested that a fourth way could be explored, which weaves together elements of all three. It finally put forward the idea of a hypertext authoring-environment where the articulation of discourse structure is regulated by basic relational principles, and discourse relations are marked by visual and spatial features. Chapter by chapter, we then saw the different aspects and implications of this idea.

Moving from the assumption that natural language is the backbone of scholarly argumentation, Chapter 2 looked at psycholinguistic theories of discourse coherence in text, which conceive discourse as a hierarchical structure whose constituting units are related through basic cognitive concepts. The distinction was made between coherence and cohesion in text, by specifying the former as grammatical elements that work as indicators of relational concepts, and therefore facilitate the construction of a coherent mental representation of the text content. A small number of these relational concepts were discussed that are generally established among theoreticians, and it was suggested that these primitive relational concepts could be used in hypertext as principles of discourse articulation, that is, as principles to define systematic rendering schemas.

Following this idea, Chapter 3 showed how cognitive coherence relations can account for link types that are used in hypertext argumentation, and mapping a primitive set of relations onto two published link taxonomies from hypertext research systems. This showed that cognitive coherence relations could provide useful a reference point when creating link taxonomies to use in hypertext argumentation systems. Cognitive coherence relations were also used to analyse links in a scholarly hypertext essay by David Kolb, which constituted a coherence relation based verification of the author's theoretical approach to structuring argument in hypertext.

Chapter 4 then discussed the use of visual and spatial features to provide cohesion in hypertext discourse. Adhering to the school of thought that considers hypertext an essentially cinematic medium, and therefore regards cinematic theory as a powerful lens through which to view its linguistic potentialities, the connection between cinematic and hypertext discourse was analysed. We saw how cinematic discourse cohesion is provided through the use of a conventional set of rhetorical patterns, which help the viewer construct a coherent mental representation of the film's contents. We also saw how the cinematic viewer infers rhetorical connections on the basis of visual clues that shape the different discourse patterns. This motivated the proposal that, in hypertext, visual and spatial features could be used to mark discourse coherence relations and shape recognisable rhetorical patterns.

Extrapolating the idea that if coherence relations have cognitive reality, they should also hold between discourse units in other media with a discourse structure similar to text, Chapter 5 described the classical set of cinematic rhetorical patterns in terms of coherence relations. Two examples of cinematic sequences were analysed, interpreting in terms of coherence relations the shot connections as the sequence's visual elements suggest the viewer to make them. This showed how coherence relations are indeed applicable to cinematic discourse, and how they can in fact account for a certain use of visual features.

Having established a parallel between textual and cinematic coherence, Chapter 6 discussed the cognitive similarities between text discourse processing and visual discourse processing. This showed how certain principles of text cohesion have an equivalent in Gestalt principles of visual cohesion, which provides a theoretical basis to represent the cohesive elements of text coherence in a graphic form. In order to produce a visual representation of discourse coherence relations in which graphic components could consistently work together as cohesive elements, we then looked at representational guidelines deriving from the semiology of graphics.

With this theoretical foundation in place, the work moved into a design phase. In Chapter 7, for experimental purposes, a set of eight coherence relations was defined and motivated, comprising *causality*, *conditionality*, *conjunctiveness*, *disjunctiveness*, *similarity*, *contrast*, *elaboration* and *background* relations. Taking into account the principles of perception and the semiotic guidelines previously discussed, we looked at the representation of the relations that had been rendered using a minimum number of graphic parameters, in order to minimise the complexity of the representation and any visual 'noise', and so enhance the representations' distinctiveness.

Finally, Chapter 8 described and motivated the design process of the empirical study for which the relation renderings had been designed, in order to evaluate the expressiveness of the configurations obtained from the application of the principles of visual cohesion and from the use of the graphic variables previously discussed. The execution of the experiment was described and its results analysed, which largely support this work's approach to discourse shaping in hypertext argumentation and in hypertext in general. Whilst recognising its limitations, this study motivates the continuation of this kind of research with further theoretical investigation and new empirical studies.

2. Proposals of this Research Work

The investigation conducted within this work results in four proposal, three of which are theoretical and on of which is applied.

Cognitive coherence relations and hypertext connections. Firstly, this work proposes that text coherence theory should be considered as a resource for understanding hypertext connectivity, and specifically that Cognitive Coherence Relations (CCR) provide a valuable reference point when defining relations for hypertext applications. That is, it proposes to refer to a set of primitive relational concepts, which are hypothesised to characterise cognitively relevant processes from which other more specific relational concepts derive - and we have seen how these primitive relational concepts can in fact be used to analyse existing hypertext link taxonomies and hypertext dissertations.

As we have seen, text coherence theory or coherence relations have been previously used in hypertext to define links. However, while the general tendency is to *differentiate* relations to express the variety of possible hypertext links, this approach seeks to minimise this differentiation, which is why CCR are so appealing. This is because the final goal here is to use relations as regulating principles for the consistent and congruent use of graphic features to connote the role of nodes with respect to one another and to allow the emerging of visual meta-discourse in hypertext.

Cinematic theory and hypertext's linguistic potentialities. Secondly, this work proposes cinematic theory as a new framework for understanding the hypertext medium and its linguistic potentialities. Based on the fundamental commonalities between the two visual media, it proposes that discourse relations between hypertext nodes could be expressed following the same principles according to which discourse relations between cinematic shots are signalled through the consistent and concurrent use of visual features.

As we have seen, cinematic theory has been also applied by others to account for certain characteristics of hypertext as a medium and as a language, namely concerning the aspect of the transition from one discourse unit to the other. The specificity of this work, however, consists of the fact that it focuses on the cohesive aspects of cinematic discourse. That is, it looks at the way in which cinema represents discourse coherence through the use of formal features, cohesive elements that play the role of textual connectives and lead the viewer to establish meaningful connections between the film's shots. In this perspective, the way in which cinema uses formal features as cohesive elements and the way in which formal features could be used in hypertext with the same function constitutes the focus of the connection between the two media.

The concept of 'cinematic hypertext'. Thirdly, this work proposes the notion of 'cinematic hypertext', as a distinct graphically enriched and animated form of hypertext that finds itself at the intersection between spatial hypertext, semantic hypertext, and page-based hypertext. That is, it proposes to use primitive relational concepts to define connections between hypertext nodes and to use graphic and animation features to represent those relations, both in a node-to-node and in an anchor-to-page type of hypertext. These features do not have denotative signified in themselves, but if they are used consistently and concurrently to signal discourse connections, they can shape local visual languages to express discourse cohesion at the connotative level.

In fact, the concept of cinematic hypertext is essentially based on the consistent and concurrent use of the medium's formal features with some structuring principle in order to allow the emergence of regularities and therefore of a structuring language. From this, it derives that, if CCR could be very good structuring principles in 'cinematic hypertext', in principle they only constitute one 'possible' approach to representing connections, just as scholarly discourse constitutes one 'possible' use for hypertext. In other words, if the approach to discourse structuring presented in this book particularly addresses the issue of coherence representation in argumentative hypertext, in effect this work proposes that the concept of 'cinematic hypertext' goes beyond argumentative discourse and the problem of discourse coherence, to explore the very *affordances* of the medium.

A prototype visual language for hypertext discourse relations. Finally, at the application level, this work proposes a prototype visual language to render hypertext links as discourse relations. Based on parallels existing between textual and visual processing, and based on certain principles of perception and elementary linguistic criteria for the use of graphical components, it proposes the graphic design of a first set of hypertext relations in order to initiate a testing process. In the attempt to 'translate' cognitive coherence relations into a graphic language, it motivates the use of certain variables and shows their expressive potentialities when they are used concurrently and consistently to signify relational concepts through visual relationships. As a systematic approach to the representation of the relations, it proposes a design method in which each relational parameter is attributed features, so that the final rendering of each relation derives from the combination of the features that characterise the parameters defining the relation.

The results obtained from the first empirical testing of this prototype language support the assumptions on which its definition is based and suggest that the investigation of a visual language for expressing hypertext discourse relations should continue at the theoretical, at the design and at the empirical level.

3. Continuing the Investigation on 'Cinematic Hypertext'

Building on these results, numerous questions arise of a theoretical, design and empirical nature.

3.1. Theoretical Work

It would be interesting to investigate further the conceptual relationship between *causality* and *conditionality*. As we have seen, the difference between the two is that the first expresses actuality whereas the second expresses hypotheticality. We have also seen that hypotheticality might be difficult to represent visually, since visual languages are based on the act of monstration, whose only temporality is the present, and whose only spatiality is the visual field of the screen. Deepening the investigation on this problem, looking at how cinematic language deals with it in different circumstances might help to find effective ways of representing the concept of hypotheticality that differentiates *conditionality* from *causality*. As a consequence, the representation of conditional relations, so relevant in argumentative discourse, might become more intuitive and straightforward.

Another aspect is the definition of the conceptual relationship between *conditionality* and *background*. We have seen that there are similarities between the two relations, but for the moment these similarities have been observed in an intuitive manner. In this respect, a more theoretically grounded explanation would provide a more rigorous definition of the extent to which the two relations are similar. This should in turn help in seeking the best representation for each when designing them for further studies.

Deepening the exploration of Cognitive Coherence Relations' theory would also make it easier to find ways of representing relations both at a *semantic* and at a *pragmatic* level. In the first study, we have only worked with semantic relations, since working with both semantic and pragmatic relations would have introduced a considerable degree of complexity. In fact, representing both within a single hypertext might produce unintelligible results. However, pragmatic relations have a very relevant role in argumentation, so in one way or another the distinction should be accounted for (if not expressed) in a relational visual language. It might be that the best solution would be to let the author choose whether he wants to represent relations at a semantic or at a pragmatic level and ignore the other, or ignore the distinction altogether, but it might also be possible to find ways of representing both. In this respect, both theoretical as well as design considerations might be determinant.

3.2. Design Work and Empirical Studies

In general, all relation representations produced for the first study could be revisited and their design parameters varied and experimented with: there is certainly space for improvement. In fact, after deepening the reflection on the use of graphic elements to express relational concepts in general, several versions of each relation's representation could be designed in order to test their efficacy. For this study, new design parameters could be introduced, for instance one or two colours in addition to the grey scale; or minor animation features, for instance the scrolling of a text box instead of its appearing or sliding in.

After refining the relation design aspect, another study could be carried out on the model of the original one, to find out whether conceptual similarities between different relations have correspondence in the way their graphical representations are perceived. In such a study, as in the one reported, for each relation to be examined there could be different design solutions to chose from, one of which would be the graphic solution designed to express that particular relation, whereas the others would correspond to the graphic solutions designed to express other relations. In contrast to the first study, however, these other solutions could be selected according to specific criteria: one could be the graphical solution corresponding to a relation that is conceptually very close to the one being examined; another one could be the graphical solution corresponding to a relation that is conceptually distant from the one being examined. For instance, with *causality*, *conditionality* could be associated as a conceptually close relation, while *conjunctiveness* could be associated as a conceptually distant relation. With *conjunctiveness*, *similarity* could be associated as a conceptually close relation, while *causality* could be associated as a conceptually distant relation.

If the design solutions used to represent the various relations are accurate and have passed the design test described above, the choices that people will make should reflect the conceptual closeness and distance existing between the relations whose graphic design solutions have been proposed as alternative representations for the examined relation. For instance, for *causality*, the configuration expressly designed to represent the relation should obtain the majority of votes, the configuration designed to represent *conditionality* should attract fewer votes, whereas the configuration designed to express *conjunctiveness* should receive still fewer votes. Similarly, for *conjunctiveness*, the configuration expressly designed to represent the relation should obtain the majority of votes, the configuration designed to represent *similarity* should obtain fewer votes, and the configuration designed to represent *causality* should reasonably obtain fewer votes still. And so on.

This would certainly be a very interesting result, but such a study to be meaningful a number of conditions would need to be satisfied. First of all, the research on relations design should be more advanced than it is at this stage, that is, the configuration produced to represent each relation in the study should have been previously validated in terms of design quality. Second, a large enough number of relations (certainly larger than in the original study) should be examined, in order to allow an appropriate sorting and matching of the various configurations per relation. Third, rigorous criteria should be established at the theoretical level that define what constitutes conceptual 'closeness' and conceptual 'distance', to make sure that, for each examined relation, the respective configuration is appropriately associated to other alternative configurations. Finally, a larger number of subjects should be involved in the study to enhance the significance of the vote distribution: in this case the object of verification would not simply be the fact that people are sensitive and responsive to the visualisation of relational concepts, but it would also be the fact that people can discriminate between different solutions in a 'scalar' way.

A quite different type of study, ideally to be carried out after the ones described above, would consist of building a small working example of 'cinematic hypertext' to be tested among a large number of subjects. A short hypertext essay would be a good example of a small, self-contained scholarly hypertext whose link system could be expressed in terms of discourse relations dynamically visualised through the use of graphic features. Otherwise, other examples might be found or even built from scratch.

Three different versions of the same hypertext could be created: one that follows the structuring and representational conditional rules suggested by the results of the previous studies; one that breaks the same conditional rules, that is, that makes use of visual features with no consistency and that makes use of 'weak' configurations; finally, one that works as a control condition making no use of any structuring or representational rule. Three different groups of people could be asked to perform the same tasks respectively on the three different versions: navigate the hypertext, answer some comprehension questions, answer some recall questions, provide sketches of the argument structure, and so on. The prediction would be that the group expected to perform most efficiently would work on the 'cinematic' version; the group that should perform the worst would work on the 'wrong' version; whereas the group that worked on the control condition version would be expected to produce intermediate results.

4. Towards a 'Cinematic Hypertext' Authoring Environment

A design objective of these studies would be to define good parameters and design guidelines, which could then be implemented in a hypertext authoring-environment, a 'cinematic hypertext editor'. Since it is the tools available to writers that define to some extent the form of their writing, implementing tools that support the easy creation of 'cinematic' hypertext would be the first step towards the development of its language. The description that follows sketches a vision of how such an authoring tool would work.

The system should work like any other hypertext authoring tool and share aspects with applications like Storyspace, ClaiMaker and PowerPoint, respectively characterising three different modalities of interaction. In writing modality, the system should work similarly to Story Space, allowing the author to create nodes and to link them (either in the node-to-node or in the anchor-to-node way), and maybe also to define constraints on the navigation order. In editing modality, firstly the author should be allowed to define the links between nodes as discourse relations, and secondly to design each relation by attributing it visual and animation features.

For the first task, the system should work similarly to ClaiMaker, which allows the user to define the semantics of the links created between objects. Furthermore, the author should be free to use the sets of Cognitive Coherence Relations available in the system, to differentiate and specify them further, or even to create her set of relations from scratch, as long as she has a set of at least two relations to use.

The author should be able to define her relations in different ways: parametrical or taxonomical. In the first option, she should be able to provide a parametrical definition of the relations, in which she was required to attribute binary values to each parameter that defines the relation: *basic operation* (*causal* or *additive*), *polarity* (*positive* or *negative*), *source of coherence* (*semantic* or *pragmatic*), *directionality* (*forward-backwards-bidirectional*), and additional criteria like *temporality*, *hypotheticality*, *comparativeness*, etc. Since this option would allow the author to work with all or only some of the parameters, she could keep her definitions as general as she wishes, for instance, by using only the discrimination *additive-causal*, *positive-negative*, and *forward-backwards*, and disregarding the other ones.

Alternatively, the author should be able to provide a taxonomical definition of the relations and directly choose from a structured menu between definitions like *cause-consequence*, *claim-argument*, *contrastive cause-consequence*, *contrastive argument-cause*, *list*, *opposition*, *enumeration*, *concession*, *similarity*, *contrast*, *condition-consequence*, *contrastive condition-consequence*, *background*, *elaboration*, and so on. This option maybe quicker to work with but requires a higher degree of commitment to the specificity of the relations' semantics.

Once all the links of her hypertext were defined in terms of coherence relations, the author would have to specify how each relation was rendered using visual and animation features. For this second task, the system could work similarly to PowerPoint, allowing the author to define what the different relations between discourse parts will look like in presentation modality.

If the author had chosen to give her relations a parametrical definition, she would be requested to shape each parameter by associating them with graphical and animated features (as seen in Chapter 7), and the system would then integrate the features that connote the parameters defining each relation. This means that, for instance, all the causal relations would present some common features, whether they are positive or negative, pragmatic or semantic, forward or backward, etc. All negative causal relations would present the features that express causality plus the features that express negativity, and so on, according to the prioritisation that the user gave to the parameters.

If the author had chosen to give her relations a taxonomical definition, when shaping the relations, she would have to make sure that her choices are not incongruent, for instance, that the visualisation of a similarity relation and the visualisation of a contrast relation express the fact that the first is positive and the second is negative, but that they are both additive relations.

In both cases, as a form of assistance, the system could provide predefined templates for the rendering of the relations, however the author should be able to modify any of them, or create new representational schemes altogether. She should even be able to break her own rules: after the completion of the connection definition and shaping process, she could still select and manually modify any one link, defining what the look, position, animation, etc. of the connected nodes should be once that link was activated.

Finally, it is in this phase of the work that the author should also be able to define how many and which nodes should appear on the screen at the same time as part of an animated configuration, constituting single discourse patterns. When in presentation modality, as readers navigated the hypertext, clicking links here and there, new nodes would keep coming in and distributing with the others on the screen, while older nodes would go. They would see animated configurations of nodes taking shape before their eyes.

The system should also allow readers to go beyond what they have seen and read and to access the architecture of the hypertext with constituting principles and rules. This could be very important in collaborative contexts, in which each participant should be able to see and manipulate the hypertext structure both at the writing and editing level, and both at the relation definition and rendering design level. Each intervention should be recorded, maintained and made retrievable as such by the system.

5. 'Cinematic Hypertext' and Argumentative Functions

Throughout the book, hypertext argumentation has been referred to mainly from the point of view of writers - scholarly authors - and their need to maintain the integrity of their argument, on the one hand, and find effective ways to present it, on the other. However, the point of view of the readers - and specifically learners - needs to be taken into account when thinking of hypertext systems, and languages that address the issue of coherence in interactive argumentative discourse. This section looks at how 'cinematic hypertext' could support the integration of these two roles in a creatively productive way. In the absence of a software environment at present, these ideas are necessarily at a preliminary stage of development, and await empirical validation.

5.1. Cinematic Hypertext for Scholars

Summarising the characteristics outlined above, 'cinematic hypertext' could support the scholar's writing, like many other authoring environments. However, in this case she would benefit from working with a tool that allows her to take advantage of the formal features that characterise the medium and integrating them in the construction of her arguments. For this purpose, the system would offer her a set of basic argumentative relations that she can use to define (and subsequently shape) the connections between her hypertext's nodes. However, it would also allow her to use connective principles of her own choice, offering her the maximum flexibility in creating juxtaposition effects that are functional to her type of argument and to her expressive goals. In the process of shaping discourse relations, then, the system would make sure that the scholar is consistent and congruent with the use of the available formal features, by constraining them to the relational definitions previously used by the author, or by providing predefined representational schemes. However, even in this case the scholar would retain control, as ultimately it would be always up to her what features to use and in what way. Finally, the system should even allow the scholar the expressive freedom of breaking her own rules.

In sum, these characteristics of 'cinematic hypertext' could provide the scholar with a tool that would allow her to create her own enriched hypertext language, and to achieve the best trade off between expressive capabilities and communicative efficacy. This is particularly important from the point of view of collective argumentation. We have seen how certain hypertext paradigms, such as spatial hypertext, can be difficult to use for collaboration, because no consistency is required for the use of formal features and no explicit semantics is relied upon (see Chapter 1, § 4.3.). As previously discussed, to open any possibility of collaboration in hypertext systems, the use of representational conditional rules is very important to create expressive regularities and achieve - at least at the local level - some kind of recognisable language. Moreover, if somewhere the system allows a scholar to define her personal semantics and conditional rules, then the definition of that semantic and of those conditional rules could be accessed by other scholars. They could in turn manipulate the original semantics and conditional rules and reformulate (re-shape) the hypertext contents in terms of their own point of view, by creating new connections, eliminating old ones, redefining and reshaping them, creating and connecting new nodes, etc. In so doing, their own semantics and conditional rules would in turn be accessible to the original author. In other words, scholars could use this authoring tool to debate with one another, which they could do by inventing and re-inventing, defining and re-defining, shaping and re-shaping discourse relations.

5.2. Cinematic Hypertext for Students

But, in different ways, 'cinematic hypertext' could also offer support to students' work. The use of argumentation in computer-supported collaborative learning (CSCL) is becoming a major research topic. Andriessen et al. (2003) distinguish three different situations in which argumentation may be part of a student's learning process: when *from* argumentation they gain a deeper understanding about a topic and the associated concepts; when they learn *about* the various points of view and arguments with respect to a topic; and when they learn *to* argue, that is, when they acquire the skills (language and the techniques) to be able to engage in argumentation. Cinematic hypertext might prove a useful tool in all the situations mentioned above.

In the first situation, the focus is on the contents of the argument, of which students are meant to achieve a better understanding. In this respect, understanding the concepts that constitute the argument is the most important thing, that is, the fact that certain concepts are there, and that they are expressed clearly and in depth is very important, since they constitute its building blocks. However, to gain understanding of a topic, understanding the connections holding between its related concepts is fundamental. The connections between these concepts could be explicitly labelled, as in semantic hypertext, or they could be suggested implicitly, as in spatial hypertext. In the first, the student is being told what connections he is supposed to recognise, so he does not have to make any effort to interpret them himself; whereas, in the second, he is almost being provoked to establish connections, but he cannot rely on a consistent codification of them, so he has no access key to facilitate the understanding of their intended meaning.

However, if the students were presented with a 'cinematic hypertext argument', they would have (initially, at least) to navigate it in presentation mode and would have to interpret the patterns that appear in front of them on the screen, that is, they would have to invest cognitive effort to understand the relations between the content units presented by the nodes. This very work would bring them closer into the matter, whose understanding would literally constitute an achievement, as long as the students could rely on the consistent use of those formal features that, by shaping the discourse's patterns, seem to suggest certain relations between the discourse's components. In this process, the function of those visual and dynamic patterns would primarily consist of giving the students a 'sense' of structure, helping them to perceive the hierarchical organisation of the concepts that they are trying to understand and relate, even if they were not able to exactly point out what relation types are meant to hold between nodes. However, eventually students might be given access also to the underlying semantics and representational conditional rules that shape the hypertext, for them to see how it is constructed, to reshape and personalise its representation, and to reuse its components.

Cinematic hypertext could similarly be a useful support also in the second situation described by Andriessen et al.: when students are learning *about* a debate. In this scenario the focus shifts from the contents to the discourse, and gaining understanding of the different points of view about a topic becomes the most relevant aspect. From this perspective, understanding the relations between the different elements that compose the debate (claims, arguments, evidence, etc.) is essential. In this process, 'cinematic' hypertext could be used, on the one hand, to present the debate to the students, and, on the other hand, it would constitute for them an analytical and constructive tool. That is, the 'cinematic' presentation of the debate would help them to understand its structure. Gaining access to the underlying semantics and rules would allow them to establish new connections, modify the relation definitions to focus on certain particular ones, to change the representational rules to see more clearly certain juxtapositions, to add new elements over time and update their personalised picture of the debate itself, and so on.

Finally, in the third situation described by Adriessen et al. - when students learn to debate - 'cinematic hypertext' could prove to be a useful learning tool, because it would constantly exercise their awareness about two fundamental aspects of arguing: establishing connections and shaping discourse. The tool could provoke reflection on the cognitive processes involved in arguing, on the idea that there are primitive cognitive moves that can be articulated into more specific relations, that certain relations have certain aspects in common, that an argument is an ordered structure and has a shape which strongly impacts its effectiveness. The students could literally see their arguments take shape before their eyes, as a visualisation of the conceptual network that they have constructed, and could discover that graphics and animation are not only a decorative supplement, but can be used as a language to express what they want to say. Finally, all this might help them to gain more awareness of the hypertext medium and of its linguistic potentialities, and of the fact that ultimately constructing an argument is a creative process, as it is shooting and editing a film.

6. Conclusion

From the scholarly point of view, hypertext's connectivity appears to constitute the main attraction of the medium, since it allows scholars to reify the very process that characterises the way they think and work. Despite this, argumentation tends to make a limited use of hypertext connectivity, because fragmentation of the line of argument weakens the argumentative structure. As Lanham (1993) discusses, there tends to be a scholarly suspicion towards digital and visual media in general, and a preference for more traditional forms and paradigms of expression and communication, namely paper-based text and linearity. However, this work argues that there is a whole cinematic dimension that scholars could explore to express themselves and to communicate through this medium, if hypertext tools were available that allow the individual to fully explore the *affordances* of the medium. If we could become literate in 'cinematic hypertext' the connectivity of argumentative hypertext would greatly increase, allowing scholars to construct hypertexts that are closer and closer to "*the way they think*". To do this, they would need to work with tools that encourage and support the exploitation of the 'cinematic' dimension of the medium, as well as the exploration of new expressive paradigms.

When they write on paper, scholars always make use of the written (words, symbols, etc.) and graphic (diagrams, pictures, maps, etc.) languages that the medium supports, and to some extent they practise document design when they format their essays. In fact, the very languages that they use to shape their discourse on paper have determined the way they are able to write, as the medium always determines one's form of expression. Likewise, should scholars choose to write in hypertext, writing would not solely involve words and links, but in principle it would involve all the various languages that the medium can 'afford'. In order for this to happen, the scholar needs to become aware of the hypertext medium's inherent *affordances*, going beyond the *affordances* that he perceives at first, his perception being limited by and to the characteristics of the medium that he is most acquainted with: paper.

Throughout history, new media have always *remediated* (Bolter and Grusin, 1998) old ones, gradually achieving their particular reinterpretation of old paradigms. Every time, however, through this process of continuous remediation, the original characteristics of the new medium have determined the development of new languages and forms of expression. When the first cine cameras were invented, cinematic language as such did not exist yet, and the reference paradigm was theatre: an entire film consisted of what we would call today a long *sequence-shot*. It took a couple of decades for cinematic language to start developing with the work of pioneers like Griffin and Eisenstein. They taught cinema to 'speak' through the articulation of filmic chunks that could be finally achieved with montage, and soon the ubiquity of the *cinema-eye* (Vertov, 1984), made the theatrical paradigm only one of the many possible references that cinematic language could make use of.

Bibliography

Andriessen, J., Baker, M., Suthers, D. (2003). Argumentation, Computer Support, and the Educational Context of Confronting Cognitions. In Andriessen, J., Baker, M., Suthers, D. (Eds.) *Arguing to Learn. Confronting Cognitions in Computer-Supported Collaborative Learning Environments.*, Kluwer Academic Publishers, Dordrecht- Boston-London, pp.1-25

Bannon, L. and Bødker, S. (1997). Constructing Common Information Spaces. In *Proceedings ECSCW'97*, Lancaster, September, pp.81-96

Baptista, A. A., Rodrigues, E. and Barbosa Machado, A. (1999). Online Publishing as a Support for Scholarly Communication in Dynamic Knowledge Communities. In *Electronic Publishing*, Ronneby, ICCC Press, Washington DC, pp.236-249

Baron, L., Tague-Sutcliffe, J., Kinnucan, M.T. (1996). Labeled, Typed Links as Cues when Reading Hypertext Documents. In *Journal of the American Association for Information Science*, 47 (12), pp.896-908

Barthes, R. (1960). Scrittori e Scriventi. In Barthes, R. *Essais Critiques*, Seuil, Paris

Benveniste, E. (1970). L'Appareil Formel de l'Énonciation. In *Langages*, 5(17), March, pp.12-18

Bernstein, M. (1998). Patterns of Hypertext. In *Proceedings of ACM Hypertext'98:* Pittsburgh, PA, ACM Press, New York, pp.21-29

Bernstein, M. (2003). Collage, Composites, Construction. In *Proceedings of ACM Hypertext'98*, ACM Press, New York, pp.122-123

Bertin, J. (1967). *Semiologie Graphique.* English translation (1983). *Semiology of Graphics: Diagrams, Networks, Maps.* University of Wiscounsin Press, Madison

Bertin, J. (1977). *La Graphique et le Traitement Graphique del l'Information.* English translation (1981). *Graphics and Graphic Information Processing.* Walter de Gruyter, Berlin

Bertin, J. (2000/2001). Matrix Theory of Graphics. In *Information Design Journal*, 10(1), pp.5-19

Biro, Y. (1982). *Profane Mythology: The Savage Mind of the Cinema.* Indiana University Press, 1982

Bolter, D.J. (1991). Topographic Writing: Hypertext and the Electronic Writing Space. In Delany, P., Landow, G.P. (Eds.) *Hypermedia and Literary Studies*, MIT Press, Cambridge, MA, pp.105-118

Bolter, J.D. (1991). *Writing Space: The Computer, Hypertext, and the History of Writing*, Eastgate Systems, Cambridge MA

Bolter, J.D., Grusin, R. (1998). *Remediation. Understanding New Media.* MIT Press, Cambridge, MA

Bordwell, D., Staiger, J., Thompson, K. (1985). *The Classical Hollywood Cinema. Film Style and Mode of Production to 1960,* Columbia University Press, New York

Branigan, E. (1992). *Narrative Comprehension and Film.* Routledge, London

Brent, D. (1997). Rhetorics of the Web: Implications for Teachers of Literacy. *Kairos: A Journal for Teachers of Writing in Webbed Environments.* 2(1), Spring, http://english.ttu.edu/kairos/2.1/features/brent/bridge.html

Brewer, C.A. (1992). *Color Selection for Geographic Data Analysis and Visualisation.* Paper presented at GIS/LIS, 12 November, San Jose, CA

Bublitz, W. (1999). Introduction: Views of Coherence. In Bublitz, W., Lenk, U., Ventola, E. (Eds.), *Coherence in Spoken and Written Discourse. How to Create It and How to Describe It.* John Benjamins Publishing Co., Amsterdam, pp.1-7

Buckingham Shum, S., Uren, V., Li, G., Sereno, B. and Mancini, C. (2004). Modelling Naturalistic Argumentation in Research Literatures: Representation and Interaction Design Issues. In *International Journal of Intelligent Systems* (IJIS), special issue on Computational Models of Natural Argument . Chris Reed and Floriana Grasso Eds.

Buckingham Shum, S. (2003). The Roots of Computer Supported Argument Visualisation. In Kirschner, P.A., Buckingham Shum, S., Carr, Ch.S. (Eds.) *Visualising Argumentation. Software Tools for Collaborative and Educational Sense-Making.* Springer-Verlag, London, pp.3-24

Buckingham Shum, S. and Sumner, T. (2001). JIME: An Interactive Journal for Interactive Media. In *First Monday*, 6(2), February 2001, http://www-jime.open.ac.uk/99/1/

Buckingham Shum, S. Hammond, N. (1994). Argumentation-Based Design Rationale: What Use at What Cost? In *International Journal of Human Computer Studies*, 40(4), pp. 603-652

Buckingham Shum, S., Motta, E., Domingue, J. (2000). ScholOnto: An Ontology-Based Digital Library Server for Research Documents and Discourse. In *International Journal on Digital Libraries,* 3(3), pp. 237-248

Buckingham Shum, S., Uren, V., Li, G., Domingue, J., Motta, E., Mancini, C. (2002). *Designing Representational Coherence into an Infrastructure for Collective Sensemaking.* Invited Discussion

Paper, 2nd International Workshop on Infrastructures for Distributed Collective Practices, San Diego, 6-9 February 2002
Buckingham Shum, S., Uren, V., Li, G., Domingue, J., Motta, E. (2003). Visualizing Argumentation. In Kirschner, P.A., Buckingham Shum, S., Carr, Ch.S. (Eds) *Software Tools for Collaborative and Educational Sense-Making*. Springer-Verlag, London
Burch, N., (1969). *Praxis du cinema*. Gallimard, Paris
Bush, V. (1945). As We May Think. In *Atlantic Monthly*, July 1945 (157), pp.106-107
Buziek, D. (1995). Kartographische Visualisierung von Geo-Daten under Berücksichtigung Moderner Technischer Entwicklungen. In Buziek, D. (Ed.), *GIS in Forschung un Praxis*, Stuttgart, pp.234-250
Campbell, K.S. (1995). *Coherence, Continuity, and Cohesion. Theoretical Foundations for Document Design*. Lawrence Erlbaum Associates Publishers, Hillsdale (NJ), Hove (UK)
Carr, L., Hall, W., Miles-Board, T. (2000). *Writing and Reading Hypermedia on the Web*. Technical Report ECSTR-IAM00-1, University of Southampton, Southampton, UK
Carter, L.M. (2000). Arguments in Hypertext: A Rhetorical Approach. In *Proceedings of ACM Hypertext '00*, ACM Press, New York, pp.87-91
Casetti, F., Di Chio, F., (1990). *Analisi del film*. Bompiani, Milano
Chatman, S., (1978). *Story and Discourse. Narrative Structure in fiction and film*. Cornell University Press, Ithaca (USA) and London
Chatman, S., (1990). *Coming to Terms: the Rhetoric of Narrative in Fiction and Film*. Cornell University Press, Ithaca and New York
Chomsky, N. (1957). *Syntactic Structures*. Mouton, The Hague
Citeseer. http://citeseer.nj.nec.com/
Conklin, J. and Begeman, M.L. (1988). *gIBIS: A Hypertext Tool for Exploratory Policy Discussion*. MCC Technical Report Number STP-082-88, Austin, Texas
Cuccu, L. (1990). *Antonioni. Il discorso dello Sguardo*. EDS Editrice, Pisa
D3E. http://d3e.sourceforge.net/
Dancygier, B., Sweetser, E. (2000). Constructions with If, Since, and Because: Causality, Epistemic Stance, and Clause Order. In Couper-Kuhlen, E., Kortmann, B. (Eds.), *Cause, Condition, Concession, Contrast. Cognitive and Discourse Perspectives*. Mouton de Gruyter, Berlin and New York, pp.111-141
De Saussure, F. (1922). *Cours de Linguistique Générale*. Editions Payot, Paris
Derrida, J. (1972). *La Dissémination*, Collection "Tel Quel", Seuil, Paris
Dijk, T. van (1977). *Text and Context. Explorations in Semantics and Pragmatics of Discourse*. Longman, London
Dransch, D. (1995). *Temporale und Nontemporale Computer-Animation in der Kartographie*. Berliner Geograph. Abh., R.C., Bd. 15. Berlin, FU, TU, TFH
Eisenstein, S.M. (1964). *Neravnodusnaja Priroda*. Iskusstvo, Moscow
EJournal. http://www.ucalgary.ca/ejournal/
Electronic Encyclopedia. http://www.columbia.edu/cu/cup/cee/cee.html
Encarta Encyclopedia. http://microsoft.com/products/encarta/products/encarta_ee.asp
Engelbart, D. (1963). A Conceptual Framework for the Augmentation of the Human Intellect. In Howerton, P.D., Weeks, D.C. (Eds.) *Vistas in Information Handling*, Vol. 1, Spartan Books, Washington DC
Ess, Ch. (1996). Modernity and Postmodernism in 'Hypertext Notes': A Call for Theoretical Consistency and Completeness. In *EJournal*, 6(3) http://www.hanover.edu/philos/ejournal/archive/v6n3/ess/ess.html
Foltz, P. W. (1996). Comprehension, Coherence, and Strategies in Hypertext and Linear Text. In J. Levonen, J. F. Rouet, A. Dillon, & R. Spiro (Eds.), *Hypertext and Cognition*. Lawrence Erlbaum, Hillsdale, NJ
Foucault, M. (1966). *Les Mots et Les Choses*, Gallimard, Paris
Fritz, G. (1982). Kohärenz: *Grundfragen der Dialoganalyse*. Tübingen, Narr
Gardies, A. (1981) L'espace du Récit Filmique: Propositions. In D.Chateau, A. Gardies, F.Jost (Eds.), *Cinémas de la Modernité. Films, Théories. Colloque de Cerisy*. Paris, Klincksieck, pp.75-92
Gardies, A. (1984). Le Su et le Vu. *Hors Cadre*, 2, pp.45-65
Gardies, A. (1993). *L'espace au Cinema*. Méridiens Klincksieck, Paris
Gaudreault, A. (1989). *Du Littéraire au Filmique. Système du Récit*. Méridiens Klincksieck, Paris
Gaver, W. (1991). Technology Affordances. In *Proceedings of ACM CHI Conference '91*, ACM Press, New York, pp.79-84
Gelder, van T. (2003). Enhancing Deliberation Through Computer Supported Argument Visualization. In Kirschner, P.A., Buckingham Shum, S., Carr, Ch.S. (Eds.) *Visualising Argumentation. Software Tools for Collaborative and Educational Sense-Making*. Springer-Verlag, London, pp. 97-115
Genette, G. (1972). *Figure III*. Éditions du Seuil, Paris
Genin, C. (1998). *Mémoire réticulaire et hypertexte*, Université Paris3, Hubert de Phalèse. http://www.cavi.univ-paris3.fr/phalese/rdf7.htm

Gibson, J. J. (1977). The theory of affordances. In R. E. Shaw & J. Bransford (Eds.), *Perceiving, Acting, and Knowing*. Lawrence Erlbaum Associates, Hillsdale, NJ

Gibson, J. J. (1979). *The Ecological Approach to Visual Perception*. Mifflin, Houghton, Boston

Givón, T. (1995). Coherence in Text vs. Coherence in Mind. In Gernsbacher, M.A., Givón, T. (Eds.), *Coherence in Spontaneous Text. Typological Studies in Language*, 31, John Benjamins. Amsterdam, pp.59-115

Glenny, M., Taylor, R. (Eds). (1991). *Eisenstein, Volume 2 - Towards a Theory of Montage*. Translation by Michael Glenny, British Film Institute, London

Grice, H.P. (1975). Logic and Conversation. In Cole, P., Morgan, J. (Eds.), *Syntax and Semantics*. Academy Press of New York, Vol. 3, pp.41-58

Gruber, T. R. (1993). Toward Principles for the Design of Ontologies Used for Knowledge Sharing. In *International Journal of Human-Computer Studies*, 43(5-6), pp.907-928

Haas, S.W., Grams, E.S. (1998). A Link Taxonomy for Web Pages. In *Proceedings of the 61st Annual Meeting of the American Society for Information Science*, Cecilia Preston, pp.485-495

Halasz, F.G., Moran, Th.P., Trigg, R.H. (1987). NoteCards in a Nutshell. In *Proceedings of ACM and GI'87 Conference on Human Factors in Computing Systems and Graphic Interface*, pp.45-52

Halliday, M.A.K., Hasan, R. (1976). *Cohesion in English*. Longman

Hammond, N., Allison, L. (1987). The Travel Metaphor as Design Principle and Training Aid for Navigating around Complex Systems. In *Proceedings of the 3rd Conference of the British Computer Society HCI Specialist Group*, pp. 75-90

Harnad, S., 1991, Post-Gutenberg Galaxy: The Fourth Revolution in the Means of Production of Knowledge. In *Public-Access Computer Systems (PACS) Review*, 2(1), pp.39–53

Harnad, S. (1997). Learned Inquiry and the Net: The Role of Peer Review, Peer Commentary and Copyright. *Learned Publishing*, 11(4), pp.283-292

Harnad, S. (1997). The Paper House of Cards (And Why It Is Taking So Long To Collapse). In *Ariadne*, vol. 8, pp.6-7

Hobbs, J.R. (1985). *On the Coherence and Structure of Discourse*. Technical Report CSLI-85-37, Stanford, CA

Horn, R.E. (2003). Infrastructure for Navigating Interdisciplinary Debates: Critical Decisions for Representing Argumentation. In *Visualizing Argumentation: Software Tools for Collaborative and Educational Sense-Making*. Kirschner, P. A., Buckingham Shum, S. and Carr, C. (Eds.) Springer-Verlag: London

HyperCard, Apple Systems. http://www.wired.com/news/mac/0,2125,54365,00.html

Jackson, M.H. (1997). Assessing the Structure of Communication on the World Wide Web. In *Journal of Computer-Mediated Communication*, 3(1), June, http://www.ascusc.org/jcmc/vol3/issue1/jackson.html

Jost, F. (1987). *L'Oeil-Caméra. Entre Film et Roman*. Presses Universitaires de Lyon

Journal of Digital Information (JoDI). http://jodi.ecs.soton.ac.uk/

Kanizsa, G. (1955). Margini Quasi-Percettivi in Campi con Stimolazione Omogenea. In *Rivista di Psicologia*, 49(1), pp 7-30

Kaplan, N. (1995). E-literacies: Politexts, Hypertexts, and Other Cultural Formations in the Late Age of Print. In *Computer-Mediated Communication Magazine*, 2(3), March, http://sunsite.unc.edu/cmc/mag/1995/mar/toc.html

Kepes, G. (1944). *Language of Vision*. Paul Theobold, Chicago

Kerne, A., Mistrot, J.M., Khandelwal, M., Sundaram, V., Koh, E. (2004). Using Composition to Re-Present Personal Collections of Hypersigns. In *Proceedings of COSIGN 2004*, Split, CRO, Sep 14-16, pp.72-81

Kinneavy, J. (1980). *A Theory of Discourse*. Norton, New York

Knott, A., Dale, R. (1994). Using Linguistic Phenomena to Motivate a Set of Coherence Relations. In *Discourse Processes*, 18(1), pp.35-62

Knott, A., Mellish, C. (1996). A feature-based account of the relations signalled by sentence and clause connectives. In *Language and Speech*, 39(2/3), pp.142-183

Knott, A. (1998). Similarity and Contrast Relations and Inductive Rules. In *Proceedings of the ACL Workshop on Discourse Relations and Discourse Markers*. Association for Computational Linguistics, pp.54-57

Knott, A., Sanders, T.J.M (1998). The Classification of Coherence Relations: An Exploration of Two Languages. In *Journal of Pragmatics*, 30(2), pp.135-175

Knott, A. (1999). Semantic and pragmatic relations and their intended effects. In Sanders, T.J.M., Schilperoord, J., Spooren, W. (Eds.), *Text Representation. Linguistic and Psycholinguistic Aspects*. University of Utrecht, University of Tilburg, Free University of Amsterdam, pp.127-152

Koch, W.G. (2000/2001). Jaques Bertin's Theory of Graphics and its Development and Influence on Multimedia Cartography. In *Information Design Journal*, 10(1), pp.37-43

Kolb D. (1997). Scholarly Hypertext: Self-Represented Complexity. In *Proceedings of ACM Hypertext '97*, ACM Press, New York, pp.29-37

Kolb, D. (1995). *Socrates in the Labyrinth: Hypertext, Argument, Philosophy*. Eastgate Systems, Cambridge

Kolb, D. (2004). *Sprawling Places*. http://www.dkolb.org/sprawlingplaces/suburbsa.html

Kopak, R.W. (1999). Functional Link Typing in Hypertext. In *ACM Computing Surveys*, 31(4), Article n.16

Kraak, M.J. (1990). Theoretical Aspects of Three-Dimensional Cartography. In *International Yearbook of Cartography*, vol. 30, Ulm, pp.81-91

Krygier, J.B. (1994). Sound and Geographic Visualisation. In Mac-Eachren, A.M., Taylor, D.R.F. (Eds.) *Visualisation on Modern Cartography*, Oxford, pp.149-166

Kuleshov, L. (1974). Kuleshov on Film. In *Writings of Lev Kuleshov*. University of California Press, Berkeley

Kumpf, E.P. (2000). Visual Metadiscourse: Designing the Considerate Text. In *Technical Communication Quarterly*, 9(4), pp.401-24

Landow, G.P. (1991). The Rhetoric of Hypermedia: Some Rules for Authors. In Delany, P., Landow, G.P. (Eds.) *Hypermedia and Literary Studies*, MIT Press, Cambridge, MA, pp.81-104

Landow, G. P. (1992). *Hypertext: The Convergence of Contemporary Critical Theory and Technology*. Johns Hopkins Press, Baltimore

Lanham, R.A. (1993). The Electronic Word: Literary Study and the Digital Revolution. In Lanham, R.A. *The Electronic Word. Democracy. Technology and the Arts*, The University of Chicago Press, Chicago-London, pp.3-28

Laurillard, D., Stratfold, M., Luckin, R., Plowman, L. & Taylor, J. (2000). Affordances for Learning in a Non-Linear Narrative Medium. In *Journal of Interactive Media in Education*, 2000(2), http://www-jime.open.ac.uk/00/2

Li, G., Uren, V., Motta, E., Buckingham Shum, S., John Domingue, J. (2002). ClaiMaker: Weaving a Semantic Web of Research Papers. In *Proceedings of the 1st International Semantic Web Conference*. (ISWC2002), Ian Horrocks and James Hendler Editors, pp. 436-441

Louwerse, M. (2001). An Analytic and Cognitive Parametrization of Coherence Relations. In *Cognitive Linguistics*, 12 (3), pp. 291-315

MacEachren, A.M. (2000/2001). An Evolving Cognitive-Semiotic Approach to Geographic Visualisation and Knowledge Construction. In *Information Design Journal*, 10(1), pp.26-36

Mancini, C. (2003). *Towards Cinematic Hypertext. A Theoretical and Empirical Investigation*. Ph.D. Thesis, Knowledge Media Institute, The Open University

Mancini, C. (2000). From Cinematographic to Hypertext Narrative. In *Proceedings of ACM Hypertext '00*, New York, pp. 236-237

Mancini, C., Buckingham Shum, S. (2004). Towards Cinematic Hypertext. In *Proceeding of ACM Hypertext '04*, Santa Cruz, CA, USA, Aug 9-13, ACM Press, New York, pp.115-124

Mancini, C., Buckingham Shum, S. (2001). Cognitive Coherence Relations and Hypertext: from Cinematic Patterns to Scholarly Discourse. In *Proceedings of ACM Hypertext '01*, ACM Press, New York, pp.165-174

Mann, W.C., Thompson, S.A. (1988). Rhetorical Structure Theory: Toward a Functional Theory of Text Organisation. In *Text*, 8 (3), pp.243-281

Marshall, C.C., Halasz, F.G., Rogers, R.A., Janssen, W.C. Jr. (1991). Aquanet: a Hypertext Tool to Hold your Knowledge in Place. In *Proceedings of ACM Hypertext '91*, ACM Press, New York, pp. 261-275

Marshall, C.C., Rogers, R.A. (1992). Two Years Before the Mist: Experiences with Aquanet. In *Proceedings of ACM Hypertext '92*, ACM Press, New York, pp. 53-62

Marshall, C.C., Shipman, F.M. III. (1993). Searching for the Missing Link: Discovering Implicit Structure in Spatial Hypertext. In *Proceedings of ACM Hypertext '93*, ACM Press, New York, pp.217-230

Marshall, C.C., Shipman, F.M. III, and Coombs, J.H. (1994). VIKI: Spatial Hypertext Supporting Emergent Structure In *Proceedings of ACM European Conference on Hypermedia Technologies*. Sept. 18-23, Edinburgh, Scotland. ACM Press, New York, pp. 13-23

Marshall, C.C., Shipman, F.M. III (1997). Spatial Hypertext and the Practice of Information Triage. In *Proceedings of UK Conference on Hypertext*, pp. 124-133

Martin, J.R. (1992). *English Text. System and Structure*. John Benjamins Publishing Co., Amsterdam, pp. 286-288

Metz, Ch. (1968). *Essai sur la Signification au Cinéma -I*. Editions Klincksieck, Paris.

Metz, Ch. (1972). *Essai sur la Signification au Cinéma -II*. Editions Klincksieck, Paris.

Metz, Ch. (1991). *L'Énunciation Impersonnelle, ou le Site du Film*. Méridien Klincksieck, Paris

Meyer, P.G. (2000). The Relevance of Causality. In Couper-Kuhlen, E., Kortmann, B. (Eds.), *Cause, Condition, Concession, Contrast. Cognitive and Discourse Perspectives*. Mouton de Gruyter, Berlin and New York, pp.9-33

Miles, A. (1999). Cinematic Paradigms of Hipertext. In *Continuum: Journal of Media & Cultural Studies*, 13(2), pp. 217-226
Miles, A. (2000). Hypertext Syntagmas: Cinematic Narration with Links. In *Journal of Digital Information*, 1(7). http://jodi.ecs.soton.ac.uk/Articles/v01/i07/Miles/
Miles, A. (2001). Hypertext Structure as the Event of Connection. In *Proceedings of ACM Hypertext '01*, ACM Press, New York, pp.61-68
Miles-Board, T., Carr, L., Hall, W. (2002). Looking for Linking: Associative Links on the Web. In *Proceedings of ACM Hypertext '02*, ACM Press, New York, pp.76-77
Miles-Board, T., (2003). *Everything Integrated: A Framework for Associative Writing in the Web*. Ph.D. Thesis, Faculty of Engineering and Applied Science, Department of Electronics and Computer Science, University of Southampton
Moulthrop, S. (1992). Toward a Rhetoric of Informating Texts. In *Proceedings of ACM Hypertext '99*, ACM Press, New York, pp.171-180
Nack, F., Hardman, L. (2001). Denotative and Connotative Semantics in Hypermedia: Proposal for a Semiotic-Aware Architecture. In *New Review of Hypermedia and Multimedia*, vol. 7, pp.7-37
Nelson, T. (1981). *Literary Machines*. Swardmore
Nelson, T. (1987). *Computer Lib and Dream Machines*. Microsoft Press, Redmond, Wash
Nielsen, J. (1999). *When Bad Design Elements Become the Standard*. http://www.useit.com/alertbox/991114.html
Nielsen, J. (2002). *Deep Linking Is Good Linking*. http://www.useit.com/alertbox/20020303.html
Noordman, L.G.M., Blijzer, F. de (2000). On the Processing of Causal Relations. In Couper-Kuhlen, E., Kortmann, B. (Eds.), *Cause, Condition, Concession, Contrast. Cognitive and Discourse Perspectives*. Mouton de Gruyter, Berlin and New York, pp.35-57
Not, E., Zancanaro, M. (2000). The MacroNode Approach: Mediating Between Adaptive and Dynamic Hypermedia. In *AH 2000*, pp.167-178
Open Archive Initiative. http://www.openarchives.org/
Open Citation Project. http://opcit.eprints.org/
Pander Maat, H. (1994). Coherentie-relaties Hebben Zowel Semantische als Pragmatische Aspecten. In Maes, A., Hauwermeiren, P. van, Waes, L. van (Eds.), *Perspectiven in Taabeheersingsonderzoek*. Dordrecht: ICG, pp.118-129
Pander Maat, H. (1999). The Differential Linguistic Realisation of Comparative and Additive Coherence Relations. In *Cognitive Linguistics*, 10(2), pp.147-184
Pander Maat, H., Degand, L. (2001). Scaling Causal Reations and Conectives in terms of Speaker Involvement. In *Cognitive Linguistics*, 12(3), pp.211-245
Pander Maat, H., Sanders, T.J.M. (2001). Subjectivity in Causal Connectives: An Empirical Study of Language in Use. In *Cognitive Linguistics*, 12(3), pp.247-237
Parunak, H. van D. (1991). Ordering the information graph. In Emily Berk and Joseph Devlin (Eds.), *Hypertext / Hypermedia Handbook*, McGraw-Hill Publishing Company, New York, pp.299-325
Peirce, C. (1931-1935). *Collected Papers*. The Belknap Press of Harvard University Press, Cambridge, MA
Penrose, L. S. and Penrose, R. (1958). Impossible objects: A special type of illusion. In *British Journal of Psychology* 49, 31-33
Pinker, S. (1994). *The Language Instinct. How the Mind Creates Language*. William Morrow & Co.
Riley, K., Parker, F. (1998). Parallels Between Visual and Textual Processing. In *IEEE Transactions on Professional Communication*, 41(3), pp.175-185
Ropars-Wuilleumier, M.C. (1970). *L'Écran de la Mémoire. Essais de Lecture Cinématographique*. Édition du Seuil, Paris
Rosenberg, J. (2001). And *And*: Conjunctive Hypertext and the Structure Acteme Juncture. In *Proceedings of ACM Hypertext '02*, New York, pp.51-60
Rosenberg, J. (2002). *Conditional Spatiality*. Second Workshop on Spatial Hypertext, ACM Hypertext '02, 12 June, University of Maryland, Maryland, US
Rubin, E. (1921). *Visuell Wahrgenommene Figuren*, Copenhagen, Gyldendals
Rutledge, L., Bailey, B., Ossenbruggen, J. van, Hardman, L., Geurts, J. (2000). Generating Presentation Constraints from Rhetorical Structure. In *Proceedings ACM Hypertext '00*, ACM Press, New York, pp.19-28
Sanders, T.J.M., Spooren, W.P.M., Noordman, L.G.M. (1992). Towards a Taxonomy of Coherence Relations. In *Discourse Processes*, 15, pp.1-35
Sanders, T.J.M., Spooren, W.P.M., Noordman, L.G.M. (1993). Coherence Relations in a Cognitive Theory of Discourse Representation. In *Cognitive Linguistics*, 4(2), pp.93-133
Sanders, T.J.M. (1997). Semantic and Pragmatic Sources of Coherence: On the Categorisation of Coherence Relations in Context. In *Discourse processes*, 24, pp.119-147

Sanders, T.J.M., Spooren, W. (1999). Communicative intentions and coherence relations. In: W. Bublitz & U. Lenk & E. Ventola (Eds.), *Coherence in spoken and written discourse*. Benjamins, Amsterdam, pp.235-251

Sanders, T.J.M, Noordman, L.G.M. (2000). The Role of Coherence Relations and Their Linguistic Markers in Text Processing. In *Discourse Processes*, 29(1), pp.37-60

Sanders, T.J.M, Spooren, W. (2001). Text Representation as an Interface Between Language and its Users. In Sanders, T.J.M., Schilperoord, J., Spooren, W. (Eds.), *Text Representation. Linguistic and psycholinguistic aspects*. University of Utrecht, University of Tilburg, Free University of Amsterdam Press, pp.1-26

Sawhney, N., Balcom, D. and Smith, I. (1996). HyperCafé: Narrative and Aesthetic Properties of Hypervideo. In *Proceedings of ACM Hypertext '96*, ACM Press, New York, pp. 1-10

Selvin, A., Buckingham Shum, S., Sierhuis, M., Conklin, J., Zimmermann, B., Palus, C., Drath, W., Horth, D., Domingue, J., Motta, E. and Li, G. (2001). Compendium: Making Meetings into Knowledge Events. In *Knowledge Technologies*, March 4(7), Austin, TX

Shipman, F., Hsieh, H., Airhart, R., Maloor, P., Moore, J.M. (2001). The Visual Knowledge Builder: A Second Generation Spatial Hypertext. In *Proceedings of the ACM Hypertext '01*, ACM Press, New York, pp. 113-122

Shipman, F.M. III, Marshall, C.C. (1999). Spatial Hypertext: An Alternative to Navigational and Semantic Links. In *ACM Computing Surveys*. 31(4), Article n.14

Shum, S. (1990). Real and Virtual Spaces: Mapping from Spatial Cognition to Hypertext. In *Hypermedia*, 2(2), pp.133-158

Slatin, J. (1991). Reading Hypertext: Order and Coherence in a New Medium. In Delany, P., Landow, G.P. (Eds.) *Hypermedia and Literary Studies*, MIT Press, Cambridge, MA, pp.153-170

Storyspace, Eastgate Systems. http://www.eastgate.com/Storyspace.html

Streitz, N.A., Haake, J.M., Hannemann, J., Lemke, A., Schuler, W., Schütt, H., Thüring, M. (1992). SEPIA: A Cooperative Hypermedia Authoring Environment. In *Proceedings of ACM Conference on Hypertext '92*, ACM Press, New York, 1992, pp.11-22

Sumner, T., Buckingham Shum, S. (1998). From Documents to Discourse: Shifting Conceptions of Scholarly Publishing. In *Proceedings of CHI '98*, ACM Press, New York, pp.95-102

Sweetser, E. (1990). *From Etymology to Pragmatics. Metaphorical and Cultural Aspects of Semantic Structure*. Cambridge University Press.

Theall, D.F. (2000). Joyce's Practice of Intertextuality: The Anticipation of Hypermedia and Its Implications for Textual Analysis of "Finnegans Wake". In *CHWP* A.19. Jointly published with *TEXT Technology*, 9(2), Article n.19

Thüring, M., Haake, J.M., Hannemann, J. (1991). What's Eliza Doing in the Chinese Room? Incoherent Hyperdocuments - and How to Avoid Them. In *Proceedings of ACM Hypertext '91*, ACM Press, New York, pp.161-177

Tinderbox, Estgate Systems Inc. http://www.eastgate.com/Tinderbox/

Tolva, T. (1996). Ut Pictura Hyperpoesis: Spatial Form, Visuality, and the Digital Word. In *Proceedings of ACM Hypertext '96,* ACM Press, New York, pp.66-73

Trigg, R.H. (1983). *A Networked Approach to Text Handling for the Online Scientific Community*, Ph.D. Thesis, University of Maryland

Trigg, R.H., Weiser, M. (1986). TEXTNET: A Network-Based Approach to Text Handling. In *ACM Transactions on Office Information Systems*, 4(1), pp. 1-23

Trigg, R.H. (1988). Guided Tours and Tabletops: Tools for Communicating in a Hypertext Environment. *ACM Transactions on Office Information Systems*, 6 (4), pp.216-226

Vande Kopple, W.J. (1988). Metadiscourse and the Recall of Modality Markers. In *Visible Language*, 22 (1988), pp.233-272

Vasconcellos, R. (1993). Representing the Geographical Space for Visually Handicapped Students: A Case Study on Map Use. In *Proceedings of the 16th International Cartographic Conference*, vol. 2, pp.993-1004

Verhoeven, A. and Warendorf, K. (1999). External Navigation Control and Guidance for Learning with Spatial Hypermedia. In *Journal of Interactive Media in Education*, 1999(1), http://www-jime.open.ac.uk/99/1

Vertov, D. (1984). *Kino-Eye: the Writings of Dziga Vertov*. Translation by Kevin O'Brien, Berkeley, University of California Press

Walker, J. (1999). Piecing Together and Tearing Apart: Finding the Story in "Afternoon". In *Proceedings of ACM Hypertext '99*, ACM Press, New York, pp.111-117

Wertheimer, M. (1938). Laws of organization in perceptual forms. In Ellis, W.B. (Eds), *A Sourcebook of Gestalt Psycychology*. Routledge and Kegan Paul, London, pp. 71-88

Cinematic Hypertext
C. Mancini
IOS Press, 2005

Appendix: CCR Analysis of a Scholarly Hypertext

Chapter 3 comments on the results of a CCR analysis of the scholarly dissertation 'Hypertext and Suburbs', from *Sprawling Places*, by David Kolb (http://www.dkolb.org/sprawlingplaces/suburbsa.html). This appendix reports the text of the thirteen nodes composing the dissertation, the map of the hypertext and the results of the three types of analyses, in which CCR were respectively used to identify the discourse relations holding between discourse parts at the level of the connections between nodes, at the level of the connections between paragraphs within a node, and at the level of connections between the text spans within a paragraph of a node.

1. 'Hypertext and Suburbs': the Hypertext

Parallel and Not

We can make, but also qualify, a parallel between suburbs [-> **Places in General**] and hypertexts, as a way of emphasizing that the meaning of a given chunk of suburban building or real estate usually depends on its linkages to distant items. The basic comparison with hypertext is that the form of the text is not the same as the form visible on any one page or screen. It reaches beyond, just as form of the suburb is not the same as the immediately visible spatial connections. Immediate architectural form is not the same as the place form of suburban locations, because they reach out beyond the local horizon, and form wholes and networks that are not architecturally obvious. We are not sure how to express this linkage architecturally, and most suburban architectural types celebrate isolation rather than connection.

The parallel is useful, because the armature of links in a hypertext creates a "spatiality" that has more complex interrelations and dimensions than linear one-thing-after-another of physical space, or of pages in a novel. The analogy with hypertext shows how the reality of a suburb can be more complex than appears locally [-> **Horizons**], with more dimensions of movement and connection. There are other parallels [-> **Other Parallels**] as well. But the parallel between hypertext and suburbs is not perfect, for a number of reasons. The most important difference has to do with the two kinds of spatialities [-> **Two Spatialities**] formed by grammatical and spatial connection. This also has to do with the way meaning is created by adjacency [-> **Meaning and Intentions**].

Places in General

The parallel between suburbs and hypertexts can be generalized to a parallel between linkage and connection in any place and any text. Places, of whatever kind, and texts, hyper or not, get their unity through sets of meaning connections some of which are made normative. Both places and texts have their normative grammar(s) within fields of possibilities that exceed [-> **Horizons**] that grammar and which that grammar cannot control. Both places and texts exist as structures embedded within an ongoing process of re-creation and re-interpretation.

The point of the specific comparison of suburbs and hypertexts is to emphasize that the being of a suburb is not exhausted by its immediate visible vicinity. There are so many pictures of ghastly uniform suburbs stretching off to infinity, and I don't mean to deny such spiritless repetition and uniformity. But I do mean to say that that ghastly aspect is not the whole reality of the suburbs being viewed, that the motions of people's lives [-> **Changing Connections**] and the networks that intersect the visible array make of the suburb a more complex place. We need to learn how to mitigate the ghastly aspects by making those complexities and connections and networks more salient in everyday experience.

Horizons

What something is revealed to be, what it means, depends on the horizon of possibilities [-> **Rhetorical Connections**] (actions, inferences, things it might have been or done, etc.) within which it stands in contrasts. Explicit hypertext links are part of that standing within the horizon, but the items a text chunk, or a region of a place, are linked to stand close by, surrounded by a farther horizon. We can distinguish a variety of horizons for a thing, for a text, for a hypertext, for a suburban building, or for part of any place:

items the thing or place or textual fragment is linked to explicitly (the factory in the next town, the head bank, the vacation home, other parts of a machine, matching items (tables with chairs), grammatical connections, explicit textual references, and so on.); the horizon visible behind these closely linked items. In places this is still mostly the result of design; "farther out": the phenomenological horizon that is not a visible object linked to, not a visible object since it is composed of absences linked by rules of possibility; the wilder possibilities that are on that horizon but not according to rules, that break or bend or defy rules; nearby adjacencies, not themselves necessarily designed for contrast but standing in contrasts that will influence meaning and affect function; the space of possible routes toward the horizon: other ways of reading the text or acting in the space, either according to the rules or running against them; the contour of meaning surrounding this text or this place or this action, as a relatively definite perspectival construct out of surrounding possibilities.

Other Parallels

There are other parallels between suburbs and hypertexts [-> **Parallel and Not**] that could be discussed: issues of diversity, issues of justice, as the rich (in resources or links or attention) get richer, the need to open walls and gates, the need to see current structures (and walls, and links, as well as open spaces) as effects within a larger field that they don't rule over. There are also issues having to do with space and time (collage and montage) in both suburbs and hypertext design, issues of density and complexity, timing, and availability, the need for multiple maps that deny any single Official map, and, finally the way that multiple borders effect different unities, breaking down the community or textual analogues to the nation state that grabs and demands to supervise all borders.

Two Spatialities

Grammatical connections create an action space of linked areas that are "next to" one another in the sense that geographies or trajectories of action do one phase here and another phase there. For instance in an auditorium the stage and the audience area are "next to" one another in terms of action definitions even though they may be physically separated by the orchestra pit, or, in a large office building two offices on different floors may be "next to" one another for a sequence of actions that are done first here then there.

But in addition to grammatical next-to-ness, there is normal physical proximity [-> **Virtual Spatialities**]. This may or may not be grammatically important, but it will have meaning effects. The office just next door to mine may be "miles away" in terms of its function, so that trajectories of action that pass through my office never go through the one next door, but because the two offices are physically adjacent, other kinds of interaction will develop. Even if the employees never eat lunch together, or never speak to one another, the contrast between the two offices will still function as an overtone of meaning [-> **Meaning and Intention**] on their official grammatical places. Physical connection also allows the exploration of new kinds of relations that begin [-> **Travels and New Paths**] outside of grammatical links.

In a hypertext [-> **Kinds of Adjacencies**] the difference between these two kinds of connection collapses because the only connections are the links. In that sense, while the hypertext can be a useful analogue for pointing out the presence of the distant in the near, and the ways in which suburbs violate the expectations of visible architectural unity, suburbs are in fact a more complex kind of object because their physicality provides another mode of access and another kind of connection/unity.

Meaning and Intention

What makes the "spatiality" or connectivity of a hypertext different from a suburb is that in the hypertext all connections are intentional. Links are *made*. There is no parallel to the chance juxtapositions and chance meaning effects that occur in physical space [-> **Embodiment**] (and could occur in a large enough virtual space [-> **Virtual Spatialities**]). So all hypertext connections take on intentional meaning and effects [-> **Rhetorical Connections**].

If I build a McDonalds next to a music store, I may have no intention that the relation between the two be meaningful. The site for my restaurant became available through causes that have nothing to do with the adjacent music store. However, though unintended, the association and contrast of the two will still be meaningful. Philosophers from Hobbes to Derrida have pointed out that there is no stopping the generation of meaning by contiguity [-> **Horizons**]. Such meaning effects may not have been specially intended, nor need they be taken as rhetorically or normatively important (unless the local store owner wants to use them in some way, perhaps for publicity). But the effects will be there nonetheless.

On the other hand, in a standard node-and-link hypertext, nothing is next to anything else until a link is created. There are no unavoidable and uncontrollable adjacencies such as occur in physical space [-> **Kinds of Adjacencies**].

Yet, even in a hypertext, we do have to distinguish between links that are intentional and which, though they have some meaning effects, had been made for other purposes, perhaps to ease navigation, from links that have particular rhetorical effects [-> **Rhetorical Connections**], and both of these need to be distinguished from links that are normatively important.

Suburbs are more like established texts with normative readings. But our places are never totally set, in part because of spatial possibilities exceed any link or normative structure. In addition, some contemporary places are becoming especially fluid, made on the fly, more like temporary work groups than the settled institutions.

Changing Connections

Because items in (physical or virtual [-> **Virtual Spatialities**]) places are available independently of their normative grammatical connections, those connections can be altered by patterns of action that develop new accesses and connections. Living in the suburb can change its connections and grammatical norms. Such flexibility is harder to find in a hypertext, where there is no way to other parts of the text except through intentionally established connecting links. Neither on the web nor in separately published hypertexts can the reader make new connections [-> **New Connections**] that will be publicly available.

In the suburb, some intentional links are carried in quasi-permanent pipes (highways, wiring, conduits), while others exist in alterable habits and practices. Of course the fixed pipes such as highways can carry many different kinds of connections at once, or over time, and their existence will encourage certain kinds of connections and discourage others.

A communally created hypertext might be arranged to receive added links, so that there would not be a single permanent armature but an ongoing process of linking. In this case some mechanism would have to be set up for the elimination of links, or at least for their grouping into separate path sets, or else the text would become so cluttered that its links would be useless. (Such a text would be one way of emphasizing the non-finality of structure and embeddedness of formal systems within a process of reinterpretation.)

We are more used to the change of connections over time in physical space, though sometimes the relative permanence of physical adjacencies and architectural effects can fool us into thinking that a place's meaning and use are more stable than they really are.

Rhetorical Connections

It is not the same to say that a connection is meaningful, or that it is intentional, or that it creates a rhetorical effect, or that it is normative.

Each of these can each be true without the others being true. Meaningful connections need not be intentional, rhetorical effects need not be normative, meaningful connections might not have any noticeable rhetorical effect, and so on. A major distinction lies between normativity and the other terms. Norms legitimize a selection from among possible or actual meaningful, rhetorical, or intentional connections [-> **Meaning and Intention**].

Place grammars legitimize only certain kinds of actions and connections and divisions in the place. But all grammars remain surrounded by wilder possibilities and connections.

In a hypertext it may be that there are many links, but only some of them are normative: these might be suggested or even forced by the author, with the others remaining as a reserve for further exploration. But whether or not the authorial links are so divided, there will always be yet other unlinked potential connections, as there are in any text, which have their effects as you travel on the links. Echoes and contrasts will happen even among items that are not linked.

Despite this excess, we cannot do without normative connections. Echoes and similarities and contrasts will have their effects whether or not there are explicit links. But there still have to be specific links, because if everything links to everything, or nothing links to anything, the echoes and contrasts will themselves have nothing to work against and with, and this will neutralize their effects. Although a given definition will never succeed in dominating the flow of meaning, if there were no place for a horizon to form around, there would be no way to distinguish any of the infinite echoes. We cannot read "the general text." The space of difference cannot be made to purely appear, since appearance is always as something definite against the space of difference.

Travels and New Paths

Here is one problematic aspect to the comparison of place linkage and hypertext linkage: In a hypertext there is the structure of the set of links in the text, and there is also the envisioned structure and history created on the occasion of a particular reading of the text. The link structure provides possible paths but not an actual journey. Some literary hypertext theorists argue that it is the unique event of a particular reading, which creates "the text." I find this view unsatisfactory for the same reasons that it would be unsatisfactory to argue that a symphony or a play exists uniquely in each performance and not also in the score or script. The full reality of the work must involve both, so that each can provide ways to criticize the other. A performance of a play or a reading of a hypertext could be inadequate to what is there in the text; on the other hand a script could be unperformable, or a hypertext structure so convoluted that it was unreadable.

The point in relation to suburbs is that a suburban place is structured by its skein of normative connections, not just by the itineraries of your or my particular life [-> **Changing Connections**] in the suburbs, which will actualize only some of the "built-in" connections. However, as with texts, each may be used to criticize the other: my daily life might not take adequate advantage of the connections available, or, as too often happens, the poverty of daily living might show up the thinness of the normative connections. As with art, density of available connection is important for the richness of life.

Kinds of Adjacencies

Books provide an intermediate case for two kinds of connection. Parts of the book will be "linked" by intentional connection to distant parts: one page may contain a reference to a distant page, or a sentence contain a footnote number linking to note in the back of the book. Then there is the linear sequence of materials from page to page, which is both a physical and an intentional connection. There is, also, the physical availability of the pages at the edge of the book; I can stick my finger in two-thirds of the way through, or turn thirty pages at once to see what comes up; this allows abrupt non-intentional juxtapositions of different parts of the book, somewhat like finding something uncontrollably next-door [-> **Meaning And Intention**] to where you build.

Hypertexts seldom have any analogue to this physical availability [-> **Embodiment**], though something like it can be built in, for instance, by providing a map of the hypertext that allows one to jump to another part of the text without following any intentional link. Such maps are, however, labelled, so that the jump is not quite as unintentional as jumping through book pages might be.

Something more like the abrupt nonintentional adjaciencies of physical space could be built into a hypertext by introducing randomized contacts, or a skein of built-in connectors independent of meaning or order of creation, etc. Such connectors could be random, or partly intentional, as in a library or bookstore where there is some order but unexpected encounters can still happen.

Or, there could be automatic link creation. There is another paradigm of hypertext, not as linked chunks of text, but as fields of text from which search engines and algorithms create links on the fly depending on user interest. For instance, imagine software that watches what you are writing and adds links to other texts based on statistics about your use of words, or questions you ask in the text, or metaphors you create. We don't have intelligent enough software to do this well, though there are beginnings in some proposals for extending the capabilities of the Web, and there have been demonstrations of such link-on-the-fly programs. This type of hypertext does not have a fixed armature of links made intentionally by an author, though its links do represent priorities that were jointly set up by the authors of the software and observations of the behavior of the users. (It is possible, of course, that such a system might suggest a link based on regularities in my writing or word use that I was totally unaware of and might find very helpful.)

Embodiment

In contrasting a kind of place with a kind of hypertext, we need to remember that our embodiment, our being-in-place, is far stronger and denser than our being-in-texts, even though places can be seen as a kind of text-ure. Being in position and being oriented in place can be oppressive or liberating in ways that text cannot manage. (The two may tend to come together as texts become multimedia and then mutate toward virtual realities.) Because embodiment is unavoidable (even virtual places are such because they offer some analogue to embodiment), design in the traditional sense remains very important amid all the talk about linkage and virtualities.

New Connections

Many hypertext implementations that are richer in features than the Web make use of link servers, so that different sets of links can be set up on the same base text. Most of these are only laboratory demonstration projects, but there are some annotation services that let readers add comments or links to web pages, though the results are available only to those who subscribe to the same link servers. While link servers enrich the hypertextual features of texts, they tend to create individualized sets of links, which make it more difficult to change normative textual connections for a community. What they can do is alter the *idea* of normative textual connections, replacing them with published sets of links, some of which may become accepted and normative.

It is difficult to envision a place analogue to this process, because physical adjacency and architectural effects are "there" whether or not they are intended. Their effects on my building and my activities are not intentional links, nor are they avoidable. The car wash next door, or the threateningly large office building down the block, cannot be wished away or made invisible by linking around them. On the other hand, physical adjacencies and architectural effects provide possibilities for exploration and new connection in an intermediate zone [-> **Two Spatialities**] between invisibility and fully intentional linkage.

Virtual Spatialities

It might seem that in virtual places there would be a collapse of the distinction [-> **Meaning and Intention**] between physical proximity and intentional linkage. The grammatical place-connections would be the same as the virtual spatial connections establishing the virtual world. However, this is not so; the distinction does hold for virtual places, because a virtual place does not have to occupy the whole of a virtual area. It's true that the underlying connections in a virtual world are intentionally designed, but that does not make them the same as the normative or grammatical connections that select out certain areas [-> **Rhetorical Connections**] within that virtual world as parts of a socially grammatized place.

For instance, if a virtual world made available virtual real estate for development, my virtual place could find itself next to new places outside my control -- I didn't want a virtual McDonald's next door -- and this would affect the meaning of my place and also allow non-grammatical explorations and connections, just as happens in physical space.

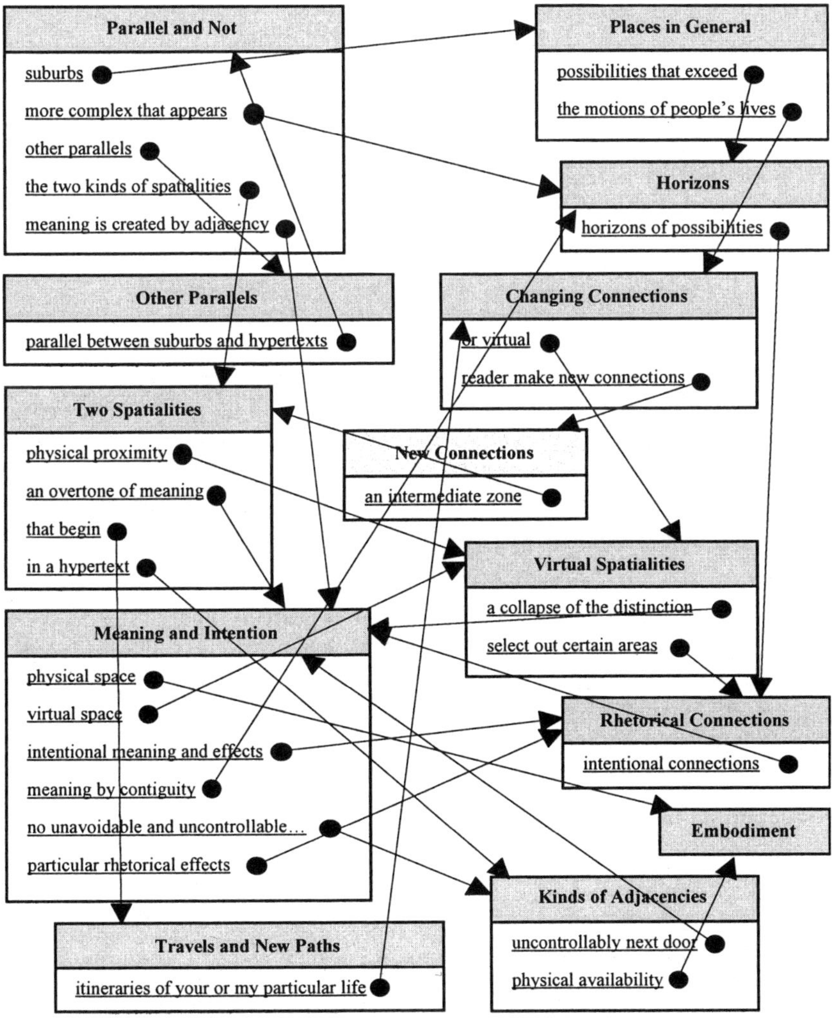

Figure App.1. Map of Hypertext and Suburbs, from *Sprawling Places* (Kolb, 2004)

2. Analysis of the relations between nodes

Parallel and Not

We can make, but also qualify, a parallel between suburbs [-> **Places in General**] and hypertexts, as a way of emphasizing that the meaning of a given chunk of suburban building or real estate usually depends on its linkages to distant items. The basic comparison with hypertext is that the form of the text is not the same as the form visible on any one page or screen. It reaches beyond, just as form of the suburb is not the same as the immediately visible spatial connections. Immediate architectural form is not the same as the place form of suburban locations, because they reach out beyond the local horizon, and form wholes and networks that are not architecturally obvious. We are not sure how to express this linkage architecturally, and most suburban architectural types celebrate isolation rather than connection.

The parallel is useful, because the armature of links in a hypertext creates a "spatiality" that has more complex interrelations and dimensions than linear one-thing-after-another of physical space, or of pages in a novel. The analogy with hypertext shows how the reality of a suburb can be more complex than appears locally [-> **Horizons**], with more dimensions of movement and connection. There are other parallels [-> **Other Parallels**] as well. But the parallel between hypertext and suburbs is not perfect, for a number of reasons. The most important difference has to do with the two kinds of spatialities [-> **Two Spatialities**] formed by grammatical and spatial connection. This also has to do with the way meaning is created by adjacency [-> **Meaning and Intentions**].

suburbs -> (<< *elaboration*) **Places in General**
more complex that appears locally -> (<< *argument*) **Horizons**
other parallels -> (<< *elaboration*) **Other Parallels**
the two kinds of spatialities -> (<< *argument*) **Two Spatialities**
meaning is created by adjacency -> (<< *argument*) **Meaning and Intentions**

Places in General

The parallel between suburbs and hypertexts can be generalized to a parallel between linkage and connection in any place and any text. Places, of whatever kind, and texts, hyper or not, get their unity through sets of meaning connections some of which are made normative. Both places and texts have their normative grammar(s) within fields of possibilities that exceed [-> **Horizons**] that grammar and which that grammar cannot control. Both places and texts exist as structures embedded within an ongoing process of re-creation and re-interpretation.

The point of the specific comparison of suburbs and hypertexts is to emphasize that the being of a suburb is not exhausted by its immediate visible vicinity. There are so many pictures of ghastly uniform suburbs stretching off to infinity, and I don't mean to deny such spiritless repetition and uniformity. But I do mean to say that that ghastly aspect is not the whole reality of the suburbs being viewed, that the motions of people's lives [-> **Changing Connections**] and the networks that intersect the visible array make of the suburb a more complex place. We need to learn how to mitigate the ghastly aspects by making those complexities and connections and networks more salient in everyday experience.

possibilities that exceed -> (<< *elaboration*) **Horizons**
the motions of people's lives -> (<< *background*) **Changing Connections**

Horizons

What something is revealed to be, what it means, depends on the horizon of possibilities [-> **Rhetorical Connections**] (actions, inferences, things it might have been or done, etc.) within which it stands in contrasts. Explicit hypertext links are part of that standing within the horizon, but the items a text chunk, or a region of a place, are linked to stand close by, surrounded by a farther horizon. We can distinguish a variety of horizons for a thing, for a text, for a hypertext, for a suburban building, or for part of any place:

items the thing or place or textual fragment is linked to explicitly (the factory in the next town, the head bank, the vacation home, other parts of a machine, matching items (tables with chairs), grammatical connections, explicit textual references, and so on.); the horizon visible behind these closely linked items. In places this is still mostly the result of design; "farther out": the phenomenological horizon that is not a visible object linked to, not a visible object since it is composed of absences linked by rules of possibility; the wilder possibilities that are on that horizon but not according to rules, that break or bend or defy rules; nearby adjacencies, not themselves necessarily designed for contrast but standing in contrasts that will influence meaning and affect function; the space of possible routes toward the horizon: other ways of reading the text or acting in the space, either according to the rules or running against them; the contour of meaning surrounding this text or this place or this action, as a relatively definite perspectival construct out of surrounding possibilities.

horizons of possibilities -> (<< *background*) **Rhetorical Connections**

Other Parallels

There are other parallels between suburbs and hypertexts [-> **Parallel and Not**] that could be discussed: issues of diversity, issues of justice, as the rich (in resources or links or attention) get richer, the need to open walls and gates, the need to see current structures (and walls, and links, as well as open spaces) as effects within a larger field that they don't rule over. There are also issues having to do with space and time (collage and montage) in both suburbs and hypertext design, issues of density and complexity, timing, and availability, the need for multiple maps that deny any single Official map, and, finally the way that multiple borders effect different unities, breaking down the community or textual analogues to the nation state that grabs and demands to supervise all borders.

parallel between suburbs and hypertexts -> (<< *enumerated*) **Parallel And Not**

Two Spatialities

Grammatical connections create an action space of linked areas that are "next to" one another in the sense that geographies or trajectories of action do one phase here and another phase there. For instance in an auditorium the stage and the audience area are "next to" one another in terms of action definitions even though they may be physically separated by the orchestra pit, or, in a large office building two offices on different floors may be "next to" one another for a sequence of actions that are done first here then there.

But in addition to grammatical next-to-ness, there is normal physical proximity [-> **Virtual Spatialities**]. This may or may not be grammatically important, but it will have meaning effects. The office just next door to mine may be "miles away" in terms of its function, so that trajectories of action that pass through my office never go through the one next door, but because the two offices are physically adjacent, other kinds of interaction will develop. Even if the employees never eat lunch together, or never speak to one another, the contrast between the two offices will still function as an overtone of meaning [-> **Meaning and Intention**] on their official grammatical places. Physical connection also allows the exploration of new kinds of relations that begin [-> **Travels and New Paths**] outside of grammatical links.

In a hypertext [-> **Kinds of Adjacencies**] the difference between these two kinds of connection collapses because the only connections are the links. In that sense, while the hypertext can be a useful analogue for pointing out the presence of the distant in the near, and the ways in which suburbs violate the expectations of visible architectural unity, suburbs are in fact a more complex kind of object because their physicality provides another mode of access and another kind of connection/unity.

physical proximity -> (<< *elaboration*) **Virtual Spatialities**
an overtone of meaning -> (<< *elaboration*) **Meaning and Intention**
that begin -> (<< *elaboration*) **Travels and New Paths**
in a hypertext -> (<< *elaboration*) **Kinds of Adjacencies**

Meaning and Intention

What makes the "spatiality" or connectivity of a hypertext different from a suburb is that in the hypertext all connections are intentional. Links are *made*. There is no parallel to the chance juxtapositions and chance meaning effects that occur in physical space [-> **Embodiment**] (and could occur in a large enough virtual space [-> **Virtual Spatialities**]). So all hypertext connections take on intentional meaning and effects [-> **Rhetorical Connections**].

If I build a McDonalds next to a music store, I may have no intention that the relation between the two be meaningful. The site for my restaurant became available through causes that have nothing to do with the adjacent music store. However, though unintended, the association and contrast of the two will still be meaningful. Philosophers from Hobbes to Derrida have pointed out that there is no stopping the generation of meaning by contiguity [-> **Horizons**]. Such meaning effects may not have been specially intended, nor need they be taken as rhetorically or normatively important (unless the local store owner wants to use them in some way, perhaps for publicity). But the effects will be there nonetheless.

On the other hand, in a standard node-and-link hypertext, nothing is next to anything else until a link is created. There are no unavoidable and uncontrollable adjacencies such as occur in physical space [-> **Kinds of Adjacencies**].

Yet, even in a hypertext, we do have to distinguish between links that are intentional and which, though they have some meaning effects, had been made for other purposes, perhaps to ease navigation, from links that have particular rhetorical effects [-> **Rhetorical Connections**], and both of these need to be distinguished from links that are normatively important.

Suburbs are more like established texts with normative readings. But our places are never totally set, in part because of spatial possibilities exceed any link or normative structure. In addition, some contemporary places are becoming especially fluid, made on the fly, more like temporary work groups than the settled institutions.

physical space -> (<< *background*) **Embodiment**
virtual space -> (<< *elaboration*) **Virtual Spatialities**
intentional meaning and effects -> (<< *elaboration*) **Rhetorical Connections**
meaning by contiguity -> (<< *elaboration*) **Horizons**
no unavoidable and ... -> (<< *elaboration*) **Kinds Of Adjacencies**
particular rhetorical effects -> (<< *background*) **Rhetorical Connections**

Changing Connections

Because items in (physical or virtual [-> **Virtual Spatialities**]) places are available independently of their normative grammatical connections, those connections can be altered by patterns of action that develop new accesses and connections. Living in the suburb can change its connections and grammatical norms. Such flexibility is harder to find in a hypertext, where there is no way to other parts of the text except through intentionally established connecting links. Neither on the web nor in separately published hypertexts can the reader make new connections [-> **New Connections**] that will be publicly available.

In the suburb, some intentional links are carried in quasi-permanent pipes (highways, wiring, conduits), while others exist in alterable habits and practices. Of course the fixed pipes such as highways can carry many different kinds of connections at once, or over time, and their existence will encourage certain kinds of connections and discourage others.

A communally created hypertext might be arranged to receive added links, so that there would not be a single permanent armature but an ongoing process of linking. In this case some mechanism would have to be set up for the elimination of links, or at least for their grouping into separate path sets, or else the text would become so cluttered that its links would be useless. (Such a text would be one way of emphasizing the non-finality of structure and embeddedness of formal systems within a process of reinterpretation.)

We are more used to the change of connections over time in physical space, though sometimes the relative permanence of physical adjacencies and architectural effects can fool us into thinking that a place's meaning and use are more stable than they really are.

or virtual -> (<< *elaboration*) **Virtual Spatialities**
reader make new connections -> (<< *elaboration*) **New Connections**

Rhetorical Connections

It is not the same to say that a connection is meaningful, or that it is intentional, or that it creates a rhetorical effect, or that it is normative.

Each of these can each be true without the others being true. Meaningful connections need not be intentional, rhetorical effects need not be normative, meaningful connections might not have any noticeable rhetorical effect, and so on. A major distinction lies between normativity and the other terms. Norms legitimize a selection from among possible or actual meaningful, rhetorical, or intentional connections [-> **Meaning and Intention**].

Place grammars legitimize only certain kinds of actions and connections and divisions in the place. But all grammars remain surrounded by wilder possibilities and connections.

In a hypertext it may be that there are many links, but only some of them are normative: these might be suggested or even forced by the author, with the others remaining as a reserve for further exploration. But whether or not the authorial links are so divided, there will always be yet other unlinked potential connections, as there are in any text, which have their effects as you travel on the links. Echoes and contrasts will happen even among items that are not linked.

Despite this excess, we cannot do without normative connections. Echoes and similarities and contrasts will have their effects whether or not there are explicit links. But there still have to be specific links, because if everything links to everything, or nothing links to anything, the echoes and contrasts will themselves have nothing to work against and with, and this will neutralize their effects. Although a given definition will never succeed in dominating the flow of meaning, if there were no place for a horizon to form around, there would be no way to distinguish any of the infinite echoes. We cannot read "the general text." The space of difference cannot be made to purely appear, since appearance is always as something definite against the space of difference.

intentional connections -> (<< *elaboration*) **Meaning and Intention**

Travels and New Paths

Here is one problematic aspect to the comparison of place linkage and hypertext linkage: In a hypertext there is the structure of the set of links in the text, and there is also the envisioned structure and history created on the occasion of a particular reading of the text. The link structure provides possible paths but not an actual journey. Some literary hypertext theorists argue that it is the unique event of a particular reading, which creates "the text." I find this view unsatisfactory for the same reasons that it would be unsatisfactory to argue that a symphony or a play exists uniquely in each performance and not also in the score or script. The full reality of the work must involve both, so that each can provide ways to criticize the other. A performance of a play or a reading of a hypertext could be inadequate to what is there in the text; on the other hand a script could be unperformable, or a hypertext structure so convoluted that it was unreadable.

The point in relation to suburbs is that a suburban place is structured by its skein of normative connections, not just by the itineraries of your or my particular life [-> **Changing Connections**] in the suburbs, which will actualize only some of the "built-in" connections. However, as with texts, each may be used to criticize the other: my daily life might not take adequate advantage of the connections available, or, as too often happens, the poverty of daily living might show up the thinness of the normative connections. As with art, density of available connection is important for the richness of life.

itineraries of your or my particular life -> (<< *elaboration*) **Changing Connections**

Kinds of Adjacencies

Books provide an intermediate case for two kinds of connection. Parts of the book will be "linked" by intentional connection to distant parts: one page may contain a reference to a distant page, or a sentence contain a footnote number linking to note in the back of the book. Then there is the linear sequence of materials from page to page, which is both a physical and an intentional connection. There is, also, the physical availability of the pages at the edge of the book; I can stick my finger in two-thirds of the way through, or turn thirty pages at once to see what comes up; this allows abrupt non-intentional juxtapositions of different parts of the book, somewhat like finding something uncontrollably next-door [-> **Meaning And Intention**] to where you build.

Hypertexts seldom have any analogue to this physical availability [-> **Embodiment**], though something like it can be built in, for instance, by providing a map of the hypertext that allows one to jump to another part of the text without following any intentional link. Such maps are, however, labelled, so that the jump is not quite as unintentional as jumping through book pages might be.

Something more like the abrupt nonintentional adjaciencies of physical space could be built into a hypertext by introducing randomized contacts, or a skein of built-in connectors independent of meaning or order of creation, etc. Such connectors could be random, or partly intentional, as in a library or bookstore where there is some order but unexpected encounters can still happen.

Or, there could be automatic link creation. There is another paradigm of hypertext, not as linked chunks of text, but as fields of text from which search engines and algorithms create links on the fly depending on user interest. For instance, imagine software that watches what you are writing and adds links to other texts based on statistics about your use of words, or questions you ask in the text, or metaphors you create. We don't have intelligent enough software to do this well, though there are beginnings in some proposals for extending the capabilities of the Web, and there have been demonstrations of such link-on-the-fly programs. This type of hypertext does not have a fixed armature of links made intentionally by an author, though its links do represent priorities that were jointly set up by the authors of the software and observations of the behavior of the users. (It is possible, of course, that such a system might suggest a link based on regularities in my writing or word use that I was totally unaware of and might find very helpful.)

uncontrollably next-door -> (<< *elaboration*) **Meaning and Intention**
physical availability -> (<< *elaboration*) **Embodiment**

New Connections

Many hypertext implementations that are richer in features than the Web make use of link servers, so that different sets of links can be set up on the same base text. Most of these are only laboratory demonstration projects, but there are some annotation services that let readers add comments or links to web pages, though the results are available only to those who subscribe to the same link servers. While link servers enrich the hypertextual features of texts, they tend to create individualized sets of links, which make it more difficult to change normative textual connections for a community. What they can do is alter the *idea* of normative textual connections, replacing them with published sets of links, some of which may become accepted and normative.

It is difficult to envision a place analogue to this process, because physical adjacency and architectural effects are "there" whether or not they are intended. Their effects on my building and my activities are not intentional links, nor are they avoidable. The car wash next door, or the threateningly large office building down the block, cannot be wished away or made invisible by linking around them. On the other hand, physical adjacencies and architectural effects provide possibilities for exploration and new connection in an intermediate zone [-> **Two Spatialities**] between invisibility and fully intentional linkage.

an intermediate zone -> (<< *background*) **Two Spatialities**

Virtual Spatialities

It might seem that in virtual places there would be a collapse of the distinction [-> **Meaning and Intention**] between physical proximity and intentional linkage. The grammatical place-connections would be the same as the virtual spatial connections establishing the virtual world. However, this is not so; the distinction does hold for virtual places, because a virtual place does not have to occupy the whole of a virtual area. It's true that the underlying connections in a virtual world are intentionally designed, but that does not make them the same as the normative or grammatical connections that select out certain areas [-> **Rhetorical Connections**] within that virtual world as parts of a socially grammatized place.

For instance, if a virtual world made available virtual real estate for development, my virtual place could find itself next to new places outside my control -- I didn't want a virtual McDonald's next door -- and this would affect the meaning of my place and also allow non-grammatical explorations and connections, just as happens in physical space.

a collapse of the distinction -> (<< *background*) **Meaning and Intention**
select out certain areas -> (<< *background*) **Rhetorical Connections**

3. Analysis of the relations between paragraphs within a node

Parallel and Not

elaboration

We can make, but also qualify, a parallel between suburbs [-> **Places in General**] and hypertexts, as a way of emphasizing that the meaning of a given chunk of suburban building or real estate usually depends on its linkages to distant items. The basic comparison with hypertext is that the form of the text is not the same as the form visible on any one page or screen. It reaches beyond, just as form of the suburb is not the same as the immediately visible spatial connections. Immediate architectural form is not the same as the place form of suburban locations, because they reach out beyond the local horizon, and form wholes and networks that are not architecturally obvious. We are not sure how to express this linkage architecturally, and most suburban architectural types celebrate isolation rather than connection.

The parallel is useful, because the armature of links in a hypertext creates a "spatiality" that has more complex interrelations and dimensions than linear one-thing-after-another of physical space, or of pages in a novel. The analogy with hypertext shows how the reality of a suburb can be more complex than appears locally [-> **Horizons**], with more dimensions of movement and connection. There are other parallels [-> **Other Parallels**] as well. But the parallel between hypertext and suburbs is not perfect, for a number of reasons. The most important difference has to do with the two kinds of spatialities [-> **Two Spatialities**] formed by grammatical and spatial connection. This also has to do with the way meaning is created by adjacency [-> **Meaning and Intentions**].

Places in General

elaboration

The parallel between suburbs and hypertexts can be generalized to a parallel between linkage and connection in any place and any text. Places, of whatever kind, and texts, hyper or not, get their unity through sets of meaning connections some of which are made normative. Both places and texts have their normative grammar(s) within fields of possibilities that exceed [-> **Horizons**] that grammar and which that grammar cannot control. Both places and texts exist as structures embedded within an ongoing process of re-creation and re-interpretation.

The point of the specific comparison of suburbs and hypertexts is to emphasize that the being of a suburb is not exhausted by its immediate visible vicinity. There are so many pictures of ghastly uniform suburbs stretching off to infinity, and I don't mean to deny such spiritless repetition and uniformity. But I do mean to say that that ghastly aspect is not the whole reality of the suburbs being viewed, that the motions of people's lives [-> **Changing Connections**] and the networks that intersect the visible array make of the suburb a more complex place. We need to learn how to mitigate the ghastly aspects by making those complexities and connections and networks more salient in everyday experience.

Horizons

elaboration

What something is revealed to be, what it means, depends on the horizon of possibilities [-> **Rhetorical Connections**] (actions, inferences, things it might have been or done, etc.) within which it stands in contrasts. Explicit hypertext links are part of that standing within the horizon, but the items a text chunk, or a region of a place, are linked to stand close by, surrounded by a farther horizon. We can distinguish a variety of horizons for a thing, for a text, for a hypertext, for a suburban building, or for part of any place:

items the thing or place or textual fragment is linked to explicitly (the factory in the next town, the head bank, the vacation home, other parts of a machine, matching items (tables with chairs), grammatical connections, explicit textual references, and so on.); the horizon visible behind these closely linked items. In places this is still mostly the result of design; "farther out": the phenomenological horizon that is not a visible object linked to, not a visible object since it is composed of absences linked by rules of possibility; the wilder possibilities that are on that horizon but not according to rules, that break or bend or defy rules; nearby adjacencies, not themselves necessarily designed for contrast but standing in contrasts that will influence meaning and affect function; the space of possible routes toward the horizon: other ways of reading the text or acting in the space, either according to the rules or running against them; the contour of meaning surrounding this text or this place or this action, as a relatively definite perspectival construct out of surrounding possibilities.

Two Spatialities

enumeration

Grammatical connections create an action space of linked areas that are "next to" one another in the sense that geographies or trajectories of action do one phase here and another phase there. For instance in an auditorium the stage and the audience area are "next to" one another in terms of action definitions even though they may be physically separated by the orchestra pit, or, in a large office building two offices on different floors may be "next to" one another for a sequence of actions that are done first here then there.

contrast

similarity

But in addition to grammatical next-to-ness, there is normal physical proximity [-> **Virtual Spatialities**]. This may or may not be grammatically important, but it will have meaning effects. The office just next door to mine may be "miles away" in terms of its function, so that trajectories of action that pass through my office never go through the one next door, but because the two offices are physically adjacent, other kinds of interaction will develop. Even if the employees never eat lunch together, or never speak to one another, the contrast between the two offices will still function as an overtone of meaning [-> **Meaning and Intentions**] on their official grammatical places. Physical connection also allows the exploration of new kinds of relations that begin [-> **Travels and New Paths**] outside of grammatical links.

In a hypertext [-> **Kinds of Adjacencies**] the difference between these two kinds of connection collapses because the only connections are the links. In that sense, while the hypertext can be a useful analogue for pointing out the presence of the distant in the near, and the ways in which suburbs violate the expectations of visible architectural unity, suburbs are in fact a more complex kind of object because their physicality provides another mode of access and another kind of connection/unity.

Meaning and Intention

contrast

What makes the "spatiality" or connectivity of a hypertext different from a suburb is that in the hypertext all connections are intentional. Links are *made*. There is no parallel to the chance juxtapositions and chance meaning effects that occur in physical space [-> **Embodiment**] (and could occur in a large enough virtual space [-> **Virtual Spatialities**]). So all hypertext connections take on intentional meaning and effects [-> **Rhetorical Connections**].

similarity

enumeration

If I build a McDonalds next to a music store, I may have no intention that the relation between the two be meaningful. The site for my restaurant became available through causes that have nothing to do with the adjacent music store. However, though unintended, the association and contrast of the two will still be meaningful. Philosophers from Hobbes to Derrida have pointed out that there is no stopping the generation of meaning by contiguity [-> **Horizons**]. Such meaning effects may not have been specially intended, nor need they be taken as rhetorically or normatively important (unless the local store owner wants to use them in some way, perhaps for publicity). But the effects will be there nonetheless.

contrast

On the other hand, in a standard node-and-link hypertext, nothing is next to anything else until a link is created. There are no unavoidable and uncontrollable adjacencies such as occur in physical space [-> **Kinds of Adjacencies**].

contrast

contrast

Yet, even in a hypertext, we do have to distinguish between links that are intentional and which, though they have some meaning effects, had been made for other purposes, perhaps to ease navigation, from links that have particular rhetorical effects [-> **Rhetorical Connections**], and both of these need to be distinguished from links that are normatively important.

Suburbs are more like established texts with normative readings. But our places are never totally set, in part because of spatial possibilities exceed any link or normative structure. In addition, some contemporary places are becoming especially fluid, made on the fly, more like temporary work groups than the settled institutions.

similarity

Changing Connections

contrast

Because items in (physical or virtual [-> **Virtual Spatialities**]) places are available independently of their normative grammatical connections, those connections can be altered by patterns of action that develop new accesses and connections. Living in the suburb can change its connections and grammatical norms. Such flexibility is harder to find in a hypertext, where there is no way to other parts of the text except through intentionally established connecting links. Neither on the web nor in separately published hypertexts can the reader make new connections [-> **New Connections**] that will be publicly available.

contrast

contrast

In the suburb, some intentional links are carried in quasi-permanent pipes (highways, wiring, conduits), while others exist in alterable habits and practices. Of course the fixed pipes such as highways can carry many different kinds of connections at once, or over time, and their existence will encourage certain kinds of connections and discourage others.

A communally created hypertext might be arranged to receive added links, so that there would not be a single permanent armature but an ongoing process of linking. In this case some mechanism would have to be set up for the elimination of links, or at least for their grouping into separate path sets, or else the text would become so cluttered that its links would be useless. (Such a text would be one way of emphasizing the non-finality of structure and embeddedness of formal systems within a process of reinterpretation.)

similarity

contrast

We are more used to the change of connections over time in physical space, though sometimes the relative permanence of physical adjacencies and architectural effects can fool us into thinking that a place's meaning and use are more stable than they really are.

Rhetorical Connections

elaboration

It is not the same to say that a connection is meaningful, or that it is intentional, or that it creates a rhetorical effect, or that it is normative.

enumeration

elaboration

Each of these can each be true without the others being true. Meaningful connections need not be intentional, rhetorical effects need not be normative, meaningful connections might not have any noticeable rhetorical effect, and so on. A major distinction lies between normativity and the other terms. Norms legitimize a selection from among possible or actual meaningful, rhetorical, or intentional connections [-> **Meaning and Intention**].

Place grammars legitimize only certain kinds of actions and connections and divisions in the place. But all grammars remain surrounded by wilder possibilities and connections.

elaboratio

concession

elaboration

In a hypertext it may be that there are many links, but only some of them are normative: these might be suggested or even forced by the author, with the others remaining as a reserve for further exploration. But whether or not the authorial links are so divided, there will always be yet other unlinked potential connections, as there are in any text, which have their effects as you travel on the links. Echoes and contrasts will happen even among items that are not linked.

Despite this excess, we cannot do without normative connections. Echoes and similarities and contrasts will have their effects whether or not there are explicit links. But there still have to be specific links, because if everything links to everything, or nothing links to anything, the echoes and contrasts will themselves have nothing to work against and with, and this will neutralize their effects. Although a given definition will never succeed in dominating the flow of meaning, if there were no place for a horizon to form around, there would be no way to distinguish any of the infinite echoes. We cannot read "the general text." The space of difference cannot be made to purely appear, since appearance is always as something definite against the space of difference.

concession

Travels and New Paths

Here is one problematic aspect to the comparison of place linkage and hypertext linkage: In a hypertext there is the structure of the set of links in the text, and there is also the envisioned structure and history created on the occasion of a particular reading of the text. The link structure provides possible paths but not an actual journey. Some literary hypertext theorists argue that it is the unique event of a particular reading, which creates "the text." I find this view unsatisfactory for the same reasons that it would be unsatisfactory to argue that a symphony or a play exists uniquely in each performance and not also in the score or script. The full reality of the work must involve both, so that each can provide ways to criticize the other. A performance of a play or a reading of a hypertext could be inadequate to what is there in the text; on the other hand a script could be unperformable, or a hypertext structure so convoluted that it was unreadable.

similarity

The point in relation to suburbs is that a suburban place is structured by its skein of normative connections, not just by the itineraries of your or my particular life [-> **Changing Connections**] in the suburbs, which will actualize only some of the "built-in" connections. However, as with texts, each may be used to criticize the other: my daily life might not take adequate advantage of the connections available, or, as too often happens, the poverty of daily living might show up the thinness of the normative connections. As with art, density of available connection is important for the richness of life.

Kinds of Adjacencies

Books provide an intermediate case for two kinds of connection. Parts of the book will be "linked" by intentional connection to distant parts: one page may contain a reference to a distant page, or a sentence contain a footnote number linking to note in the back of the book. Then there is the linear sequence of materials from page to page, which is both a physical and an intentional connection. There is, also, the physical availability of the pages at the edge of the book; I can stick my finger in two-thirds of the way through, or turn thirty pages at once to see what comes up; this allows abrupt non-intentional juxtapositions of different parts of the book, somewhat like finding something uncontrollably next-door [-> **Meaning And Intention**] to where you build.

contrast

similarity

Hypertexts seldom have any analogue to this physical availability [-> **Embodiment**], though something like it can be built in, for instance, by providing a map of the hypertext that allows one to jump to another part of the text without following any intentional link. Such maps are, however, labelled, so that the jump is not quite as unintentional as jumping through book pages might be.

contrast

Something more like the abrupt nonintentional adjaciencies of physical space could be built into a hypertext by introducing randomized contacts, or a skein of built-in connectors independent of meaning or order of creation, etc. Such connectors could be random, or partly intentional, as in a library or bookstore where there is some order but unexpected encounters can still happen.

alternative

Or, there could be automatic link creation. There is another paradigm of hypertext, not as linked chunks of text, but as fields of text from which search engines and algorithms create links on the fly depending on user interest. For instance, imagine software that watches what you are writing and adds links to other texts based on statistics about your use of words, or questions you ask in the text, or metaphors you create. We don't have intelligent enough software to do this well, though there are beginnings in some proposals for extending the capabilities of the Web, and there have been demonstrations of such link-on-the-fly programs. This type of hypertext does not have a fixed armature of links made intentionally by an author, though its links do represent priorities that were jointly set up by the authors of the software and observations of the behavior of the users. (It is possible, of course, that such a system might suggest a link based on regularities in my writing or word use that I was totally unaware of and might find very helpful.)

New Connections

Many hypertext implementations that are richer in features than the Web make use of link servers, so that different sets of links can be set up on the same base text. Most of these are only laboratory demonstration projects, but there are some annotation services that let readers add comments or links to web pages, though the results are available only to those who subscribe to the same link servers. While link servers enrich the hypertextual features of texts, they tend to create individualized sets of links, which make it more difficult to change normative textual connections for a community. What they can do is alter the *idea* of normative textual connections, replacing them with published sets of links, some of which may become accepted and normative.

contrast

It is difficult to envision a place analogue to this process, because physical adjacency and architectural effects are "there" whether or not they are intended. Their effects on my building and my activities are not intentional links, nor are they avoidable. The car wash next door, or the threateningly large office building down the block, cannot be wished away or made invisible by linking around them. On the other hand, physical adjacencies and architectural effects provide possibilities for exploration and new connection in an intermediate zone [-> **Two Spatialities**] between invisibility and fully intentional linkage.

Virtual Spatialities

It might seem that in virtual places there would be a collapse of the distinction [-> **Meaning and Intention**] between physical proximity and intentional linkage. The grammatical place-connections would be the same as the virtual spatial connections establishing the virtual world. However, this is not so; the distinction does hold for virtual places, because a virtual place does not have to occupy the whole of a virtual area. It's true that the underlying connections in a virtual world are intentionally designed, but that does not make them the same as the normative or grammatical connections that select out certain areas [-> **Rhetorical Connections**] within that virtual world as parts of a socially grammatized place.

elaboration

For instance, if a virtual world made available virtual real estate for development, my virtual place could find itself next to new places outside my control -- I didn't want a virtual McDonald's next door -- and this would affect the meaning of my place and also allow non-grammatical explorations and connections, just as happens in physical space.

4. Analysis of relations between text spans within a paragraph of a node

Parallel and Not

[1.a.1]We can make, [1.a.2]but also qualify, a parallel between suburbs and hypertexts, [1.b]as a way of emphasizing that the meaning of a given chunk of suburban building or real estate usually depends on its linkages to distant items. [2]The basic comparison with hypertext is that the form of the text is not the same as the form visible on any one page or screen. [3.a]It reaches beyond, [3.b]just as form of the suburb is not the same as the immediately visible spatial connections. [4.a]Immediate architectural form is not the same as the place form of suburban locations, [4.b.1]because they reach out beyond the local horizon, [4.b.2]and form wholes and networks that are not architecturally obvious. [5.a]We are not sure how to express this linkage architecturally, [5.b]and most suburban architectural types celebrate isolation rather than connection.

The parallel is useful, because the armature of links in a hypertext creates a "spatiality" that has more complex interrelations and dimensions than linear one-thing-after-another of physical space, or of pages in a novel. The analogy with hypertext shows how the reality of a suburb can be more complex than appears locally, with more dimensions of movement and connection. There are other parallels as well. But the parallel between hypertext and suburbs is not perfect, for a number of reasons. The most important difference has to do with the two kinds of spatialities formed by grammatical and spatial connection. This also has to do with the way meaning is created by adjacency.

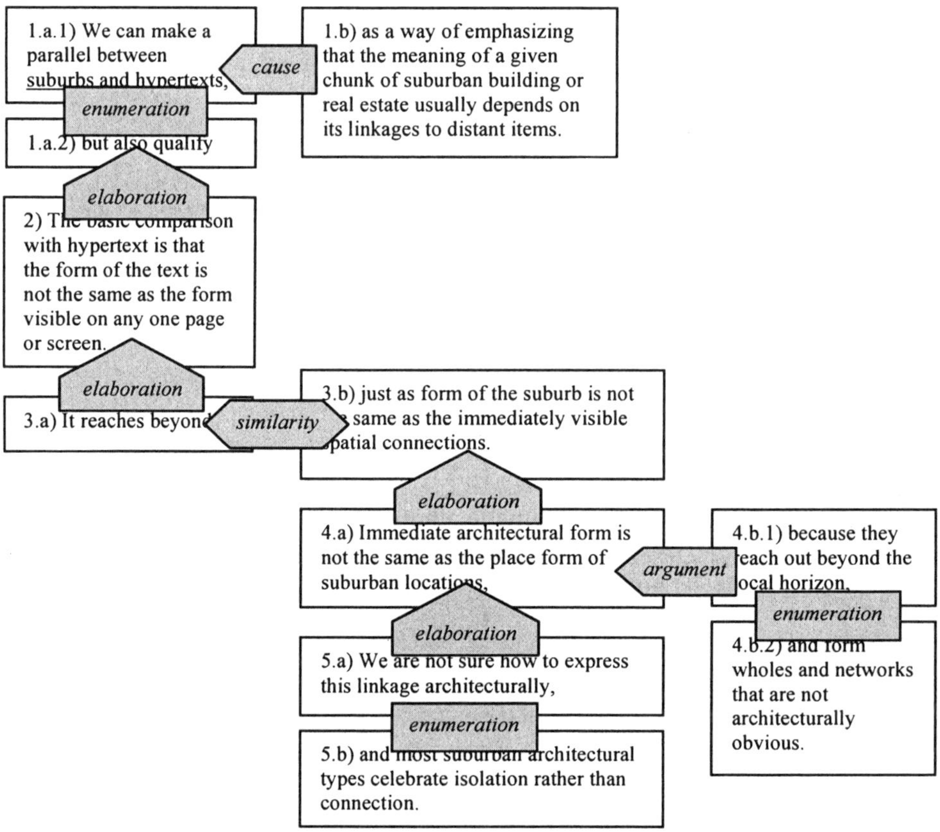

suburbs -> (<< *elaboration*) **Places in General**

Parallel and Not

We can make, but also qualify, a parallel between suburbs and hypertexts, as a way of emphasizing that the meaning of a given chunk of suburban building or real estate usually depends on its linkages to distant items. The basic comparison with hypertext is that the form of the text is not the same as the form visible on any one page or screen. It reaches beyond, just as form of the suburb is not the same as the immediately visible spatial connections. Immediate architectural form is not the same as the place form of suburban locations, because they reach out beyond the local horizon, and form wholes and networks that are not architecturally obvious. We are not sure how to express this linkage architecturally, and most suburban architectural types celebrate isolation rather than connection.

[1.a]The parallel is useful, [1.b]because the armature of links in a hypertext creates a "spatiality" that has more complex interrelations and dimensions than linear one-thing-after-another of physical space, or of pages in a novel. [2]The analogy with hypertext shows how the reality of a suburb can be more complex than appears locally, with more dimensions of movement and connection. [3]There are other parallels as well. [4]But the parallel between hypertext and suburbs is not perfect, for a number of reasons. [5]The most important difference has to do with the two kinds of spatialities formed by grammatical and spatial connection. [6]This also has to do with the way meaning is created by adjacency.

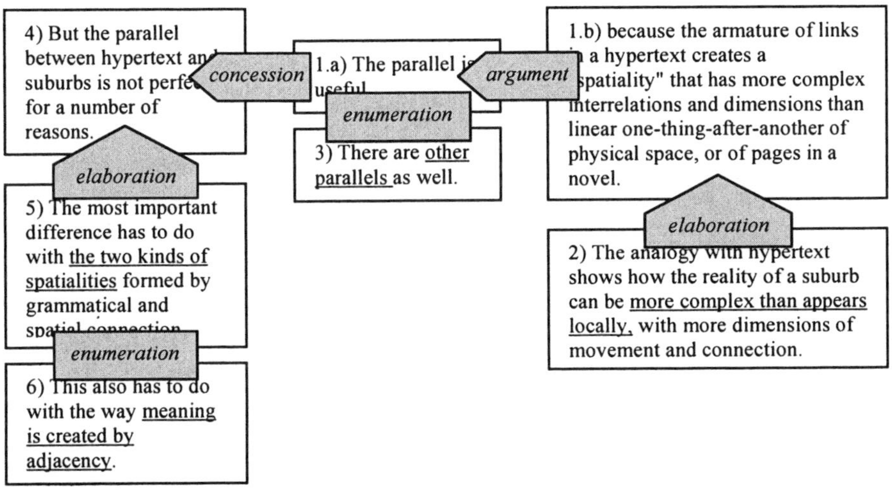

more complex that appears locally -> (<< *argument*) **Horizons**
other parallels -> (<< *elaboration*) **Other Parallels**
the two kinds of spatialities -> (<< *argument*) **Two Spatialities**
meaning is created by adjacency -> (<< *argument*) **Meaning and Intentions**

Places in General

[1]The parallel between suburbs and hypertexts can be generalized to a parallel between linkage and connection in any place and any text. [2]Places, of whatever kind, and texts, hyper or not, get their unity through sets of meaning connections some of which are made normative. [3]Both places and texts have their normative grammar(s) within fields of possibilities that exceed that grammar and which that grammar cannot control. [4]Both places and texts exist as structures embedded within an ongoing process of re-creation and re-interpretation.

The point of the specific comparison of suburbs and hypertexts is to emphasize that the being of a suburb is not exhausted by its immediate visible vicinity. There are so many pictures of ghastly uniform suburbs stretching off to infinity, and I don't mean to deny such spiritless repetition and uniformity. But I do mean to say that that ghastly aspect is not the whole reality of the suburbs being viewed, that the motions of people's lives and the networks that intersect the visible array make of the suburb a more complex place. We need to learn how to mitigate the ghastly aspects by making those complexities and connections and networks more salient in everyday experience.

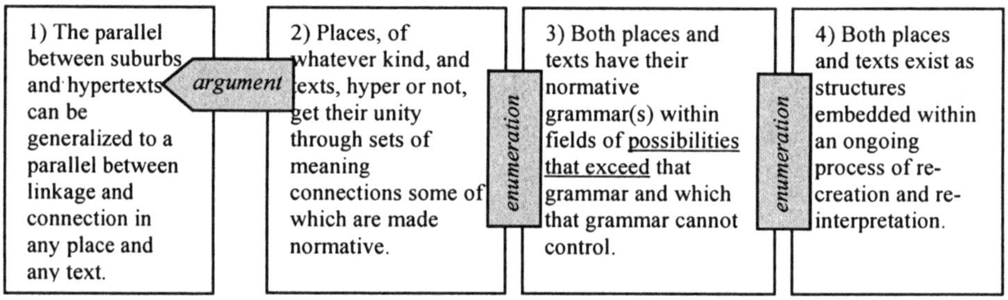

possibilities that exceed -> (<< *elaboration*) **Horizons**

Places in General

The parallel between suburbs and hypertexts can be generalized to a parallel between linkage and connection in any place and any text. Places, of whatever kind, and texts, hyper or not, get their unity through sets of meaning connections some of which are made normative. Both places and texts have their normative grammar(s) within fields of <u>possibilities that exceed</u> that grammar and which that grammar cannot control. Both places and texts exist as structures embedded within an ongoing process of re-creation and re-interpretation.

[1]The point of the specific comparison of suburbs and hypertexts is to emphasize that the being of a suburb is not exhausted by its immediate visible vicinity. [2.a]There are so many pictures of ghastly uniform suburbs stretching off to infinity, [2.b]and I don't mean to deny such spiritless repetition and uniformity. [3.a]But I do mean to say that that ghastly aspect is not the whole reality of the suburbs being viewed, [3.b]that <u>the motions of people's lives</u> and the networks that intersect the visible array make of the suburb a more complex place. [4]We need to learn how to mitigate the ghastly aspects by making those complexities and connections and networks more salient in everyday experience.

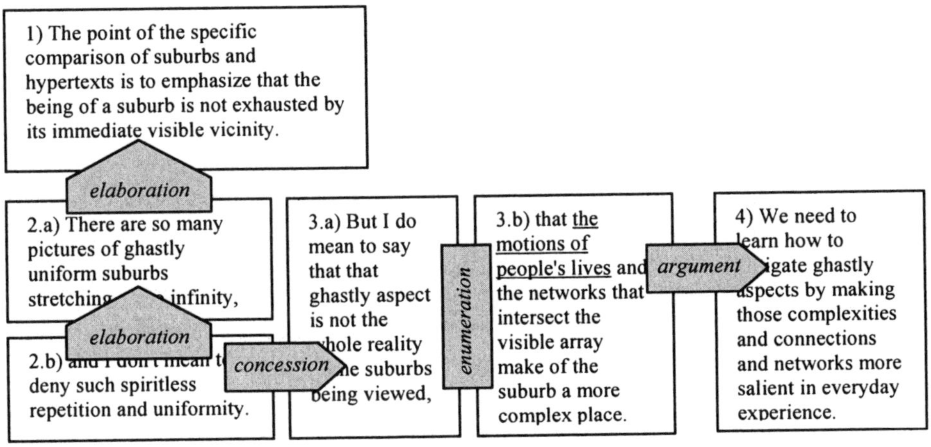

<u>the motions of people's lives</u> -> (<< *background*) **Changing Connections**

Horizons

[1]What something is revealed to be, what it means, depends on the <u>horizon of possibilities</u> (actions, inferences, things it might have been or done, etc.) within which it stands in contrasts. [2.a]Explicit hypertext links are part of that standing within the horizon, [2.b]but the items a text chunk, or a region of a place, are linked to stand close by, surrounded by a farther horizon. [3]We can distinguish a variety of horizons for a thing, for a text, for a hypertext, for a suburban building, or for part of any place:

items the thing or place or textual fragment is linked to explicitly (the factory in the next town, the head bank, the vacation home, other parts of a machine, matching items (tables with chairs), grammatical connections, explicit textual references, and so on.); the horizon visible behind these closely linked items. In places this is still mostly the result of design; "farther out": the phenomenological horizon that is not a visible object linked to, not a visible object since it is composed of absences linked by rules of possibility; the wilder possibilities that are on that horizon but not according to rules, that break or bend or defy rules; nearby adjacencies, not themselves necessarily designed for contrast but standing in contrasts that will influence meaning and affect function; the space of possible routes toward the horizon: other ways of reading the text or acting in the space, either according to the rules or running against them; the contour of meaning surrounding this text or this place or this action, as a relatively definite perspectival construct out of surrounding possibilities.

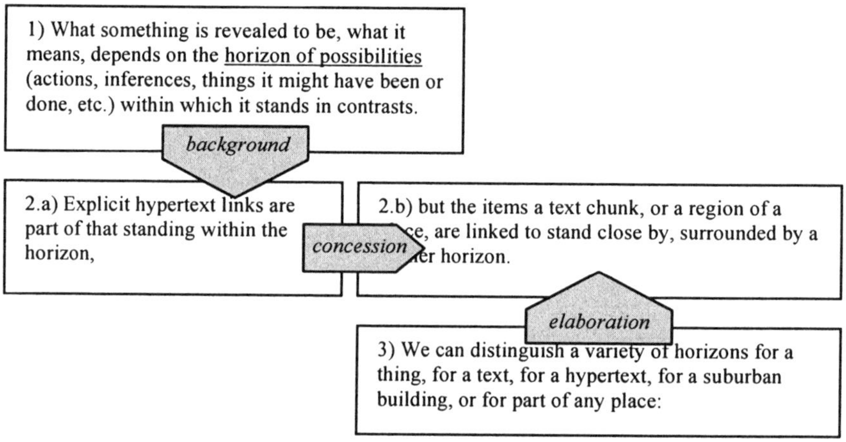

<u>horizons of possibilities</u> -> (<< *background*) **Rhetorical Connections**

Other Parallels

[1]There are other <u>parallels between suburbs and hypertexts</u> that could be discussed: [2.a.]issues of diversity, [2.b.1]issues of justice, [2.b.2]as the rich (in resources or links or attention) get richer, [2.c]the need to open walls and gates, the need to see current structures (and walls, and links, as well as open spaces) as effects within a larger field that they don't rule over. [3.a]There are also issues having to do with space and time (collage and montage) in both suburbs and hypertext design, [3.b.]issues of density and complexity, timing, and availability, [3.c]the need for multiple maps that deny any single Official map, [3.d]and, finally the way that multiple borders effect different unities, breaking down the community or textual analogues to the nation state that grabs and demands to supervise all borders.

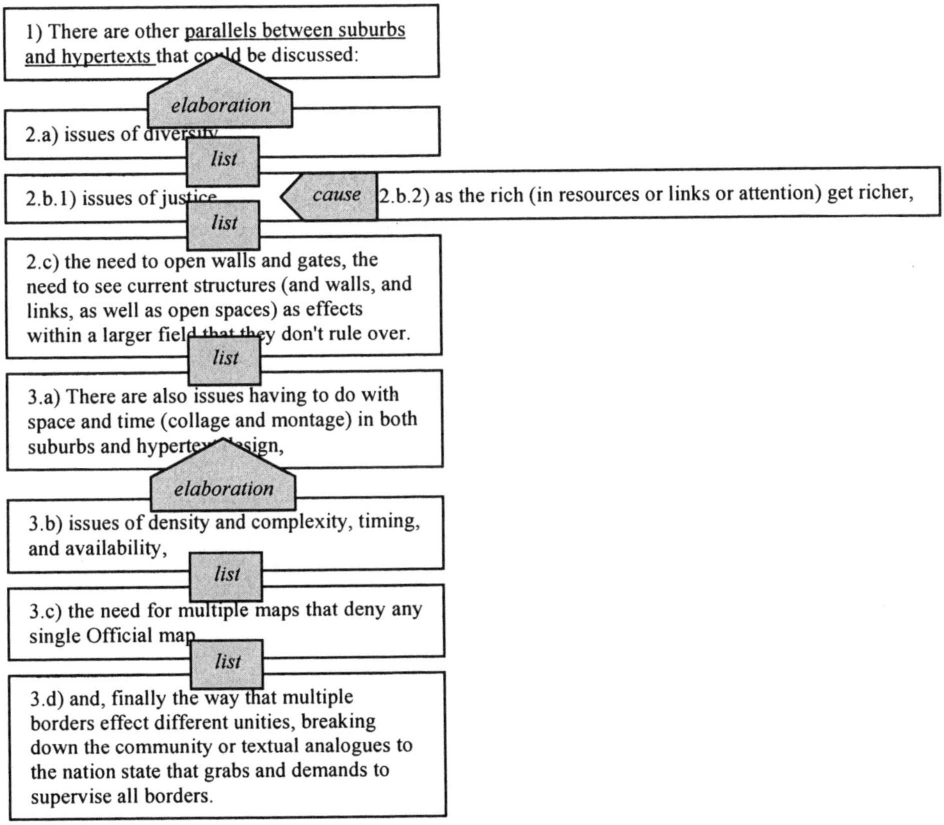

<u>parallel between suburbs and hypertexts</u> -> (<< *enumerated*) **Parallel And Not**

Two Spatialities

Grammatical connections create an action space of linked areas that are "next to" one another in the sense that geographies or trajectories of action do one phase here and another phase there. For instance in an auditorium the stage and the audience area are "next to" one another in terms of action definitions even though they may be physically separated by the orchestra pit, or, in a large office building two offices on different floors may be "next to" one another for a sequence of actions that are done first here then there.

But [1] in addition to grammatical next-to-ness, there is normal <u>physical proximity.</u> [2.a] This may or may not be grammatically important, but [2.b] it will have meaning effects. [3.a.1] The office just next door to mine may be "miles away" in terms of its function, [3.a.2] so that trajectories of action that pass through my office never go through the one next door, but [3.b.1] because the two offices are physically adjacent, [3.b.2] other kinds of interaction will develop. [4.a.1] Even if the employees never eat lunch together, [4.a.2] or never speak to one another, [4.b] the contrast between the two offices will still function as <u>an overtone of meaning</u> on their official grammatical places. [5] Physical connection also allows the exploration of new kinds of relations <u>that begin</u> outside of grammatical links.

<u>In a hypertext</u> the difference between these two kinds of connection collapses because the only connections are the links. In that sense, while the hypertext can be a useful analogue for pointing out the presence of the distant in the near, and the ways in which suburbs violate the expectations of visible architectural unity, suburbs are in fact a more complex kind of object because their physicality provides another mode of access and another kind of connection/unity.

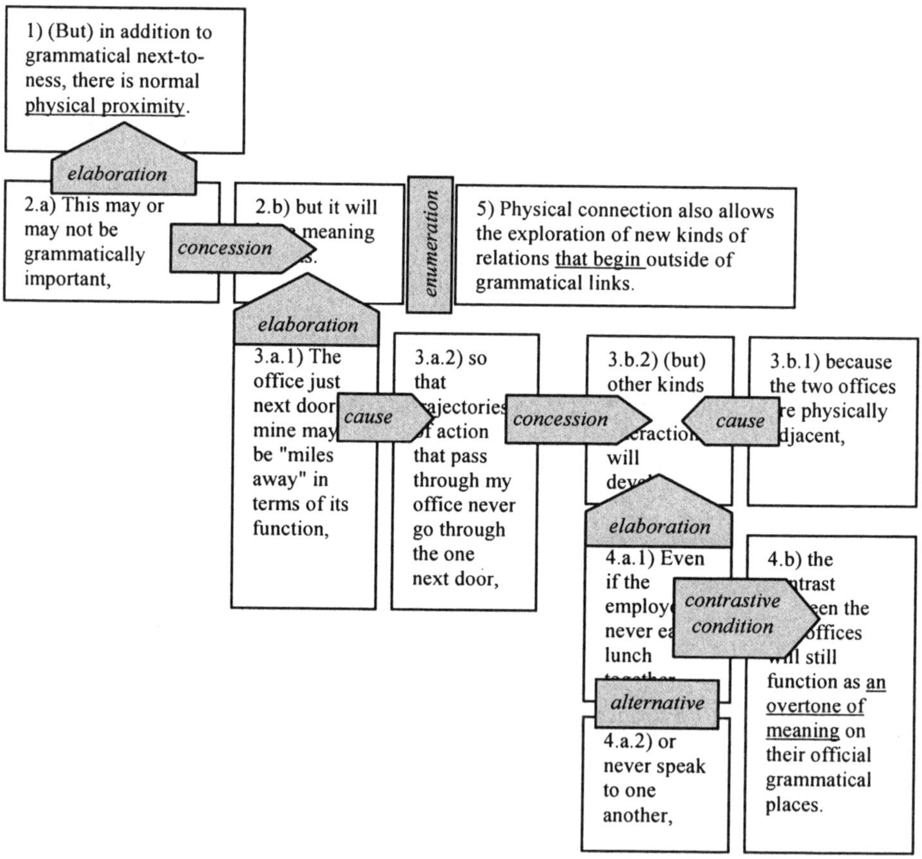

<u>physical proximity</u> -> (<< *elaboration*) **Virtual Spatialities**
<u>an overtone of meaning</u> -> (<< *elaboration*) **Meaning and Intention**
<u>that begin</u> -> (<< *elaboration*) **Travels and New Paths**

Two Spatialities

Grammatical connections create an action space of linked areas that are "next to" one another in the sense that geographies or trajectories of action do one phase here and another phase there. For instance in an auditorium the stage and the audience area are "next to" one another in terms of action definitions even though they may be physically separated by the orchestra pit, or, in a large office building two offices on different floors may be "next to" one another for a sequence of actions that are done first here then there.

But in addition to grammatical next-to-ness, there is normal physical proximity. This may or may not be grammatically important, but it will have meaning effects. The office just next door to mine may be "miles away" in terms of its function, so that trajectories of action that pass through my office never go through the one next door, but because the two offices are physically adjacent, other kinds of interaction will develop. Even if the employees never eat lunch together, or never speak to one another, the contrast between the two offices will still function as an overtone of meaning on their official grammatical places. Physical connection also allows the exploration of new kinds of relations that begin outside of grammatical links.

[1.a] In a hypertext the difference between these two kinds of connection collapses [1.b] because the only connections are the links. In that sense, [2.a.1] while the hypertext can be a useful analogue for pointing out the presence of the distant in the near, [2.a.2] and the ways in which suburbs violate the expectations of visible architectural unity, [2.b] suburbs are in fact a more complex kind of object [2.c] because their physicality provides another mode of access and another kind of connection/unity.

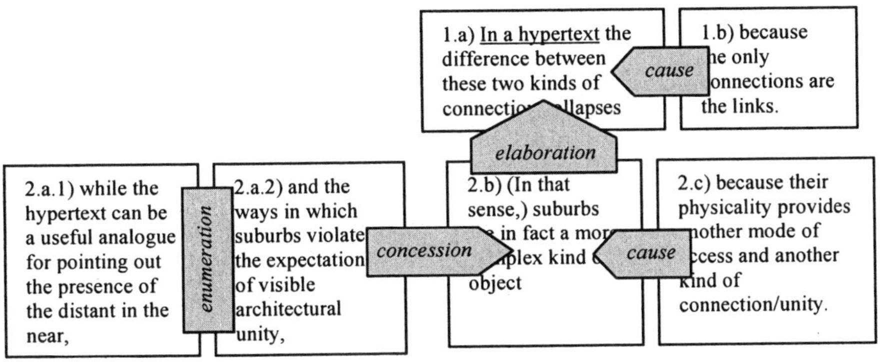

in a hypertext -> (<< *elaboration*) **Kinds of Adjacencies**

Meaning and Intention

[1]What makes the "spatiality" or connectivity of a hypertext different from a suburb is that in the hypertext all connections are intentional. [2]Links are *made*. [3.a]There is no parallel to the chance juxtapositions and chance meaning effects that occur in <u>physical space</u> [3.b](and could occur in a large enough <u>virtual space</u>). [4]So all hypertext connections take on <u>intentional meaning and effects.</u>

If I build a McDonalds next to a music store, I may have no intention that the relation between the two be meaningful. The site for my restaurant became available through causes that have nothing to do with the adjacent music store. However, though unintended, the association and contrast of the two will still be meaningful. Philosophers from Hobbes to Derrida have pointed out that there is no stopping the generation of <u>meaning by contiguity</u>. Such meaning effects may not have been specially intended, nor need they be taken as rhetorically or normatively important (unless the local store owner wants to use them in some way, perhaps for publicity). But the effects will be there nonetheless.

On the other hand, in a standard node-and-link hypertext, nothing is next to anything else until a link is created. There are <u>no unavoidable and uncontrollable adjacencies such as occur in physical space</u>.

Yet, even in a hypertext, we do have to distinguish between links that are intentional and which, though they have some meaning effects, had been made for other purposes, perhaps to ease navigation, from links that have <u>particular rhetorical effects</u>, and both of these need to be distinguished from links that are normatively important.

Suburbs are more like established texts with normative readings. But our places are never totally set, in part because of spatial possibilities exceed any link or normative structure. In addition, some contemporary places are becoming especially fluid, made on the fly, more like temporary work groups than the settled institutions.

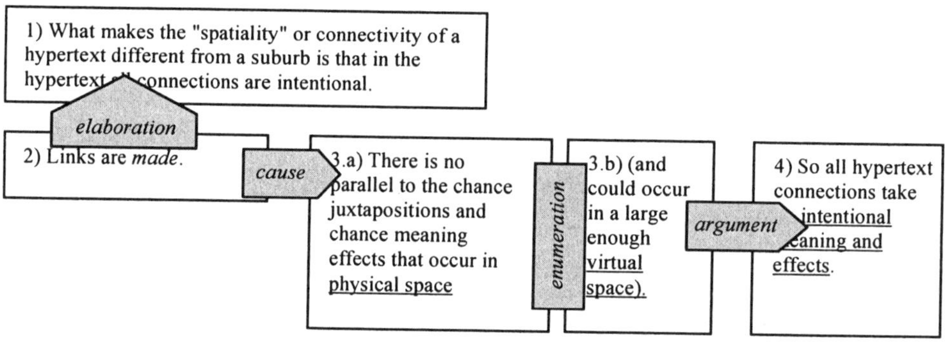

<u>physical space</u> -> (<< *background*) **Embodiment**
<u>virtual space</u> -> (<< *elaboration*) **Virtual Spatialities**
<u>intentional meaning and effects</u> -> (<< *elaboration*) **Rhetorical Connections**

Meaning and Intention

What makes the "spatiality" or connectivity of a hypertext different from a suburb is that in the hypertext all connections are intentional. Links are *made*. There is no parallel to the chance juxtapositions and chance meaning effects that occur in physical space (and could occur in a large enough virtual space). So all hypertext connections take on intentional meaning and effects.

1.a If I build a McDonalds next to a music store, 1.b I may have no intention that the relation between the two be meaningful. 2 The site for my restaurant became available through causes that have nothing to do with the adjacent music store. 3 However, though unintended, the association and contrast of the two will still be meaningful. 4 Philosophers from Hobbes to Derrida have pointed out that there is no stopping the generation of meaning by contiguity. 5.a.1 Such meaning effects may not have been specially intended, 5.a.2 nor need they be taken as rhetorically or normatively important 5.b (unless the local store owner wants to use them in some way, perhaps for publicity). 6 But the effects will be there nonetheless.

On the other hand, in a standard node-and-link hypertext, nothing is next to anything else until a link is created. There are no unavoidable and uncontrollable adjacencies such as occur in physical space.

Yet, even in a hypertext, we do have to distinguish between links that are intentional and which, though they have some meaning effects, had been made for other purposes, perhaps to ease navigation, from links that have particular rhetorical effects, and both of these need to be distinguished from links that are normatively important.

Suburbs are more like established texts with normative readings. But our places are never totally set, in part because of spatial possibilities exceed any link or normative structure. In addition, some contemporary places are becoming especially fluid, made on the fly, more like temporary work groups than the settled institutions.

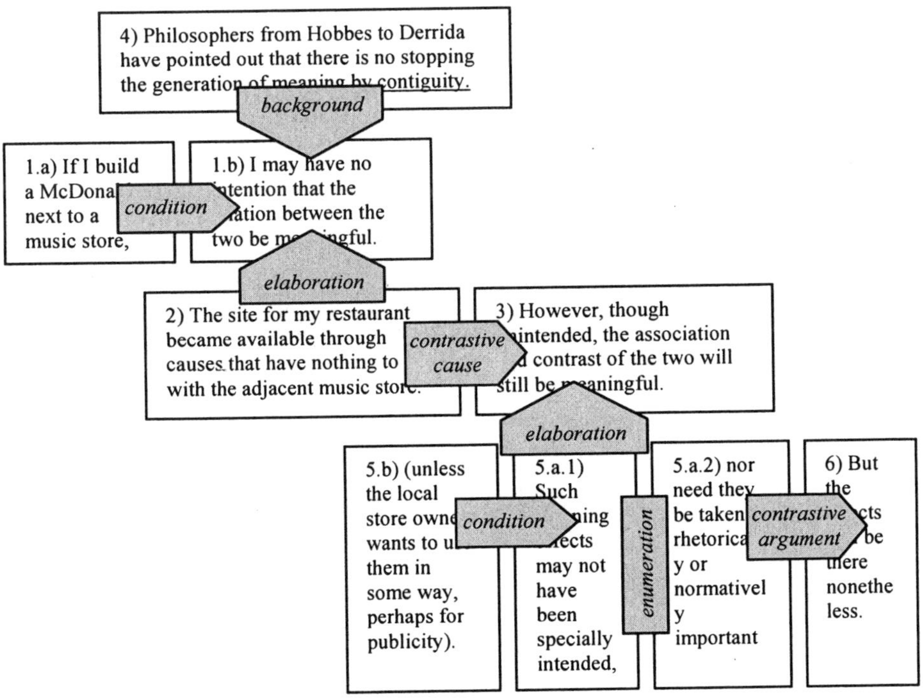

meaning by contiguity -> (<< *elaboration*) **Horizons**

Meaning and Intention

What makes the "spatiality" or connectivity of a hypertext different from a suburb is that in the hypertext all connections are intentional. Links are *made*. There is no parallel to the chance juxtapositions and chance meaning effects that occur in physical space (and could occur in a large enough virtual space). So all hypertext connections take on intentional meaning and effects.

If I build a McDonalds next to a music store, I may have no intention that the relation between the two be meaningful. The site for my restaurant became available through causes that have nothing to do with the adjacent music store. However, though unintended, the association and contrast of the two will still be meaningful. Philosophers from Hobbes to Derrida have pointed out that there is no stopping the generation of meaning by contiguity. Such meaning effects may not have been specially intended, nor need they be taken as rhetorically or normatively important (unless the local store owner wants to use them in some way, perhaps for publicity). But the effects will be there nonetheless.

On the other hand, [1] in a standard node-and-link hypertext, nothing is next to anything else until a link is created. [2] There are no unavoidable and uncontrollable adjacencies such as occur in physical space.

Yet, even in a hypertext, we do have to distinguish between links that are intentional and which, though they have some meaning effects, had been made for other purposes, perhaps to ease navigation, from links that have particular rhetorical effects, and both of these need to be distinguished from links that are normatively important.

Suburbs are more like established texts with normative readings. But our places are never totally set, in part because of spatial possibilities exceed any link or normative structure. In addition, some contemporary places are becoming especially fluid, made on the fly, more like temporary work groups than the settled institutions.

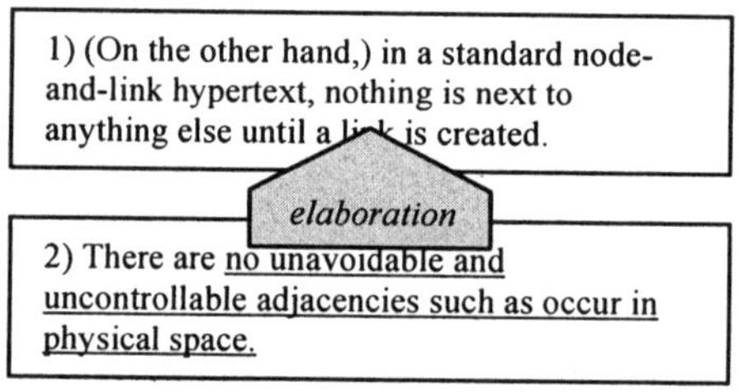

no unavoidable and ... -> (<< *elaboration*) **Kinds Of Adjacencies**

Meaning and Intention

What makes the "spatiality" or connectivity of a hypertext different from a suburb is that in the hypertext all connections are intentional. Links are *made*. There is no parallel to the chance juxtapositions and chance meaning effects that occur in physical space (and could occur in a large enough virtual space). So all hypertext connections take on intentional meaning and effects.

If I build a McDonalds next to a music store, I may have no intention that the relation between the two be meaningful. The site for my restaurant became available through causes that have nothing to do with the adjacent music store. However, though unintended, the association and contrast of the two will still be meaningful. Philosophers from Hobbes to Derrida have pointed out that there is no stopping the generation of meaning by contiguity. Such meaning effects may not have been specially intended, nor need they be taken as rhetorically or normatively important (unless the local store owner wants to use them in some way, perhaps for publicity). But the effects will be there nonetheless.

On the other hand, in a standard node-and-link hypertext, nothing is next to anything else until a link is created. There are no unavoidable and uncontrollable adjacencies such as occur in physical space.

Yet, [1.a.1] even in a hypertext, we do have to distinguish between links that are intentional [1.a.2] and which, though they have some meaning effects, had been made for other purposes, perhaps to ease navigation, [1.a.1] from links that have particular rhetorical effects, [1.b] and both of these need to be distinguished from links that are normatively important.

Suburbs are more like established texts with normative readings. But our places are never totally set, in part because of spatial possibilities exceed any link or normative structure. In addition, some contemporary places are becoming especially fluid, made on the fly, more like temporary work groups than the settled institutions.

1.a.1) (Yet,) even in a hypertext, we do have to distinguish between links that are intentional from links that have particular rhetorical effects,	*enumeration*	1.a.2) and which, had been made for other purposes, perhaps to ease navigation,	*enumeration*	1.b) and both of these need to be distinguished from links that are normatively important.

particular rhetorical effects -> (<< *background*) **Rhetorical Connections**

Changing Connections

1.a Because items in (physical <u>or virtual</u>) places are available independently of their normative grammatical connections, 1.b those connections can be altered by patterns of action that develop new accesses and connections. 2 Living in the suburb can change its connections and grammatical norms. 3.a Such flexibility is harder to find in a hypertext, 3.b where there is no way to other parts of the text except through intentionally established connecting links. 4 Neither on the web nor in separately published hypertexts can the <u>reader make new connections</u> that will be publicly available.

In the suburb, some intentional links are carried in quasi-permanent pipes (highways, wiring, conduits), while others exist in alterable habits and practices. Of course the fixed pipes such as highways can carry many different kinds of connections at once, or over time, and their existence will encourage certain kinds of connections and discourage others.

A communally created hypertext might be arranged to receive added links, so that there would not be a single permanent armature but an ongoing process of linking. In this case some mechanism would have to be set up for the elimination of links, or at least for their grouping into separate path sets, or else the text would become so cluttered that its links would be useless. (Such a text would be one way of emphasizing the non-finality of structure and embeddedness of formal systems within a process of reinterpretation.)

We are more used to the change of connections over time in physical space, though sometimes the relative permanence of physical adjacencies and architectural effects can fool us into thinking that a place's meaning and use are more stable than they really are.

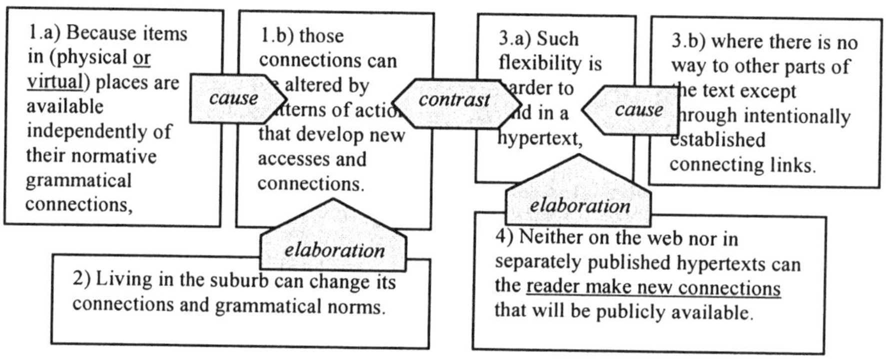

<u>or virtual</u> -> (<< *elaboration*) **Virtual Spatialities**
<u>reader make new connections</u> -> (<< *elaboration*) **New Connections**

Rhetorical Connections

It is not the same to say that a connection is meaningful, or that it is intentional, or that it creates a rhetorical effect, or that it is normative.

[1.a] Each of these can each be true [1.b] without the others being true. [2.a] Meaningful connections need not be intentional, [2.b] rhetorical effects need not be normative, [2.c] meaningful connections might not have any noticeable rhetorical effect, and so on. [3] A major distinction lies between normativity and the other terms. [4] Norms legitimize a selection from among possible or actual meaningful, rhetorical, or intentional connections.

Place grammars legitimize only certain kinds of actions and connections and divisions in the place. But all grammars remain surrounded by wilder possibilities and connections.

In a hypertext it may be that there are many links, but only some of them are normative: these might be suggested or even forced by the author, with the others remaining as a reserve for further exploration. But whether or not the authorial links are so divided, there will always be yet other unlinked potential connections, as there are in any text, which have their effects as you travel on the links. Echoes and contrasts will happen even among items that are not linked.

Despite this excess, we cannot do without normative connections. Echoes and similarities and contrasts will have their effects whether or not there are explicit links. But there still have to be specific links, because if everything links to everything, or nothing links to anything, the echoes and contrasts will themselves have nothing to work against and with, and this will neutralize their effects. Although a given definition will never succeed in dominating the flow of meaning, if there were no place for a horizon to form around, there would be no way to distinguish any of the infinite echoes. We cannot read "the general text." The space of difference cannot be made to purely appear, since appearance is always as something definite against the space of difference.

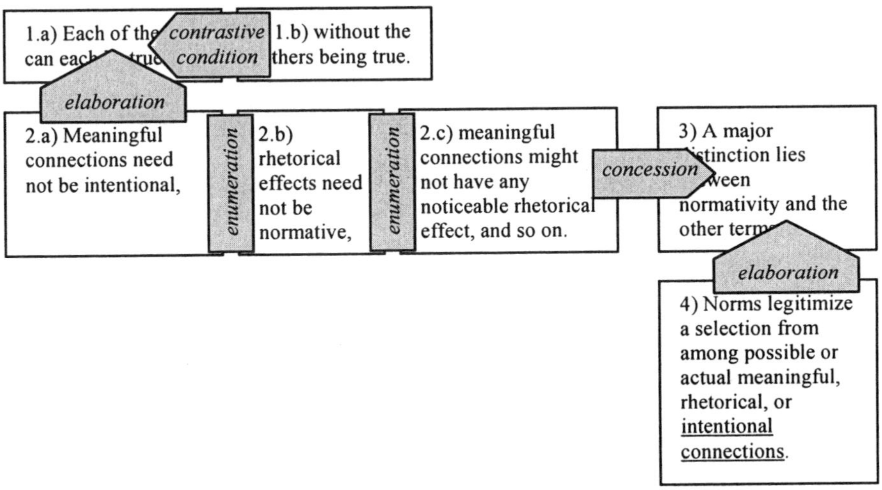

intentional connections -> (<< *elaboration*) **Meaning and Intention**

Travels and New Paths

Here is one problematic aspect to the comparison of place linkage and hypertext linkage: In a hypertext there is the structure of the set of links in the text, and there is also the envisioned structure and history created on the occasion of a particular reading of the text. The link structure provides possible paths but not an actual journey. Some literary hypertext theorists argue that it is the unique event of a particular reading, which creates "the text." I find this view unsatisfactory for the same reasons that it would be unsatisfactory to argue that a symphony or a play exists uniquely in each performance and not also in the score or script. The full reality of the work must involve both, so that each can provide ways to criticize the other. A performance of a play or a reading of a hypertext could be inadequate to what is there in the text; on the other hand a script could be unperformable, or a hypertext structure so convoluted that it was unreadable.

[1.a]The point in relation to suburbs is that a suburban place is structured by its skein of normative connections, [1.b]not just by the itineraries of your or my particular life in the suburbs, which will actualize only some of the "built-in" connections. However, [2.a]as with texts, [2.b]each may be used to criticize the other: [3.a]my daily life might not take adequate advantage of the connections available, [3.b]or, as too often happens, the poverty of daily living might show up the thinness of the normative connections. [4.a]As with art, [4.b]density of available connection is important for the richness of life.

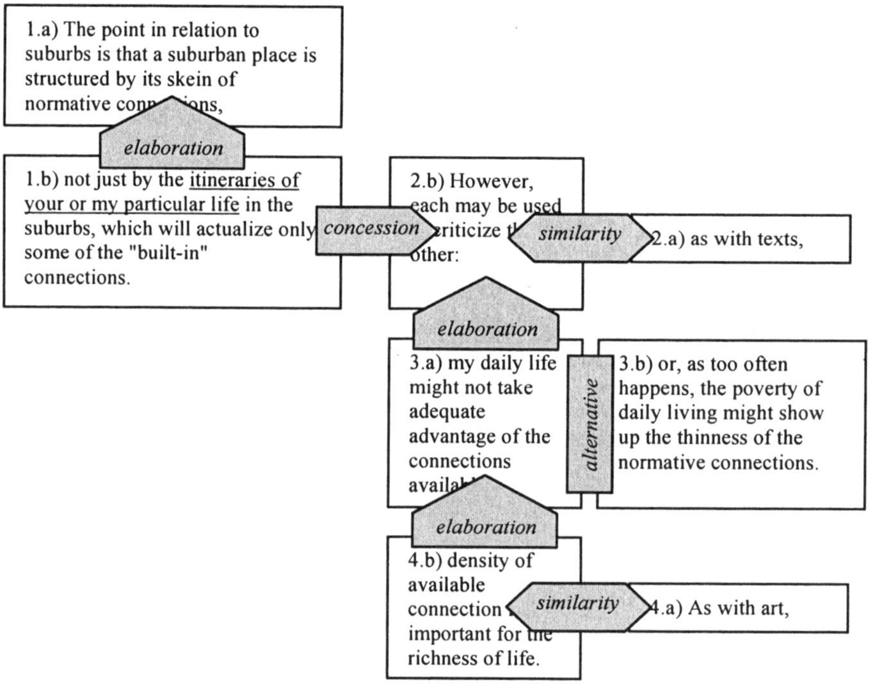

itineraries of your or my particular life -> (<< *elaboration*) **Changing Connections**

Kinds of Adjacencies

[1] Books provide an intermediate case for two kinds of connection. [2] Parts of the book will be "linked" by intentional connection to distant parts: [3.a] one page may contain a reference to a distant page, [3.b] or a sentence contain a footnote number linking to note in the back of the book. [4] Then there is the linear sequence of materials from page to page, which is both a physical and an intentional connection. [5] There is, also, the physical availability of the pages at the edge of the book; [6.a] I can stick my finger in two-thirds of the way through, [6.b] or turn thirty pages at once to see what comes up; [7.a] this allows abrupt non-intentional juxtapositions of different parts of the book, [7.b] somewhat like finding something uncontrollably next-door to where you build.

Hypertexts seldom have any analogue to this physical availability, though something like it can be built in, for instance, by providing a map of the hypertext that allows one to jump to another part of the text without following any intentional link. Such maps are, however, labelled, so that the jump is not quite as unintentional as jumping through book pages might be.

Something more like the abrupt nonintentional adjaciencies of physical space could be built into a hypertext by introducing randomized contacts, or a skein of built-in connectors independent of meaning or order of creation, etc. Such connectors could be random, or partly intentional, as in a library or bookstore where there is some order but unexpected encounters can still happen.

Or, there could be automatic link creation. There is another paradigm of hypertext, not as linked chunks of text, but as fields of text from which search engines and algorithms create links on the fly depending on user interest. For instance, imagine software that watches what you are writing and adds links to other texts based on statistics about your use of words, or questions you ask in the text, or metaphors you create. We don't have intelligent enough software to do this well, though there are beginnings in some proposals for extending the capabilities of the Web, and there have been demonstrations of such link-on-the-fly programs. This type of hypertext does not have a fixed armature of links made intentionally by an author, though its links do represent priorities that were jointly set up by the authors of the software and observations of the behavior of the users. (It is possible, of course, that such a system might suggest a link based on regularities in my writing or word use that I was totally unaware of and might find very helpful.)

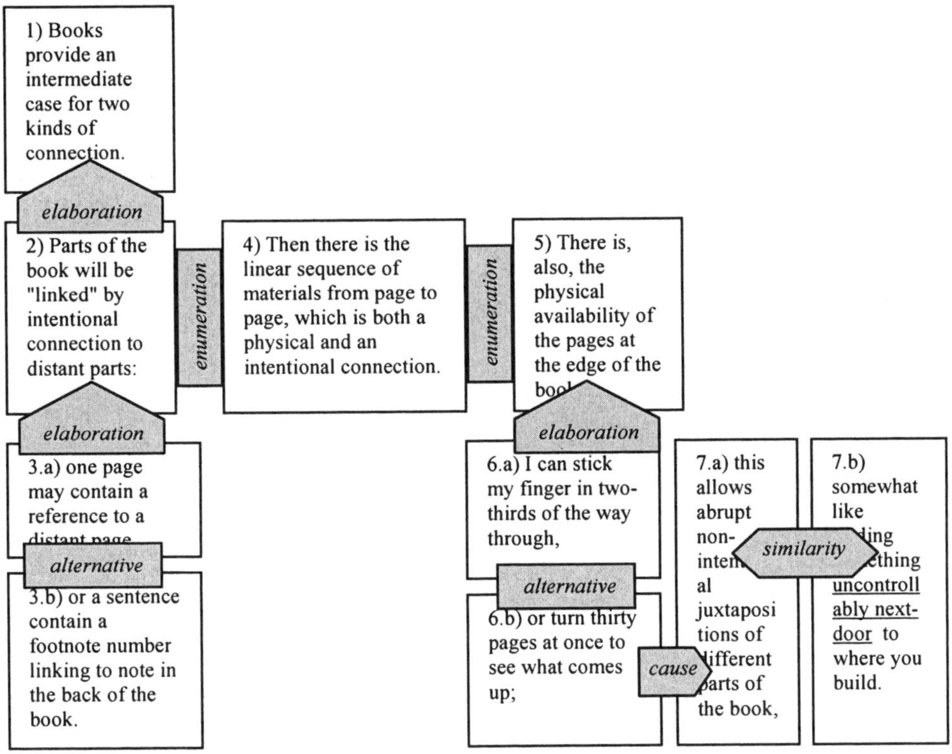

uncontrollably next-door -> (<< *elaboration*) **Meaning and Intention**

Kinds of Adjacencies

Books provide an intermediate case for two kinds of connection. Parts of the book will be "linked" by intentional connection to distant parts: one page may contain a reference to a distant page, or a sentence contain a footnote number linking to note in the back of the book. Then there is the linear sequence of materials from page to page, which is both a physical and an intentional connection. There is, also, the physical availability of the pages at the edge of the book; I can stick my finger in two-thirds of the way through, or turn thirty pages at once to see what comes up; this allows abrupt non-intentional juxtapositions of different parts of the book, somewhat like finding something uncontrollably next-door to where you build.

[1.a] Hypertexts seldom have any analogue to this physical availability, [1.b] though something like it can be built in, for instance, by providing a map of the hypertext that allows one to jump to another part of the text without following any intentional link. [2.a] Such maps are, however, labelled, [2.b] so that the jump is not quite as unintentional [2.c] as jumping through book pages might be.

Something more like the abrupt non intentional adjaciencies of physical space could be built into a hypertext by introducing randomized contacts, or a skein of built-in connectors independent of meaning or order of creation, etc. Such connectors could be random, or partly intentional, as in a library or bookstore where there is some order but unexpected encounters can still happen.

Or, there could be automatic link creation. There is another paradigm of hypertext, not as linked chunks of text, but as fields of text from which search engines and algorithms create links on the fly depending on user interest. For instance, imagine software that watches what you are writing and adds links to other texts based on statistics about your use of words, or questions you ask in the text, or metaphors you create. We don't have intelligent enough software to do this well, though there are beginnings in some proposals for extending the capabilities of the Web, and there have been demonstrations of such link-on-the-fly programs. This type of hypertext does not have a fixed armature of links made intentionally by an author, though its links do represent priorities that were jointly set up by the authors of the software and observations of the behavior of the users. (It is possible, of course, that such a system might suggest a link based on regularities in my writing or word use that I was totally unaware of and might find very helpful.)

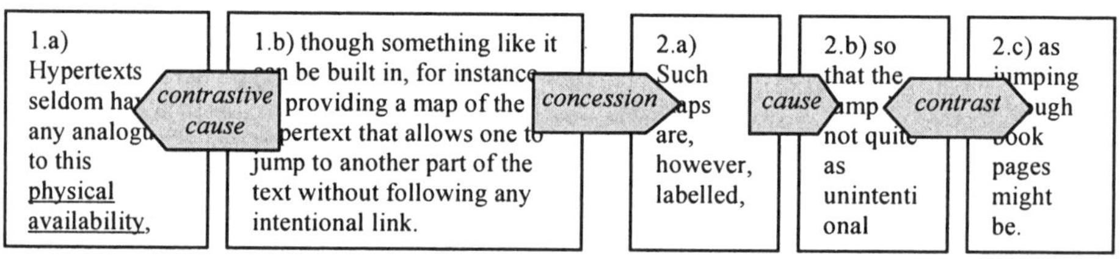

physical availability -> (<< *elaboration*) **Embodiment**

New Connections

Many hypertext implementations that are richer in features than the Web make use of link servers, so that different sets of links can be set up on the same base text. Most of these are only laboratory demonstration projects, but there are some annotation services that let readers add comments or links to web pages, though the results are available only to those who subscribe to the same link servers. While link servers enrich the hypertextual features of texts, they tend to create individualized sets of links, which make it more difficult to change normative textual connections for a community. What they can do is alter the *idea* of normative textual connections, replacing them with published sets of links, some of which may become accepted and normative.

[1.a]It is difficult to envision a place analogue to this process, [1.b]because physical adjacency and architectural effects are "there" whether or not they are intended. [2.a]Their effects on my building and my activities are not intentional links, [2.b]nor are they avoidable. [3]The car wash next door, or the threateningly large office building down the block, cannot be wished away or made invisible by linking around them. [4]On the other hand, physical adjacencies and architectural effects provide possibilities for exploration and new connection in an intermediate zone between invisibility and fully intentional linkage.

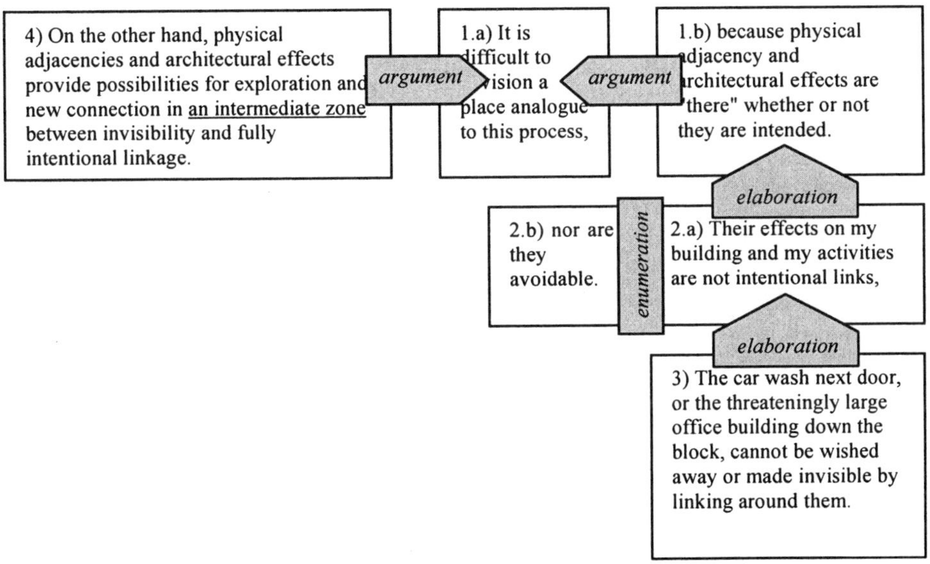

an intermediate zone -> (<< *background*) **Two Spatialities**

Virtual Spatialities

[1]It might seem that in virtual places there would be a collapse of the distinction between physical proximity and intentional linkage. [2]The grammatical place-connections would be the same as the virtual spatial connections establishing the virtual world. [3]However, this is not so; [4.a]the distinction does hold for virtual places, [4.b]because a virtual place does not have to occupy the whole of a virtual area. [5.a]It's true that the underlying connections in a virtual world are intentionally designed, [5.b]but that does not make them the same as the normative or grammatical connections that select out certain areas within that virtual world as parts of a socially grammatized place.

For instance, if a virtual world made available virtual real estate for development, my virtual place could find itself next to new places outside my control -- I didn't want a virtual McDonald's next door -- and this would affect the meaning of my place and also allow non-grammatical explorations and connections, just as happens in physical space.

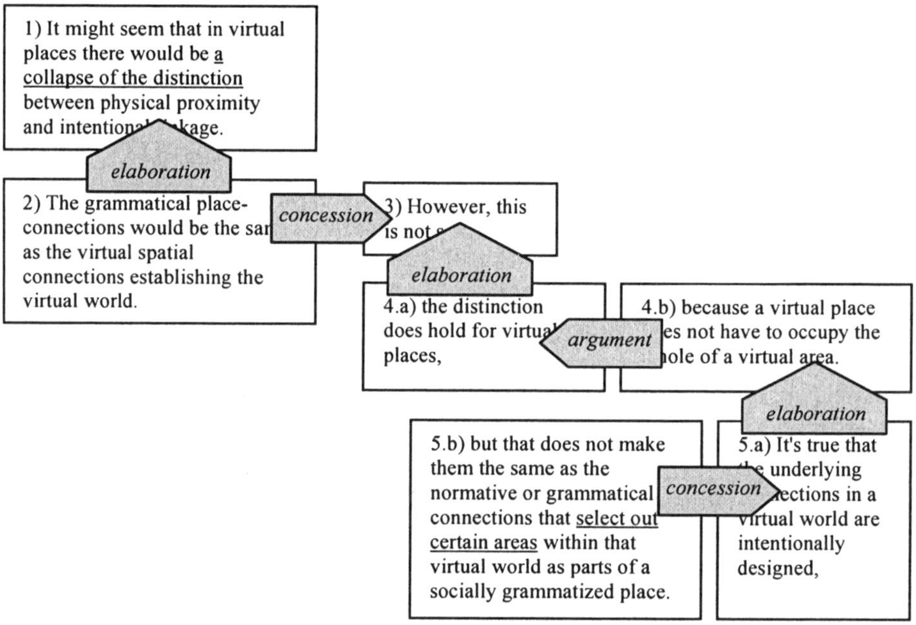

a collapse of the distinction -> (<< *background*) **Meaning and Intention**
select out certain areas -> (<< *background*) **Rhetorical Connections**